On Norms and Agency

DIRECTIONS IN DEVELOPMENT
Human Development

On Norms and Agency

*Conversations about Gender Equality with
Women and Men in 20 Countries*

Ana María Muñoz Boudet, Patti Petesch, and Carolyn Turk with Angélica Thumala

THE WORLD BANK
Washington, D.C.

Contents

Boxes

Figures

Map

Tables

Foreword (Rachel Kyte)

As part of the *World Development Report 2012: Gender Equality and Development*, the World Bank launched a new study: more than 4,000 women, men, girls, and boys from 97 communities in 20 countries across the world came together to discuss how women and men make decisions and how social norms shape everyday lives. These discussions underscored how informal gender norms, traditions, and beliefs govern and constrain behaviors and perceptions about one's place in the world. The power and freedom to take risks, seize opportunities, and shape one's life (or "agency," as it is called) can be determined as much by social norms such as gender roles as by the political and economic conditions of the communities and countries in which one lives. This book provides in-depth analysis of these rich discussions.

The findings are important for our work at the World Bank Group. It is part of our mandate to foster social inclusion for sustainable development and integrate gender considerations in the design, implementation, and monitoring of our projects. I would like to highlight in particular three findings.

First, thanks to expanding education opportunities, children today are thinking differently about their futures. This is most apparent among girls. Even in remote and poor villages of India and Togo, both girls and boys alike aspire to be scientists, lawyers, business leaders, or politicians. And girls, even in larger numbers than boys, ideally wish to earn graduate degrees. Girls and young women think that housework ought to be a responsibility shared by both sexes. The adolescents, both girls and boys, want to make their own choices in life. Their aspirations today are an invaluable resource for future gender equality outside *and* inside of households. We have to do much better than in the past to recognize and support their aspirations.

Second, and quite related, women report that they are gaining power and freedom in their lives. And when asked why, women most often refer to their own economic independence, and to taking forward new attitudes and behaviors that are more confident and purposeful. They know about their role and what they want to achieve. This can mean for some gaining a seat at the dinner table, for others sending daughters to high school, and still others the ability to thrive in a job outside the home. Women every bit as much as men consider jobs to be central to gaining more control and status for themselves. We heard this from women across the world, from Yemeni villages to Polish cities.

Finally, with the notable exception of rural men, we see from this study that most participants at least nominally say "yes" to the ideal of equality between a man and a woman. Yet, many women around the world still lack the knowledge and wherewithal to realize their rights, especially the right to be safe from physical and emotional abuse. In almost a third of the nearly 100 communities in this study, domestic violence is perceived to be a regular or frequent affair for women. We can and must do far more to safeguard women's physical and emotional integrity through actions such as making better laws and—most importantly—better enforcing them.

While the study shows how much still needs to be done, it delivers a strong message that gender equality has the potential to transform societies and place communities and countries on a trajectory toward a better, more inclusive, and sustainable development. It is up to each and every one of us to make this happen.

Rachel Kyte
Vice President of the Sustainable Development Network
World Bank

Foreword (Judith Rodin)

The *World Development Report 2012: Gender Equality and Development* offered a critical message: that effective policy making and unwavering focus on progress and persistence in achieving gender equality matter greatly for beneficial development outcomes. In the past quarter century, we have seen remarkable gains for women. Women now represent 40 percent of the global labor force. Women are living longer than men all around the world. And gender gaps in education, once prevalent, are reversing with increasing enrollment of girls and young women.

But even with this progress, gender disparities still persist in access to opportunity and resources, and in terms of individual agency. This World Bank report, *On Norms and Agency: Conversations about Gender Equality with Women and Men in 20 Countries*, provides tremendous insight on gender norms—an area that has been resistant to change, and that constrains achievement of gender equality across many diverse cultures. The report synthesizes data collected from more than 4,000 women and men in 97 communities across 20 countries. It is the largest dataset ever collected on the topic of gender and development, providing an unprecedented opportunity to examine potential patterns across communities on social norms and gender roles, pathways of empowerment, and factors that drive acute inequalities. The analysis raises the profile of persistent social norms and their impact on agency, and catalyzes discourse on the many pathways that create opportunities for women and men to negotiate transformative change.

The report is underpinned by the fact that arguably the single most important contribution to development is to unleash the full power of half the people on the planet—women. It underscores how crucial making investments in learning, supporting innovations that reduce the time costs of women's mobility, and developing a critical mass of women and men pushing the boundaries of entrenched social norms are in enhancing women's agency and capacity to aspire.

We know that women need the tools of development, but development also needs women. All the disadvantages that women experience around the world, from poverty to violence, from ill health to illiteracy, also limit the advancement of families, communities, and entire nations.

The Rockefeller Foundation is pleased to continue our collaboration with the World Bank through this report, and proud to have supported its research and production. We commend it to all who believe in building a more equitable and resilient world for the well-being of humanity.

Judith Rodin
President
The Rockefeller Foundation

Acknowledgments

This research draws on the contributions of *many* people who supported a 20-country rapid qualitative assessment titled "Defining Gender in the 21st Century: Talking with Women and Men around the World, A Multi-Country Qualitative Study of Gender and Economic Choice." First and foremost, we need to thank the 4,000 women and men and boys and girls who joined in nearly 500 focus groups. We asked very much of them, and they graciously shared their time and opinions with us.

The project was led and managed by Carolyn Turk. The core team also included Ana María Muñoz Boudet, Patti Petesch, Angélica Thumala, and Maria Beatriz Orlando. Valuable research assistance was provided by Paula Barros, Greta Gober, Gwendolyn Heaner, Rudy Herrera Marmol, Roberto Miranda, and Bethany Timmons.

We gratefully acknowledge the *World Development Report 2012* (WDR) team that initiated and supported this project throughout, including the WDR co-directors Ana Revenga and Sudhir Shetty, and the team—Luis Benveniste, Aline Coudouel, Jishnu Das, Markus Goldstein, and Carolina Sanchez Paramo. We also extend appreciation to Elisabeth Huybens of the Social Development Unit for Europe and Central Asia and Cyprian Fisiy with the Social Development Network team for hosting this publication project.

The "Defining Gender" data collection effort included national research teams from around the world led by Chona Echavez and Pierre Fallavier (AREU, Afghanistan); Ugyen Lhamo (Druk Associates, Bhutan); Jean-François Kobiané (Institut Supérieur des Sciences de la Population [ISSP], Université de Ouagadougou, Burkina Faso); Magaly Pineda and Sergia Galvan (Centro de Investigación para la Acción Femenina [CIPAF], Santo Domingo, the Dominican Republic); Priya Chattier (The University of South Pacific, Suva, Fiji); Sanjeev Sasmal and Sulbha Khanna (Sutra Consulting, India); Rizki Fillaili (SMERU, Jakarta, Indonesia); Gwendolyn Heaner (GK Consulting, research on Liberia); Dumitru Slonovschi (Magenta Consulting, Moldova); Patricia Zárate (Instituto de Estudios Peruanos, Peru); Samia M. Al-Botmeh and Lamis Abunahleh (Centre for Development Studies, Birzeit University, Ramallah, West Bank and Gaza); Paul Barker, Marjorie Andrew, and Almah Tararia (Institute of National Affairs, Papua New Guinea); Greta Gober (Centre for Gender Research, University of Oslo, research on Poland);

Hana Baronijan and Sasa Jovancevic (IPSOS, Serbia); Imraan Valodia and Kruschen Govender (School of Development Studies, University of KwaZulu-Natal, South Africa); Mohamed Braima and Khalil Al Medani (Sudanese Organization for Education, Sudan); Adalbertus Kamanzi (CORDEMA, Tanzania); Giovanna Declich (Togo); Hhuat Tha Hong and Linh Tran (Institute for Social Development Studies, Hanoi Vietnam); and Ramzia Aleryani, Sabria Al-Thwar, and Mai Abdulmalik (Yemeni Women Union, Sana'a, the Republic of Yemen).

The Institute for Women's Policy Research (IWPR) team, led by Jane Henrici and Allison Helmuth, helped with the original data coding and analysis. Amanda Lubold and Charles Ragin contributed with the qualitative comparative analysis.

Jeni Klugman, Director of Poverty Reduction and Economic Management (PREM) Gender, provided valuable support. Peer reviewers included Kathleen Beegle, Aline Coudouel, Maitreyi Das, Karla Hoff, Naila Kabeer, and Deepa Narayan. We also appreciated comments from Sarah Haddock, Dominique van de Walle, Rasmus Heltberg, and Elizaveta Perova, among others.

Getting this large research initiative off the ground in time to meet the WDR's production schedule was a major task. World Bank staff from across regions and sectors responded quickly and helpfully with guidance on research design, local research partners, data analysis, and myriad technical and administrative needs. Our very special thanks go to Dean Joliffe, Andy Kotikula, Tara Vishwanath, Nandini Krishnan, Abdalwahab Khatib, Andy Mason, Trang Nguyen, Shubha Chakravarty, Erol Graham, Iris Boutros, Mia Hyun, Yulia Immajati, Hesti Marsono, Dan Mont, Nicholas Menzies, Nora Dudwick, Owen Ozier, Andrea Gallina, Valery Vega, Roby Senderowitsch, Dan Owen, Sophia Georgieva, Hadyiat El-Tayeb Alyn, Trine Lunde, Arun Joshi, Adama Ouedrago, Sophia Georgieva, Liz Ninan, Chris Thomas, Maria Elena Garcia Mora, Elena Bardasi, Vivek Suri, and Michael Woolcock. The team also consulted experts outside the World Bank, including Lori Heise, David Crocker, Vanessa Gray, and Janice Newberry.

This publication was made possible thanks to the support of the Rockefeller Foundation. The study benefited greatly from a research workshop conducted with the lead researchers from 18 countries at the Rockefeller Foundation's Bellagio Center. A special thanks for making this possible goes to the Bellagio Center and Rockefeller Foundation teams, in particular to Heather Grady, Sundaa Bridgett-Jones, and Bethany Martin-Breen. We are also grateful for discussions with the Rockefeller Foundation's team, their relevant comments, support, and patience through the preparation of this book.

The team is also grateful for the financial support provided to the *World Development Report 2012* that made possible the collection of our unique dataset, including the Government of Norway through its Royal Ministry of Foreign Affairs, Australian Agency for International Development, Canadian International Development Agency, the Government of Sweden through its Ministry for Foreign Affairs, the Nike Foundation, and the Fast Track Initiative Education Program Development Fund.

Our great thanks go to Kristin Hunter's editorial work on successive drafts, and the Directions in Development production team. We also thank the resource management team of Sonia Joseph and Evangeline Santo Domingo, and Cecile Wodon, Rebecca Sugui, Mihaela Stangu, and Elizabeth Acul for ongoing help with coordination.

Despite our efforts to compile a comprehensive list, some who contributed may have been inadvertently omitted. The team apologizes for any oversights and reiterates its gratitude to all who contributed to this research.

Rockefeller Foundation

Innovation for the Next 100 Years

About the Authors

Ana María Muñoz Boudet is a World Bank consultant. She was a core team member of the *World Development Report 2012* and co-author of Latin America and Central America gender reports. She has worked on gender and poverty issues in the Latin America and the Caribbean, Europe and Central Asia, and Africa Regions. Prior to joining the Bank, she worked for the Inter-American Development Bank and the United Nations Development Programme (UNDP) and was a researcher at the Latin American Faculty of Social Sciences (FLACSO). Ana María holds a master's degree from the London School of Economics and is in the process of completing her PhD at the University College of London.

Patti Petesch is a World Bank consultant. She specializes in qualitative field research on poverty, gender, conflict, and participatory development. Her recent research explores factors that enlarge individual and collective empowerment at the local level, and the contribution of these processes to local democracy, poverty reduction, gender equality, and more secure and prosperous communities and nations. She was study coordinator and co-author of the World Bank's Voices of the Poor and Moving Out of Poverty global research programs, and co-author of *On Norms and Agency* companion reports on West Bank and Gaza and the Republic of Yemen. She recently published "Reflections on Global and Local Pathways to Women's Empowerment and Gender Equality: The Good, the Bad, and the Sticky" (*Ethics and Social Welfare*).

Carolyn Turk is the World Bank's country manager for Rwanda and was the Lead Social Development Specialist and Acting Sector Manager in the World Bank's Europe and Central Asia Social Development Department when this research started. She is an expert in poverty policy analysis, including quantitative and qualitative instruments, statistical capacity building, national strategic planning and budgeting processes, and design and implementation of social accountability tools. Prior to joining the Bank she was Senior Planning Officer in the Ministry of Finance in Papua New Guinea, Deputy Director of Action Aid, and Social Development Adviser at the U.K. Department for International Development (DFID). She has earned undergraduate and postgraduate degrees from Cambridge University in the economics and politics of development.

Maria Angélica Thumala is a Lecturer at the Sociology Department of the Catholic University of Chile and Research Associate at the Centre for

Criminology of the University of Oxford. She currently teaches sociology of gender and ethnographic and qualitative research methods. As a consultant for the World Bank, she has contributed to the West Bank and Gaza and the Republic of Yemen gender reports for the Middle East and North Africa Region. She has also published on consumption, cultural change, development, and religion in Latin America. Angélica holds a PhD in Sociology from the University of Cambridge and an MA in philosophy and social theory from the University of Warwick.

Abbreviations

IDP	internally displaced persons
INR	Indian rupees
NGO	nongovernmental organization
OECD	Organisation for Economic Co-operation and Development
QCA	qualitative comparative analysis
SACCOs	savings and credit cooperatives
SAR	special administrative region
SHG	self-help group
UNDP	United Nations Development Programme

The Norms of Power and the Power of Norms

Two of the many questions asked at the earliest stages of preparing the World Bank's (2012) *World Development Report 2012: Gender Equality and Development* were how do women and men make decisions about their economic participation, and how do we learn about this. To try to answer them, the World Bank launched a small qualitative field study in four countries. The objective was to find out what women and men saw as the main forces driving their decisions on economic participation—from how they used their time to their ability to start a business. The exercise quickly expanded to an unprecedented "bottom-up" exploration of how women and men make decisions in all dimensions of life; how gender differences are experienced; and how these differences, dictated by social norms, shape women's and men's everyday lives. The research covered 20 economies from all world regions and more than 4,000 participants in 97 communities—from remote and traditional villages in Papua New Guinea, the Republic of Yemen, and Liberia, to urban neighborhoods in Vietnam, Poland, and Peru (see map I.1).[1] In each country, local researchers organized about 500 focus groups to elicit information about the impact of gender norms on women and men and about the effect on their sense of agency and empowerment, and to learn about the changes in women's and men's lives as these gender norms flexed or persisted.

Gender equality in these 20 countries has increased in many domains. Like changes documented for most of the world, girls are staying in school longer than their mothers did. More women are economically active, and their participation in local networks and civic organizations has increased. And many women feel that they have more control over their lives. Yet, significant gender disparities are still evident: intrahousehold allocations of time, responsibilities, and power are unequally distributed among men and women. Almost everywhere, men remain the primary income earners in their households, as well as the main decision-makers. And there are countries and communities where income poverty, conflict situations, rurality, or distance increase these existing gender gaps.[2]

Equality means that both the husband and wife have equal rights to make choices in their lives.

—Urban woman, Fiji

[Equality for my daughter allows her] to have power, an education, and … more opportunities.

—Rural woman, Peru

Map I.1 Economies Included in the Qualitative Assessment of Gender Differences

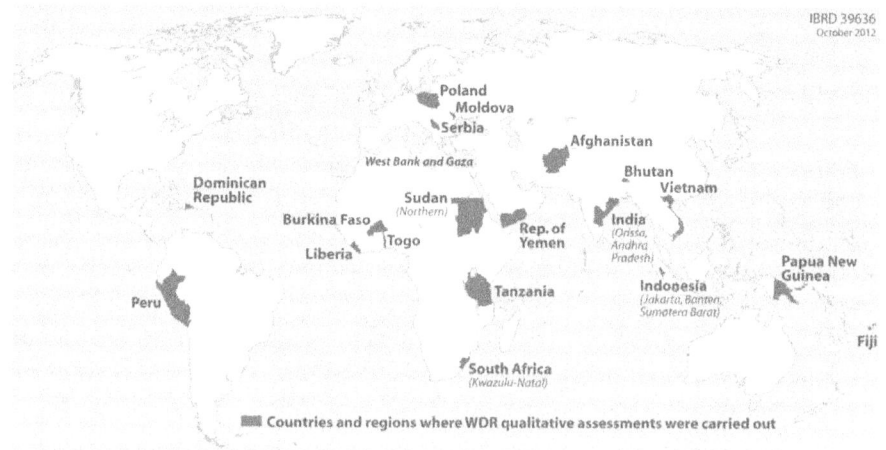

Source: World Bank.

Our study findings reveal that behind the progress toward gender equality and persistent gender gaps lies an almost universal set of factors embedded in social and gender norms, as heard in the experiences related by focus group participants. Women's and men's opportunities and actions are determined as much by social norms—including gender roles and beliefs about their abilities and capacities—as by the conditions of the communities and countries they live in.

The narratives from the sample communities show many commonalities across countries and cultures in how gender differences define women's and men's roles and dictate responsibilities in households, markets, and public life in their communities. They also reveal how innumerable social and cultural norms, traditions, beliefs, and general perceptions of the appropriate place and behavior for women and men permeate all aspects of community and individual life. These informal institutions (so named in *World Development Report 2012*) interlock with civic institutions, the institutions of the state, the market, and intrahousehold bargaining dynamics to shape and sometimes reinforce the gender inequities of power—*and* impact the choices and freedom of women and girls (and men and boys).

On Norms and Agency • http://dx.doi.org/10.1596/978-0-8213-9862-3

Social norms play a central role in the relation between people's agency and the opportunities that their communities provide. Social norms can either help or hinder an individual's capacity to take advantage of available opportunities. Certain ideas or images that reflect ideal behaviors for men and women are remarkably similar across countries and locations within countries. Adolescents participating in the study reported little variation in the different tasks and behaviors demanded in order to be seen as a "good girl" or "good boy"—whether they live in a remote highlands village in Papua New Guinea or in a busy city in the Dominican Republic. Likewise, adult views of a "good wife" or a "good husband" reiterate a clear distinction between productive and reproductive gender roles, as well as expected feminine or masculine behaviors (loving and caring versus having authority and providing well).

Yet everyday practices also include different forms of resistance to—and flexibility about—ideal gender roles. Negotiation and resistance to gender norms are evident throughout the study sample. Inasmuch as they imply a challenge to the sexual division of power, departures from the norm can sometimes be harshly punished. Among the consequences of conflict over gender roles or norm abiding, the most disempowering one is violence against women.

The change in women's ability to participate and have a voice in strategic life choices, especially in education and reproduction, is reflected both in women's achievements and in their aspirations. Education, employment, and family formation are the primary areas where women see their agency and ability to decide expanding. The autonomy of young girls and boys appears to be greater than in previous generations, and their ambitions differ from current practices in their communities, from age at marriage to number of children to level of schooling. But it is among girls and young women where these changes are most evident.

Increased agency allows women to move from enduring complete compliance with constraining and unequal gender norms, to questioning those norms in the face of potential opportunities, to changing their aspirations, as well as their ability to seek and achieve desired outcomes. While women have increased their perceived empowerment and freedom in many countries, more so than men, this change does not always alter constraining norms.

Inequalities derived from gender norms and lack of capacity to decide (agency) affect perceptions of power and freedom. The main pathways to increased perception of empowerment that we can identify from the focus group narratives combine control over material and personal life conditions with a favorable structure of opportunities. While these are equally relevant to men and women, men depend largely on the economic conditions of their communities to feel empowered, more so than women.

In a more enabling environment, which not only creates more opportunities but also changes the individual's capacity to aspire to access them, normative change is more likely. For example, women's economic participation has the potential to alter traditional definitions of gender roles, duties, and responsibilities, but it can also change the main components of both men's and women's identities.

On Norms and Agency • http://dx.doi.org/10.1596/978-0-8213-9862-3

The Study Approach

This study is based on the assumption that gender equality is a development objective in its own right as much as it is instrumental to the achievement of such development. Following Amartya Sen's (2002) notion of development as expanding freedoms equally for all people, our study assumes that the freedom to pursue a life of one's own choosing is a key component of development. In other words, we see development as connected to the freedom to enjoy a genuine set of opportunities and choices. In a similar vein, Nussbaum (1999) frames the challenge for development around liberty, but also notes that skewed preferences due to persistent gender inequalities impact girls' and women's liberty. Particularly in poor countries, this shows up in the gap between formal rights and the absence of basic material conditions necessary to realize those rights.[3] The intrinsic value of gender equality lies in increasing both women's and men's choices, autonomy, and self-efficacy, as well as their exercise and use of equal rights.

The instrumental value of gender equality—the benefits that a more equal society obtains in terms of the productivity, inclusive institutions, and well-being of future generations, among others—is rigorously explored in *World Development Report 2012*. Empowering women does indeed provide benefits for the well-being of societies. However, as Duflo (2011) notes, the relationship between economic development and women's empowerment is not always a virtuous one. Empowering women does indeed change society's and households' choices in ways that are beneficial for their members, but not in all cases: it is not always women who make the best decisions for long-term development.

If we think of gender equality as a result of gains in three dimensions—endowments, economic opportunities, and agency—then this equality is largely dependent on the interactions between four institutions: households, formal state institutions, markets, and informal institutions. Following a graphic representation of this conceptual framework from *World Development Report 2012* (figure I.1), our study zooms in on the specific interactions between social norms and agency with a focus on the household.

Women's agency, while a central element of gender equality, is an area where more research is needed and where less information is available. Several studies have been conducted on empowerment and on some agency components, but many questions remain.[4] The analysis in our report seeks to contribute to this body of literature by looking at agency and social norms together. Of all factors driving gender inequalities, these two seem to be the most elusive in helping direct policy interventions and measurement. Our findings align with Kabeer (2001) and the difficulties that appear when attempting to measure agency. First, it is not sufficient to learn about women's ability to make choices without looking at the extent their agency is reflected in their life choices and the conditions under which they exercise their agency. Second, context matters: without looking at context, it is not possible to assess the extent their agency has increased or not. The need to focus on context makes cross-country analysis more difficult. Finally,

Figure I.1 *World Development Report 2012* Analytical Framework

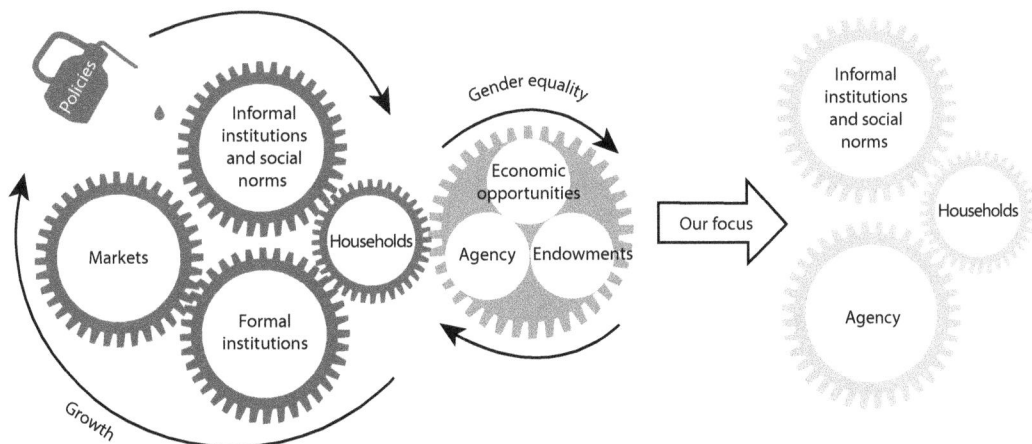

Source: Adapted from World Bank 2012, 9.

changes in agency are not clear predictors of processes of normative change if the structures of opportunities and constraints are not taken into account.

This study deals with these difficulties within the scope allowed by its cross-country sample and methodology. As presented in more detail later, we provide a foundation for a systematic exploration of agency by looking at the structures of constraint, or the norms that underpin gender inequalities, and the negotiations that surround these norms (part I). We also look at different life choices where changes in the capacity to decide are reflected (part II). And finally, we attempt to offer a more dynamic and complete view of the process and determinants of changes in power and agency, as they are perceived by individuals within their specific community setting (part III).

By exploring how gender norms and roles shape women's (and men's) agency and empowerment, their decision-making at critical junctures in their lives, their perceived ability to gain power, and their economic opportunities, new entry points for policy design can be found, as well as ways to recraft existing development policies to become more effective and better serve women's needs. The common patterns we found across countries have important implications for policy design and action.

Methodology of the Study

Our study assesses qualitatively the dynamics of gender norms and agency in the construction of gender equality. The research was designed to capture men's and women's perspectives and their own accounts of how they experience gender differences in their households and communities.

The methodology we chose builds directly on two major global studies at the World Bank, *Voices of the Poor* (Narayan, Patel, *et al.* 2000; Narayan, Chambers, *et al.* 2000; Narayan and Petesch 2002) and *Moving Out of Poverty*

(Narayan and Petesch 2007, 2010; Narayan, Pritchett, and Kapoor 2009; Narayan 2009; Narayan and Petesch 2010). These works apply primarily qualitative techniques, such as focus groups and individual interviews, to examine questions of poverty and how people move out of poverty across diverse contexts in the developing world. A guiding principle for these studies, as with this one, is the focus on learning inductively from local individuals' experiences and interpretations of their own reality. We wanted to work from a vantage point that gives primacy to local people's own perceptions and interpretations of their experiences. For this study, we aimed to capture local narratives of different situations where gender differences come into play without imposing pre-conceived concepts and models.

The research was conducted in 20 different countries, using the same data collection instruments and the same set of questions for all cases, which permitted a multi-country assessment of similarities, trends, and patterns. A set of research instruments was developed including three focus group interview guides—one for each of the three different age groups included in the study, as well as a separate questionnaire for the key informant in each community; the same set of instruments was used in all countries to ensure comparability.[5] Changes to adapt language or make additions that were more appropriate for local conditions were discussed between the local and global research teams to ensure that comparability was respected. The research strategy was flexible enough to capture bottom-up data from very different places and also to provide a reasonably adequate means for comparative analysis of the large volume of data collected.[6] The data collected was transcribed into text documents following a template provided by the global team and analyzed by a mix of techniques, including coding and interpretative analysis. To ensure validity, we verified conclusions (as suggested by Miles and Huberman 1994) and cross-checked them with the national reports by the local teams. However, it is important to note that this is, first and foremost, a subjective exploration; the samples are small and not statistically representative of each country or region.

We chose 97 communities in the 20 countries to contribute to a unique dataset made up of men's and women's focus groups with three different age groups (more than 500 focus groups), pulled from remote mountain top villages in Bhutan to refugee camps in Sudan to urban neighborhoods in Vietnam and Poland (see table I.1). Sample countries were chosen opportunistically from all world regions and, when possible, from different realities within each region.[7] However, the identification of the sample was also dependent on the availability of local research teams, funding, and time constraints determined by the production cycle of *World Development Report 2012*.

The local research teams in each study country consisted of lead researchers with extensive country knowledge and qualitative field experience, plus experienced focus group facilitators who received training and followed a detailed methodology guide to conduct the fieldwork. In each country, the research teams identified the communities to survey, following the study guidelines, which included sampling communities from rural and urban areas and from different

Table I.1 Qualitative Assessment Sample

Economy	Communities	Focus groups				Total no. of individuals (est. 8 per group)	In-depth cases
		Adults	Young adults	Adolescents	Total		
Afghanistan	4	8	8	n.a.	16	128	8
Bhutan	4	8	8	8	24	192	4
Burkina Faso	4	8	8	8	24	192	4
Dominican Republic	4	8	8	8	24	192	4
Fiji	6	12	12	12	36	288	6
India	8	16	16	16	48	384	8
Indonesia	4	8	8	n.a.	16	128	14
Liberia	9	18	18	n.a.	36	288	12
Moldova	4	8	8	n.a.	16	128	4
Papua New Guinea	6	12	12	n.a.	24	192	6
Peru	4	8	8	n.a.	16	128	5
Poland	4	8	8	n.a.	16	128	4
Serbia	5	10	10	n.a.	20	160	4
South Africa	4	8	8	n.a.	16	128	4
Sudan	5	10	10	10	30	240	4
Tanzania	4	8	8	n.a.	16	128	4
Togo	4	8	8	8	24	192	4
Vietnam	4	8	8	n.a.	16	128	4
West Bank and Gaza	6	12	12	12	36	288	6
Yemen, Rep.	4	8	8	8	24	192	4
Total	97	194	194	90	478	3,824	113

Note: n.a. = not applicable.

socioeconomic situations, and representing, when possible, different realities within the country (see the appendix). The teams were asked to sample a minimum of four communities to capture a better-off and poorer urban community, and a better-off and poorer rural community, which we hypothesized would provide a range of experiences that reflected the average situation of the country. In some countries, this was done based on household survey data; in others, it was based on representation of different country regions. The choices of regions and geographic areas were discussed with the global team, and the sampling selection was approved to ensure consistency with the global sample.

Within the communities, five different data collection tools were used: three structured focus group discussions, a key informant interview in the form of a community questionnaire with closed and open-ended questions, and a mini case study (see table I.2). The three focus groups were structured by age: adolescents (12–17 years), young adults (18–24 years), and adults (25–60 years). Each age group was then divided into men's and women's groups. Field teams also received instructions to construct the groups, as much as possible, to reflect the range of educational and livelihood experiences common for each age group in the community. The research teams invited individuals to participate in the exercise through household visits, postings, and information given to community leaders among others.

Table I.2 Summary of Methodology

Data collection method	Themes	Respondents
Community questionnaire	Information on local context and changes in the structure of opportunities.	1–2 key informants

Focus group discussion with young adults	• Happiness
	• Daily time use (included hourly time use reporting by 3–5 focus group participants)
	• Decisions: transitions from school to work and family formation
	  – Independence, cooperation, and obligations in economic decision-making processes
	  – Divorce, family dispute resolution mechanisms
	  – Local economic opportunities
	  – Savings practices
	  – Community participation
	  – Knowledge of gender-related rights
	• Role models
	• Hopes for the future
		2 groups (ages 18–24):
		• 8–12 young adult women
		• 8–12 young adult men

Focus group discussion with adults	• Happiness • Differences in the exercise of power and freedom, with a focus on economic decisions (via exercise creating a "ladder of power and freedom") • Local economic opportunities • Independence, cooperation, and obligations in economic decision-making processes • Divorce, family-dispute resolution mechanisms • Sources of economic support • Household gender relations • General patterns of domestic and community violence • Hopes for the future	2 groups (ages 25–60): • 8–12 women • 8–12 men
Focus group discussion with adolescents	• Happiness • Daily time use • Value of education • Aspirations for the future • Local economic opportunities • Savings, assets, and control of assets • Formation of families • Norms surrounding adolescent girls and boys • Domestic violence and public safety • Social networks	2 groups (ages 12–17): • 8–12 adolescent girls • 8–12 adolescent boys
Mini case study	Detailed story of a finding that emerges as important for understanding gender norms or structures shaping economic decisions in that locality	1–2 key informants

Prior to initiating the focus groups, facilitators interviewed local key informants, identified during earlier community visits by asking local authorities and people from the community. These informants completed a community questionnaire to provide extensive background information about the sample communities. A key informant might be a community leader, government official, politician, important local employer, business or financial leader, teacher, or healthcare worker. At the end of their time in the communities, the research teams also collected "mini case studies" which were unstructured interviews with a focus group participant or someone else in the community who might understand the gender gains or inequalities in the community. Local teams were free to choose their case studies based on their knowledge of the community and the country.

Each focus group, organized by sex and age, met separately. While the focus groups of young adults and adults were conducted in all 20 countries, only a sub-sample of nine countries included focus groups with adolescents. Focus groups discussed a wide range of topics, including reasons for happiness and favorite free-time activities; decisions surrounding when to leave school, where to work, and family formation; and gender differences in accumulating savings and controlling major assets. Questions also explored issues of domestic violence, public safety, and women's physical mobility. One research module charted how young adult women and men spend their days, and another explored different levels of power and freedom that adult women or men might have in their communities. Some questions were posed to all three age groups; others were specific to one group. Table I.2 summarizes the main topics that were addressed to the different groups. Each topic was covered by a set of questions and exercises.

In order to limit bias, which can be introduced by focus group dynamics, facilitators received training in additional measures to foster inclusive discussions that would capture a range of attitudes and experiences common in the specific communities. For some key questions, for instance, focus group members had opportunities to respond by "voting" in private and then volunteering to discuss their responses.

We designed the study methodology to account for the dynamics of gender relations and social norms in the study communities. Understanding that gender norms influence everyone's behaviors as much as their expectations about how the opposite sex behaves, we kept groups separated by sex. Likewise, different age groups were assessed separately to account for generational differences and avoid power imbalances. We hoped to give all participants a safe environment where they felt free to express their thoughts and interact openly about life situations that they may not normally reflect upon.[8] For example, when we asked women in Afghanistan to describe their preferences and interests regarding marriage or childbearing decisions, the research format first captured their initial accounts. Then discussion leaders posed further questions to encourage them to probe beneath the face value of their accounts—for instance, from a power perspective—so that they could begin to identify the set of values and other norms affecting their decisions. In many cases, what was accepted as the "norm" was far from what the women desired or what they considered right. Focus group participants were also invited to corroborate or refute each other's views.

In order to move beyond a static view, or a single moment in time, and capture dynamics of change, all groups were asked at different stages to compare conditions today on key study topics with conditions 10 years ago or between the current and previous generations. They also reported on their aspirations for their own future and the future of their children.

The study findings reflect the range of norms possible in the 20 countries rather than the average situation in each individual country case. However, the global findings of the research are more telling and consistent, which in many areas can be extended to other settings. The consistency of the descriptions of gender norms and associated behaviors, and the relationship between norms and agency, and how these elements interact to generate opportunities or limit equality between men and women in the communities studied, shed light on similar inequalities in other contexts and the processes behind them.

Parallel to quantitative analysis of gender dimensions in development, the insights derived from qualitative methods expand the information available on questions related to norms and to intrahousehold and community-level dynamics. In particular, contextual factors and their interactions with the deeper influences of power relations and norms on women's and men's decisions are difficult topics for even well-designed household surveys to explore effectively. Yet, the scarcity of information on the role of these complex factors limits our understanding of these issues and possible levers for policy action. This is the area where we see our research contributing the most.

Discussing and Researching Gender Equality: A Brief Introduction to the Primary Study Concepts

Throughout this report, certain concepts—social norms, agency, empowerment, and structure of opportunities, among others—appear over and over. We explore their interrelation by using the voices of the participants in the study as they reflect on the contexts and realities of their different communities. However, there is not only one way to understand these concepts. We briefly review different views of norms, agency, and power, and the reasons gender norms have such a decisive hold on women, men, and the societies where they live.

The powerful influence of gender norms on an individual's actions—a central area of concern in gender research—is one of the foundations of gender inequality. As Ridgeway (2009) notes, gender is a core frame for organizing social relations and, as such, it depends on common knowledge (i.e., cultural knowledge) that guides and coordinates individuals' actions in a given situation. But these frameworks deem women and men unequal, based on their perceived differences.

Inequality is a feature of all societies, whether it is unequal power, opportunities, outcomes, or justice. Most societies have structures and institutions whose role is to preserve the prevalent social order or organizing framework. Gender inequality is no exception. The inequalities that arise from the different roles played by women and men, the unequal power relationships between them, and the consequences of this inequality on their lives are visible in all societies. The problem is that these inequalities all too frequently pose disadvantages to women. Women face consistent differences between their opportunities and outcomes and the opportunities and outcomes of men.

The point of departure for gender inequality is our biological difference, which is visible and in most cases easily distinguishable. But it is less easy to find a cut-off point between the biological and the social distinction as a basis for gender inequality. Benhabib *et al.* (1995) rightly notes that, while equality of condition seems to be the ideal, in many societies today, the more equal conditions are, the less explanation there is for the remaining differences—to the point that inequality may end up being mistaken and merged with innate or natural qualities of men or women.[9] Preferences, needs, and constraints can differ systematically between men and women, and this may reflect both biological sexual factors and learned gender behaviors (see box I.1).

Box I.1 It's Not Sex, It's Gender: From Biology to Learned Behaviors

Researchers disagree on where gender differences come from. The observable differences between men and women, in areas such as risk aversion, trust, leadership, moral behavior, attitudes about competition, and compassion, have been attributed to biological factors, learned preferences and behaviors, and consistent differences in opportunities.[a]

Opportunities have not been equally distributed among women and men. For example, the fact that girls have achieved so much progress in education is as much a shift in the distribution of opportunities as a change in society's view of what women and men are capable of doing. Most societies at different stages have resisted educating women. For some, educating women was not "natural": the reasons have ranged from ideas that women's nature does not include the ability to learn and that women do not need education to secure their future, to the idea that there is no need for incentives for educating women. Teaching women to read and write was considered wrong because "a learned lady threatened male pride."[b] But today, most societies agree on the value of education for both girls and boys.

In school, differences in performance between girls and boys have been explained by differences in their cognitive abilities, in forms of learning, in their aspirations, in their views on the value of education, and in teacher performance, among others.[c] For example, Hoff and Pandey (2006) look at how learned discrimination, in their study of Indian students of different castes, may affect performance on tests when caste is made salient, vis-à-vis when it is not. The authors find that when caste is identified or emphasized in a given setting or situation, low-caste students perform worse, reproducing the caste gap and hierarchy. Similar studies, where race, ethnic background, and gender have been used to trigger an expected response in an experimental setting, show similar results.[d]

Gender equality, even if for the benefit of everyone's well-being, challenges the social foundation of inequality, as well as its "natural"—or biological—foundation. In the case of education, it not only contradicts the notion of who has the right to education but also challenges ideas of who can join the qualified labor force (which now includes men and women) and what constitutes women's and men's appropriate place in society.

a. Gender differences have been analyzed experimentally in different areas of economics and under very different settings. Recent reviews of this literature include Ergun, Garcia-Munoz, and Rivas (2012); Croson and Gneezy (2009); and Eckel and Grossman (2008). Lippa (2005) provides a good summary of findings from the psychological and behavioral studies field.
b. Labalme (1980, 4).
c. The Young Lives study (Dercon 2011) shows that parents have different aspirations for their children's educations than their children, and that the parents' aspirations are transmitted and adopted by children. *World Development Report 2012* cites the example of some English subject textbooks, currently in use in Australia and Hong Kong SAR, China, that tend to depict women in a limited range of social roles and present stereotyped images of women as weaker and operating primarily in domestic domains, and that may impact girls' aspirations.
d. Among others, see Steele and Aronson (1995); Shih, Pittinsky, and Ambady (1999); and Krendl *et al.* (2008).

Learned gender attributes make up gender identity and determine gender roles; they also may be valued differently, generating a power imbalance. These "gender systems" (Ridgeway and Correll 2004; Ridgeway and Smith-Lovin 1999), where gender is seen as an institutionalized system of social practices and organized social relations of inequality, are based on the different attributes associated with our biological differences. Gender systems are embedded in all societal institutions, from formal legal frameworks (such as family law or labor regulations) to religions and traditional culture. Through these systems, femininity and masculinity—the roles and patterns of behavior deemed appropriate for women and men—are constructed and defined.[10] They define the norm.

Power, Empowerment, and Agency

Power in its different expressions has always been behind gender inequalities. In fact, empowerment and agency are not only highly relevant to gender research but are essential to the questions we posed during the field work. Inasmuch as no social system exists without some divisions by gender, gender is co-substantial to the structure of power in all its forms (Caramazza and Vianello 2005):

- Power over, or *domination*, the ability to influence someone else's actions and thus determine their interests and preferences (Lukes 1974)
- Power to, or *agency*, people's enduring capacity to act (Isaac 1987; Sen 1985)
- Power with, or *solidarity*, and power within, or *consciousness* (Ibrahim and Alkire 2007; Rowlands 1997)[11]

While we saw all these different forms in the research, our focus is on power as agency and, as such, as the capacity to act to achieve desired objectives.

Our intent is to reveal men's and women's accounts of their gains in autonomy as gains in power, capacity, and potential to act, even when actions fail or are never taken. Power is not only the ability to *make* people do what they would not otherwise do but also the ability to *enable* people to do what they could not otherwise do (Hartsock 1996). It is this positive, creative notion of power that we aimed to capture in the focus groups, as well as what we stress in our analysis: a view of power as agency with individuals gaining the ability to act and decide.

Before proceeding further, it is important to visit the related elements of empowerment, agency, and opportunity structure. Probably the term most associated with gender equality is **empowerment,** *the expansion of freedom of choice and action as a result of a process of gaining power* (Narayan 2002; Narayan and Petesch 2005). It refers to the process of gaining control over resources—material and non-material—in order for individuals to gain the capacity to exercise the right to determine their own choices. Empowerment also refers to the way individuals acquire the ability to influence change in their lives (Moser 1989), and are able to take advantage of opportunities. Empowerment's departing point is a condition of disempowerment or the inability to exercise any influence.

Hence, empowerment is contingent on agency as much as it is on available resources and opportunities. In other words, it is the expansion of agency

(Ibrahim and Alkire 2007; Kabeer 2001) or the expansion of people's ability to make strategic life decisions in a context where this was previously denied to them. As with many other concepts, there is no single definition of empowerment. Ibrahim and Alkire (2007) identified over 30 different definitions of empowerment in the literature and a number of approaches to measuring it empirically.

With a development approach, **agency** *as the expansion of an individual's own power and freedom* is strongly linked to the capabilities approach.[12] According to Sen (2002), agency is part of a person's development freedoms, where one is able to choose how to use entitlements in pursuit of self-determined goals.[13] Agency, together with opportunities, is central to development. Alkire (2009) adds agency's constructive role in the creation of values and norms to its intrinsic and instrumental relevance. And Nussbaum (1998, 1999), who looks more at legal frameworks and rights, specifically addresses the gender dimensions of agency. Nussbaum argues that women's agency is different from men's due to unequal social and political circumstances that give women unequal capabilities. For Kabeer (2001), agency is a dimension of empowerment, together with resources and achievements, without which the process of women's empowerment is not possible. Agency thus is the ability to make one's own choices and act upon them.

Whether agency is seen as the ability to formulate strategic life choices or the ability to control the resources that come to bear, its relation to empowerment and decision-making (as the capacity to act and bring about change) is clear.[14] Benhabib *et al.* (1995) and Fraser (1997) include in their definitions of agency the subjective capacity for choice and also the capacity for self-determination, where women—and men—get to play an active role in the formation of their identity and do not passively absorb external determinations or constraints. As such, agency turns subjects into autonomous, purposive actors, capable of choice and self-definition, able (to attempt) to become the individual they have chosen to be through the actions that express it (Lister 1997).

Autonomy and agency are inter-related. As a necessary condition for any action, autonomy allows individuals to question the social norms, rules, and practices impacting their choices; to reflect upon these rules; and, if needed, to take action to change them (Doyal and Gough 1991; Dworkin 1988).[15] Self-efficacy, or people's belief in their ability to mobilize available resources—human, material, or social—to make their choices a reality, is autonomy, which is an essential component of agency.

Agency without access to resources is a somewhat passive capacity. As van Staveren (2013, 1) notes, "agency without resources is rather meaningless when being able to make one's own choices and having the self-confidence to do so are not matched by any real opportunities to choose from (Alkire 2002; Robeyns 2003)." **Opportunity structures**—by which we mean *resources, institutions, established processes (traditions, moral codes, gender norms), and other enabling factors*—foster the empowerment process and are necessary to create an enabling context for agency to manifest (Alsop, Bertelsen, and Holland 2006; Narayan 2005).

Formal and informal rules, state and local institutions, the market, and civil society are elements of the social structures within which choice takes place. As the context for action, the structure of opportunities for gender equality is where agency can be realized (Kabeer 2001).

Because of their characteristics, agency and empowerment are more difficult to measure than the structural factors that determine them. Research tends to focus on the opportunity structure or the prerequisites for agency (such as literacy, access to information, access to land, rights, etc., which are also opportunity structures), instead of the components of agency itself (Alkire 2009). The problem is that these prerequisites do not always translate into agency nor are they the same for all individuals.[16] Alsop (2005) argues for going beyond the mere existence of an opportunity, for a research focus on the necessary conditions of agency:[17]

• Existence of choice: whether an opportunity to make a choice exists
• Use of choice: whether a person or group actually uses the opportunity to choose
• Achievement of choice: whether the choice brings about the desired result

World Development Report 2012 opts for exploring different manifestations of agency (or lack of it), where decision-making by women can be identified,[18] similar to many of the studies surveyed by Kabeer (2001).

In our study, we attempt to look at agency and gender inequality in agency. For men and women, agency differs: they have different degrees of empowerment, different sets of choices, different opportunities, different capacities to exercise their choices, and different levels of achievement of chosen outcomes. This disparity in agency usually plays to women's disadvantage. Hence, we want to understand "inequality of agency" and its central role in perpetuating gender inequality (Rao and Walton 2004). To do this, we tried to look at agency from three angles: *the ability to act, self-efficacy or the belief that acting is possible, and the ability to control the resources to make a choice possible.*

Gender Inequality in Agency

We designed the fieldwork methods to capture different manifestations of gender inequality in agency. First, we looked at decision-making processes in households as expressions of agency and autonomy in strategic life decisions, such as marriage, childbearing, education, and job choices. Second, we assessed the dynamics of changes in perceptions of power and freedom, as accounted by men and women in the 97 sample communities, and the many dimensions they identified. Third, we looked for the necessary conditions or factors determining the ability of women to feel empowered: education, aspirations, income, lack of threat of violence, and more. We do not try to cover everything, but attempt to show how interconnected agency and empowerment are with social norms around gender, the structure of opportunities, and the community contexts of the study participants.

On Norms and Agency • http://dx.doi.org/10.1596/978-0-8213-9862-3

In the same vein, the opportunities presented in the different communities are not equally distributed or open to both sexes. In fact, a community's opportunity structure may include elements that reproduce gender inequality or women's subordination, as noted by Sen and Grown (1987), Elson (1999), and Nussbaum (2000). For the purpose of our analysis, the structure of opportunities is comprised of the formal and informal institutions, the market, and the household. For analytical purposes, social norms—normally part of the overall structure of opportunities—is treated separately to better acknowledge their role in promoting or restraining agency.

The background conditions of society governing women and men vary. Not all societies are the same, nor are the economic, cultural, social, political, religious, security, and other conditions of the 20 countries visited in the study. Within each country, communities are highly heterogeneous. Local conditions matter; they have an impact on women's choices and preferences. Women and men constantly adapt their choices to what is happening around them. If the context does not provide fair conditions for action, this inequality is registered by households and individuals, and shapes their preferences in ways that may be detrimental (particularly women).

These "adaptive preferences" have an impact on agency. What you do not see, you do not know and you cannot aspire to. For example, many of the women we interviewed reported a preference for flexible work arrangements, such as part-time work, informal sector or nonregulated work, and self-employment. It is worth asking, and we do so, if such preferences are shaped by women's prescribed (gender) role as mothers and the opportunities available for working mothers provided by local markets. Some women have the perception that the employers prefer workers without care responsibilities; others do not have public provision of childcare in their communities. And still others do not have the qualifications to get a job.

This is an example of the material and contextual preconditions to agency, in whose absence there is no real exercise of agency, merely a simulacrum of choice (Nussbaum 2006). This adaptation may lead to an inequality trap, where women's muted preferences affect their *capacity to aspire* (Appadurai 2004). In the long run, it reduces their agency because of a context that affects their ability to see the pathway to achieve their desired goals.

Creating and Enforcing Gender through Norms, Roles, and Beliefs

So how can we understand gender constructions of individuals and the strong hold of social norms on our behaviors and beliefs? Social norms are difficult to measure. If they appear as clear and concrete directives for actions, deriving from a given society's values, they are easily captured in laws and formal rules. If they refer to informal, implicit rules that govern what a person can and cannot do in the pursuit of daily life, they are more elusive (Fehr and Gachter 2000; Hechter and Opp 2001; Portes 2006). Regardless of their form, compliance with the norms—and sanctions for breaking them—are to be expected.

On Norms and Agency • http://dx.doi.org/10.1596/978-0-8213-9862-3

Norms around gender stem from a society's ideals and values of what it means to be a woman or a man. Failure to conform to these dictates can trigger strong social sanctions, such as ridiculing men for being emotional or scorning women who dress inappropriately. These norms include everything from cultural beliefs to expected behaviors and practices. Gender norms, in particular, have not changed greatly partly because they are widely held and practiced in daily life, because they often represent the interests of power holders, and because they instill unconscious learned biases about gender differences that make it easier to conform to long-standing norms than to new ones.[19]

Social norms of gender are in constant dialogue with women's agency and may determine women's capacity to act. As such, they operate as social determinants that interact with an individual's will in the form of a belief system around women and men. It is with this understanding that we observed social norms in the data collected in the 20 countries, as they appeared over and over again in women's and men's accounts of their daily lives in their communities.

Norms and Roles

For the purpose of this study, the main characteristics that define *social norms* are the following: (a) They regulate individual behavior in a society. (b) They specifically prescribe what behavior is expected and what is not allowed in specific circumstances. (c) They tell a person what to believe others expect of her behavior and tell others what to expect from that person. (d) There is an expected agreement, or belief that the agreement exists, on the content of the norm and an enforcement of such agreement or belief by whoever holds power.

Social norms are powerful forces; they are *prescriptions or dictates reflected in the formal structures of society, in its informal rules; its gender role divisions; and permeating beliefs, attitudes, and behaviors.* They hold power via emotional control (Elster 1989), social expectations (Bicchieri 2006), and prescription (Akerlof and Kranton 2000), as well as internal commitment (Alexander 2003). In many cases, particularly with gender norms, the joint presence of at least two of these forces makes the norm more binding. As Bicchieri (2006) suggests, individuals prefer to conform to the norm due to the belief that other people will also conform, to the point that a collective agreement is created between normative beliefs and behavior.[20] How people believe they should behave, what their behavior is, and how society expects them to behave are all faces of the same system that enforces a norm.

Although being a mother, a husband, or a student can be performed differently by different people, specific behaviors are associated with each. We expect mothers to care for their children and students to attend school and take exams. These behavioral regularities are what make them social roles.

Gender roles are part of these expected behaviors and, particularly, are sex-typed behaviors (Eagly, Beall, and Sternberg 2004). Gender-ascribed roles define the ideal expected behaviors for men and women in any position they occupy in society or in any activity, overlapping with other expected role behavior. In other words, gender roles define what is deemed appropriate for women and men, and define what attributes men and women should have and display in any situation. As such, gender roles are norms that women and men comply with all the time, whether in the household or on the street, in private or in public. They permeate daily life and are the basis of self-regulation, hence affecting individual agency.

The constant presence of gender as a backdrop to all other roles makes gender roles unlike others. Gender has no specific site and it is not constrained to a physical space, such as a household. Gender is constructed in relation to the opposite sex's attributes; as men and women are always present in society, so is gender. This is understood as "doing gender" (West and Zimmerman 1987; West and Fenstermaker 1995). Doing gender means being permanently accountable to what is expected that men and women will do—basically replicating and reproducing the markers of what is considered the essential differences between the sexes.

Reinforcing Norms

If gender differences are translated into gender inequalities, the constant reinforcement of these differences (when we "do gender") may lead to accepting these inequalities as the norm. If women have more disadvantages with respect to men, they will reproduce them to the point that both women and men believe that such disadvantages are not only normal but how things should be. And even when women's opportunities and resources change—women earn income, acquire assets, etc.—the belief may not change or may change more slowly (Ridgeway 1997). The beliefs that underpin these norms may even persist by adapting to new conditions.

Part of the explanation for why these beliefs are so entrenched comes from learning what it is to be a girl or a boy, or a man or a woman, from very early in life.[21] We learn the rules of the game and we then continuously reproduce them, almost as if we were following an "ethics" of gender behavior that controls our self-judging processes, as well as our awareness of judgment by others.[22]

Supporting the acquisition of gender norms is a process of social punishments for transgressing the norms. While in some cases this policing takes the form of social sanctions, such as bullying, social ostracism, and even violence, there are also more subtle strategies operating over everyone. Parents and schoolteachers, for example, perceive future disadvantages and emphasize compensating behaviors, such as teaching girls to find good husbands or boys to behave in a more masculine fashion. Adolescent girls rapidly learn the limits, such as intuiting norms about their newly developed bodies and experimenting with new ways to walk, sit, or dress. And adult women negotiate daily with different sanctions and expected behaviors.

Social norms are enforced via different mechanisms, such as coercion, overt punishment, institutional methods of control (e.g., the police), the power of the media, and more covert expectations and rules transmitted in everyday interactions. Among the covert are two powerful concepts: the normal and the deviant. Deviant is any behavior that threatens expectations and norms of individual behavior or that may challenge power. Ideas about what is normal and what is deviant are constructed by those who have the power to impose their views and have them accepted.

Gender inequality has prevented women from participating in key domains of society that define and generate the rules and definition of what is normal. The notion of the normal has been monopolized by men. The overall societal norm is male; moreover, it is a particular sort of masculinity ("hegemonic" as Connell [1987] terms it)[23] that is regarded as normal. For example, in the labor market, the "ideal" employee is free from the time constraints of running a home and caring for children. The definition of a "normal" employee enables the reproduction of gender inequality. Furthermore, this ideal is reproduced in labor codes, which established the 8-hour working day, the notion of a "family wage," and more.

Changing Norms

But there are also challenges to the norms, and norms bend, relax, evolve, and change. The communities in our research show that what was improbable 10 years ago is now possible—men help with housework and take care of children, women work for pay and manage their own money. Rather than "undoing gender" (as suggested by Butler [2004] and Deutsch [2007]), it seems that change has come through modifications in the normative frameworks associated with gender. The powerful grip of gender norms rests upon other social norms that organize society and help us live together. The collective ability to articulate alternative, oppositional norms is part of the agency of the individuals inhabiting society.

Norms are negotiated and change through a variety of channels. Ridgeway and Correll (2004) suggest that exposure to counter-stereotypical images, such as a working mother or a female politician, and the delinking of negative associations with these images can change the status of expected behavior to the point that the gender norm varies or becomes irrelevant. Our analysis explores the appearance of conflicting norms, for example, that arise from different role demands, social and technological changes that affect the cost-benefit balance of enforcing the norm, and willingness of media or information outlets (Chong, Duryea, and La Ferrara 2008; Jensen and Oster 2009) to show that other normative arrangements are possible—which are all means of negotiating norms.

Change can happen when the normative frameworks become less strict, allowing gender differences to be less of a determinant. For example, when governments revise legislation on inheritance rights to allow daughters and sons alike to inherit their parents' property, it not only weakens the social norm that says that male heirs should be given preference but also introduces variability in inheritance practices. Such legislation changes the ownership of assets in society, questions marital practices based on men being the sole land proprietors, includes women in productive decisions over land and property, and goes further.

On Norms and Agency • http://dx.doi.org/10.1596/978-0-8213-9862-3

Our analysis clearly shows how normative frameworks around gender are changing—albeit slowly—and opening space for new practices and producing more opportunities for women and men. However, this change is being contested: backlashes are common and the change is uneven. Movement in one area does not always mean movement in other areas or for everyone.

Overview of Chapters

How do agency and norms work together to increase women's and men's ability to change their lives? What do women and men need to realize the power and freedom to make choices—even when facing material or normative constraints—in their communities? Agency is as much about choice and the power to act as it is about voice. And the decisions that women and men make, their ability to act, and their voices are dependent on both the opportunities and constraints typifying the societies they live in.

Women's preferences are not independent of the social and material environment they inhabit; they are contingent on it, as economists increasingly recognize (Fehr and Hoff 2011). The sample communities in our research showcase different enabling environments in which women make choices, such as different market dynamics and different normative prescriptions on women's actions. For example, to some women in rural and isolated communities or other restricted environments, access to a road is highly strategic and liberating. For other women in a large city with public transportation, a new road may simply be practical and reduce the time or cost of their commute. For both sets of women, however, the road is a route to (gain) power.

But sometimes a road is not enough. Social norms are major factors affecting women's agency (see box I.2 for a glossary of key study terms). Their strength and ability to permeate all areas of individual action make them determinants of the context in which agency can be exercised. Due to the presence of norms, agency is not evenly distributed across spheres of life. The same road that can increase women's opportunities to engage in labor and retail markets—through

---

Box I.2 Quick Glossary

- Agency is the ability to make meaningful choices and act upon them.
- Structure of opportunities means the resources, institutions, established practices (traditions, moral codes, gender norms), and other enabling factors that foster the empowerment process and are necessary for agency to manifest (Alsop, Bertelsen, and Holland 2006; Narayan 2005).
- Social norms, the gender-ascribed formal structures, informal rules, gender role divisions, and permeating beliefs, attitudes and behaviors, are treated as a separate element, although they are a part of the structure of opportunities.

On Norms and Agency • http://dx.doi.org/10.1596/978-0-8213-9862-3

which they can increase their agency—does not always translate directly into a greater voice inside their homes. Variations in agency depend on the strength of the norms and roles that regulate each sphere.

Conversely, even with existing normative frameworks, women are seeing their power surge. They told us in the focus groups that they see themselves gaining power and freedom, more so than the men. And women's gains in economic empowerment are underpinned by more active participation in society, both of which are driving their empowerment.

This report is structured in three sections. Part I focuses on gender norms and the dynamics of negotiation, acceptance, and resistance around them. Chapter 1 sets the stage by synthesizing the range of views on gender roles found in the 20 countries. By focusing on gender ideals—the good wife and the good husband, the good girl and the good boy—the chapter reveals how little variation exists around the world in expected behavior by the sexes. Looking at different generations, however, shows that the slow change that is occurring is due more to relaxation of norms than radical upheaval.

Continuing with prevailing norms, chapter 2 presents different ways in which norms are negotiated and resisted. First, it looks at non-conflictive and negotiated practices, including incipient change to what is deemed possible or tolerable for masculine and feminine behavior. Then, the chapter moves to accepted practices for disciplining behaviors that do not conform to these norms, including domestic violence.

Part II probes how norms interact with agency in strategic life choices. Chapter 3 covers the effects of gender differences in making life-defining decisions that shape young women's and men's futures, such as why adolescent boys or girls decide to leave school and how they choose their first job. It also looks at decisions on family formation against a backdrop of reported expectations and actual practices. The discussion includes the local norms that impinge on each decision, as well as the sense of agency and power to make those decisions in the words of the focus group participants.

Moving more directly into the dynamics of empowerment, part III examines the factors that individuals identify as primarily increasing their power and freedom, as well as the opportunity structures associated with them. Chapter 4 considers the dynamics of empowerment and agency, the dynamics of individual gains in power, and the explanations behind them. It presents evidence that women see gains in their capacities to shape their lives, while men report that they are stagnating or sliding backwards. Chapter 5 looks at the community conditions associated with power loss or gain, particularly markets, formal institutions of representation, family conflict resolution, and legal regulations. The chapter especially considers how market dynamics interact with changing gender norms to shape women's perceptions of empowerment.

The concluding remarks summarize the main findings and outline future areas for research and policy action.

On Norms and Agency • http://dx.doi.org/10.1596/978-0-8213-9862-3

Notes

1. The countries included in our study are Afghanistan, Bhutan, Burkina Faso, the Dominican Republic, Fiji, India, Indonesia, Liberia, Moldova, Papua New Guinea, Peru, Poland, Serbia, South Africa, Sudan, Tanzania, Togo, Vietnam, West Bank and Gaza, and the Republic of Yemen.

2. See *World Development Report 2012: Gender Equality and Development* (World Bank 2012) for more detail and data on these trends.

3. Alkire (2002) makes similar arguments, but from a perspective of gaps in human development rather than lack of rights, and calls attention to the need to assess well-being at the individual and wider collective or societal levels, as well as the capabilities and assets needed for exercising agency.

4. Kabeer (2001), Ibrahim and Alkire (2007), and Samman and Santos (2009) provide surveys of the different studies and perspectives under which they were conducted.

5. The methodological note in the appendix includes more details on the data collection tools, as well as on the analysis techniques used.

6. At the end of the data collection effort, the team had gathered about 7,000 pages of narrative text of transcripts of focus groups and interviews. These data were structured, cleaned, and imported into qualitative analysis software.

7. Based on the World Bank's classification of regions, which includes Latin America and the Caribbean, South Asia, Sub-Saharan Africa, Middle East and North Africa, Europe and Central Asia, and East Asia and Pacific.

8. All research team members participating in each discussion were the same sex as the focus group participants.

9. Arendt's (1979) work on the origins of totalitarianism attributes this change to the appearance of the social sphere, where nothing is private or an object of political debate.

10. For example, gender differences in participation in the labor force may derive from a history of specialization due to our biological differences. As Alesina *et al.* (2010) and Alesina, Giuliano, and Nunn (2011) argue, based on the evolution of labor-intensive agriculture (before mechanization) that required physical strength, which is more common in men than women, women specialized in home production due to their lack of physical strength.

11. Robeyns (2003) also presents a detailed account of all the different approaches to power that have been used in development practice.

12. As defined by Amartya Sen. For an application of the approach to gender inequality, see Robeyns (2003) and Nussbaum (2001).

13. A person's agency freedom, for Sen, should be understood as including the individual's aims, objectives, allegiances, obligations, and—in a broad sense—the person's concept of the good. Also see Sen (1985).

14. Samman and Santos (2009) provide a good survey and summary of these two different positions.

15. Doyal and Gough (1991, 53) define autonomy as "the ability to make informed choices about what should be done and how to go about doing it. This entails being able to formulate aims and beliefs about how to achieve them, along with the ability to evaluate the success of those beliefs in the light of empirical evidence."

16. See also Ibrahim and Alkire (2007) and Kabeer (1999, 2001), who refer to studies that use measures of access to land as an indicator of empowerment. They argue that these types of studies, by focusing only on land ownership or legal capacity to own, forget the pathways by which such access translates into agency and achievements in women's lives.

17. How these three conditions are measured, however, is not clear.

18. The *World Development Report 2012* identifies freedom of movement, fertility control, freedom from domestic violence, and the ability to have a voice in society as the main components of agency. Ibrahim and Alkire (2007) propose certain "exercises of agency" areas with specific sets of indicators, including control over personal decisions, choice in household decision making, domain-specific autonomy, power to change aspects in one's life at the individual level, and power to change aspects in one's life at the community level.

19. See *World Development Report 2012* (World Bank 2012, 174, box 4.7) for an explanation of processes that make social norms very difficult to dislodge, even when the conditions that gave rise to them no longer make objective sense.

20. Bicchieri (2006) defines the expectations that underlie norm compliance as 1) empirical expectations, where individuals believe that a sufficiently large subset of the relevant group or population conforms to the norm in a given situation; 2) normative expectations, where individuals believe that a sufficiently large subset of the relevant group or population expects them to conform to the norm in a given situation; and (3) normative expectations with sanctions, where individuals believe that a sufficiently large subset of the relevant group or population expects them to conform to the norm in a given situation, prefers them to conform, and may sanction behavior.

21. Socialization is the process by which prevailing social and cultural norms of what constitutes appropriate gender behavior is transmitted to children.

22. Following the categories created by Garfinkel (1967), West and Zimmerman (1987) call this process "accountability" of our gender practice. Our everyday behavior, according to Garfinkel, is "accountable" in the sense that it is intelligible and legitimate, and observed as fitting a specific pattern so it doesn't need to be explained to anyone in order to be identified and accepted.

23. Connell (1987) uses the term hegemonic masculinity to describe ways that some forms of masculinity are more culturally exalted and socially dominant than others. "Hegemonic masculinity is constructed in relation to women and to subordinated masculinities. The other masculinities need not be as clearly defined—indeed, achieving hegemony may consist precisely in preventing alternatives gaining cultural definition and recognition as alternatives, confining them to ghettos, to privacy, to unconsciousness" (Connell 1987, 186). Connell also talks of "emphasized femininity" to describe patterns of femininity that have more cultural and ideological support than others. None can be hegemonic in a social context where women are in an overall subordinate position in relation to men—where women are not in the positions of power that enable a definition of femininity in a way that serves women's interests.

References

Akerlof, G., and R. Kranton. 2000. "Economics and Identity." *Quarterly Journal of Economics* 115 (3): 715–53.

Alesina, A. F., Y. Algan, P. Cahuc, and P. Giuliano. 2010. "Family Values and the Regulation of Labor." NBER Working Paper 15747, National Bureau of Economic Research, Cambridge, MA.

Alesina, A. F., P. Giuliano, and N. Nunn. 2011. "On the Origins of Gender Roles: Women and the Plough." NBER Working Paper 17098, National Bureau of Economic Research, Cambridge, MA.

Alexander, J. C. 2003. *The Meanings of Social Life: A Cultural Sociology*. New York: Oxford University Press.

Alkire, S. 2002. "Dimensions of Human Development." *World Development* (30) 2: 181–205.

———. 2009. "Concepts and Measures of Agency." In *Ethics, Welfare, and Measurement*. Vol. 1 of *Arguments for a Better World: Essays in Honor of Amartya Sen*, edited by K. Basu and R. Kanbur, 455–74, Oxford: Oxford University Press.

Alsop, R., ed. 2005. *Power, Rights, and Poverty: Concepts and Connections*. Washington, DC: World Bank.

Alsop, R., M. Bertelsen, and J. Holland, eds. 2006. *Empowerment in Practice: From Analysis to Implementation*. Washington, DC: World Bank.

Appadurai, A. 2004. "The Capacity to Aspire: Culture and Terms of Recognition." In *Culture and Public Action*, ed. V. Rao and M. Walton, 59–84. Stanford, CA: Stanford University Press.

Arendt, H. 1979. *The Origins of Totalitarianism*. San Diego, CA: Harcourt Brace Jovanovich.

Benhabib, S., J. Butler, D. Cornell, and N. Fraser, eds. 1995. *Feminist Contentions: A Philosophical Exchange*. New York: Routledge.

Bicchieri, C., and A. Chavez. 2010. "Behaving as Expected: Public Information and Fairness Norms." *Journal of Behavioral Decision Making* 23 (2): 161–78.

Butler, J. 2004. *Undoing Gender*. New York: Routledge.

Caramazza, E., and M. Vianello. 2005. *Gender, Space, and Power*. London: Free Association Books.

Chong, A., S. Duryea, and E. La Ferrara. 2008. "Soap Operas and Fertility: Evidence from Brazil." CEPR Discussion Paper 6785, Centre for Economic Policy Research, London.

Connell, R. W. 1987. *Gender and Power*. Oxford, U.K.: Polity Press.

Croson, R., and U. Gneezy. 2009. "Gender Differences in Preferences." *Journal of Economic Literature* 47 (2): 1–27.

Dercon, S., and A. Singh. 2011. "From Nutrition to Aspirations and Self-Efficacy: Gender Bias over Time among Children in Four Countries." Working Paper 71, Young Lives Program, Oxford. http://www.younglives.org.uk/files/working-papers/WP71_from-nutrition-to-aspirations-and-self-efficacy.

Deutsch, F. 2007. "Undoing Gender." *Gender and Society* 21: 106–27.

Doyal, L., and Gough, I. 1991. *A Theory of Human Need*. London: Macmillan.

Duflo, E. 2011. "Women's Empowerment and Economic Development." NBER Working Paper 17702, National Bureau of Economic Research, Cambridge, MA.

Dworkin, G. 1988. *The Theory and Practice of Autonomy*. Cambridge, U.K.: Cambridge University Press.

Eagly, A. H., A. Beall, and R. S. Sternberg, eds. 2004. *The Psychology of Gender*. 2nd ed. New York: Guilford Press.

Eckel, C. C, and P. J. Grossman, 2008. "Sex and Risk: Experimental Evidence." Monash Economics Working Paper 09, Department of Economics, Monash University, Victoria, Australia.

Elson, D. 1999. "Labour Markets as Gendered Institutions: Equality, Efficiency, and Empowerment Issues." *World Development* 27 (3): 611–27.

Elster, J. 1989. "Social Norms and Economic Theory." *Journal of Economic Perspectives* 3 (4): 99–117.

Ergun, S., T. Garcia-Munoz, and M. F. Rivas. 2012. "Gender Differences in Economic Experiments." Special Issue on Behavioural and Experimental Economics. *Revista Internacional de Sociologia* 70 (extra 1): 15–26.

Fehr, E., and S. Gachter. 2000. "Fairness and Retaliation: The Economics of Reciprocity." IEER Working Paper 40, Institute for Empirical Economic Research, Zurich, Switzerland.

Fehr, E., and K. Hoff. 2011. "Tastes, Castes, and Culture: The Influence of Society on Preferences." Policy Research Working Paper 5760, World Bank, Washington, DC.

Fraser, N. 1997. *Justice Interruptus: Critical Reflections on the "Postsocialist" Condition*. London: Routledge.

Garfinkel, H. 1967. *Studies in Ethnomethodology*. Englewood Cliffs, NJ: Prentice-Hall. As cited in C. West and D. Zimmerman. 1987. "Doing Gender." *Gender & Society* 1 (2): 125–51.

Hartsock, N. 1996. "Community/Sexuality/Gender: Rethinking Power." In *Revisioning the Political: Feminist Reconstructions of Traditional Concepts in Western Political Theory*, edited by N. J. Hirschmann and C. Di Stefano. Boulder, CO: Westview Press.

Hechter, M., and K.-D. Opp, eds. 2001. *Social Norms*. New York: Russell Sage Foundation.

Hoff, K., and P. Pandey. 2006. "Discrimination, Social Identity, and Durable Inequalities." *American Economic Review* 96 (2): 206–11.

Ibrahim, S., and S. Alkire. 2007. "Agency and Empowerment: A Proposal for Internationally Comparable Indicators." OPHI Working Paper 04, Oxford Poverty and Human Development Initiative, Oxford, U.K.

Isaac, J. 1987. "Beyond the Three Faces of Power: A Realist Critique." *Polity* 20 (1): 4–31.

Jensen, R., and E. Oster. 2009. "The Power of TV: Cable Television and Women's Status in India." *Quarterly Journal of Economics* 24 (3): 1057–94.

Kabeer, N. 1999. "Resources, Agency, Achievements: Reflections on the Measurement of Women's Empowerment." *Development and Change* 30: 435–64.

———. 2001. "Reflections on the Measurement of Women's Empowerment." In *Discussing Women's Empowerment: Theory and Practice*, 17–57. Sida*studies* 3. Stockholm, Sweden: Novum Grafiska AB and Sida.

Krendl, A. C., J. A. Richeson, W. M. Kelley, and T. F. Heatherton. 2008. "The Negative Consequences of Threat: A Functional Magnetic Resonance Imaging Investigation of the Neural Mechanisms Underlying Women's Underperformance in Math." *Psychological Science* 19 (2): 168–75.

Labalme, P. H., ed. 1980. *Beyond Their Sex: Learned Women of the European Past*. New York: New York University Press.

Lippa, R. A. 2005. *Gender, Nature, and Nurture.* 2nd ed. Mahwah, NJ: Lawrence Erlbaum Associates.

Lister, R. 1997. *Citizenship: Feminist Perspectives.* Basingstoke, U.K: Macmillan.

Lukes, S. 1974. *Power: A Radical View.* London: Macmillan.

Miles, M. B., and A. M. Huberman. 1994. *Qualitative Data Analysis: An Expanded Sourcebook.* 2nd ed. Thousand Oaks, CA: Sage.

Moser, C. 1989. "Gender Planning in the Third World: Meeting Practical and Strategic Gender Needs." *World Development* 17 (2): 1799–825.

Narayan, D., ed. 2005. *Measuring Empowerment: Cross-Disciplinary Perspectives.* Washington, DC: World Bank.

———., ed. 2009. *Moving Out of Poverty: The Promise of Empowerment and Democracy in India.* Vol. 3. New York: Palgrave Macmillan; Washington, DC: World Bank.

Narayan, D., R. Chambers, M. K. Shah, and P. Petesch. 2000. *Voices of the Poor: Crying Out for Change.* New York: Oxford University Press for World Bank.

Narayan, D., with R. Patel, K. Schafft, A. Rademacher, and S. Koch-Schulte. 2000. *Voices of the Poor: Can Anyone Hear Us?* New York: Oxford University Press for World Bank.

Narayan, D., and P. Petesch. 2002. *Voices of the Poor: From Many Lands.* New York: Oxford University Press for World Bank.

———. 2005. *Moving Out of Poverty: Understanding Freedom, Democracy, and Growth from the Bottom Up—Methodology Guide.* Washington, DC: Poverty Reduction and Economic Management Network, Poverty Reduction Group, World Bank.

———., eds. 2007. *Moving Out of Poverty: Cross-Disciplinary Perspectives on Mobility.* Vol. 1. New York: Palgrave Macmillan; Washington, DC: World Bank.

———. 2010. *Moving Out of Poverty: Rising from the Ashes of Conflict.* New York: Palgrave Macmillan; Washington, DC: World Bank.

Narayan D., L. Pritchett, and S. Kapoor. 2009. *Moving Out of Poverty: Success from the Bottom Up.* New York: Palgrave Macmillan; Washington, DC: World Bank.

Nussbaum, M. 2000. *Women and Human Development: The Capabilities Approach.* Cambridge, UK and New York: Cambridge University Press.

Nussbaum, M. C. 1998. "Public Philosophy and International Feminism." *Ethics* 108: 762–96.

———. 1999. *Sex and Social Justice.* Oxford, UK: Oxford University Press.

———. 2001. *Women and Human Development: The Capabilities Approach.* Cambridge, U.K.: Cambridge University Press.

———. 2006. "Capabilities as Fundamental Entitlements: Sen and Social Justice." In *Amartya Sen's Work and Ideas: A Gender Perspective,* edited by B. Agarwal, J. Humphries, and I. Robeyns. New York: Routledge.

Portes, A. 2006. "Institutions and Development: A Conceptual Re-Analysis." *Population and Development Review* 32: 233–62.

Rao, V., and M. Walton, eds. 2004. "Culture and Public Action: Relationality, Equality of Agency, and Development." In *Culture and Public Action,* 3–36. Stanford, CA: Stanford University Press.

Ridgeway, C. L. 1997. "Interaction and the Conservation of Gender Inequality: Considering Employment." *American Sociological Review* 62: 218–35.

————. 2009. "Framed Before We Know It: How Gender Shapes Social Relations." *Gender & Society* 23 (2): 145–60.

Ridgeway, C. L., and S. J. Correll. 2004. "Unpacking the Gender System: A Theoretical Perspective on Gender Beliefs and Social Relations." *Gender and Society* 18 (4): 510–31.

Ridgeway, C. L., and L. Smith-Lovin. 1999. "The Gender System and Interaction." *Annual Review of Sociology* 25: 191–216.

Robeyns, I. 2003. "Sen's Capability Approach and Gender Inequality: Selecting Relevant Capabilities." *Feminist Economics* 9 (2–3): 61–92.

Rowlands, J. 1997. *Questioning Empowerment: Working with Women in Honduras.* Oxford, U.K.: Oxfam.

Samman, E., and M. E. Santos. 2009. "Agency and Empowerment: A Review of Concepts, Indicators, and Empirical Evidence." OPHI Research Paper 10a, Oxford Poverty and Human Development Initiative, Oxford, U.K.

Sen, A. 1985. "Well-Being, Agency, and Freedom: The Dewey Lectures." *Journal of Philosophy* 82 (4): 169–221.

————. 2002. *Development as Freedom.* New York: Anchor.

Sen, G., and C. Grown. 1987. *Development, Crisis, and Alternative Visions.* New York: Monthly Review Press.

Shih, M., T. L. Pittinsky, and N. Ambady. 1999. "Stereotype Susceptibility: Identity Salience and Shifts in Quantitative Performance." *Psychological Science* 10: 80–83.

Steele, C. M., and J. Aronson. 1995. "Stereotype Threat and the Intellectual Test-Performance of African-Americans." *Journal of Personality and Social Psychology* 69 (5): 797–811.

van Staveren, I. 2013. "An Exploratory Cross-Country Analysis of Gendered Institutions." *Journal of International Development* 25 (1): 108–21.

West, C., and S. Fenstermaker. 1995. "Doing Difference." *Gender & Society* 9 (1): 8–37.

West, C., and D. Zimmerman. 1987. "Doing Gender." *Gender & Society* 1 (2): 125–51.

World Bank. 2012. *World Development Report 2012: Gender Equality and Development.* Washington, DC: World Bank.

PART I

Gender Norms

One of Sisum's most unforgettable childhood memories was an angry outburst by her father when she asked why men and boys always dined first in Samtse, her small village in southern Bhutan.[1] Sometimes this meant that Sisum had to wait to eat until late in the afternoon if her father had business in neighboring towns. "I am not so used to this," she recounted of her hunger and frustration with the delays, "because in my uncle's house [in the city] such practices are not followed. They are all educated and they feel it is not right." Sisum lives with her uncle's family in Thimphu, Bhutan's capital, during the months she is in school. She is also "sad for mother, who is always working so hard in the house and she does not even get to eat a meal together with the rest of the family."

This eventful day, Sisum found the courage to ask her mother about the mealtime tradition, but her mother only explained that it "has been followed since our ancestors' time." Searching for a reason that made more sense to her, Sisum then sought out her father for an explanation. Her father, however, responded by completely losing his temper over her question, directing his rage at her mother:

> Before our marriage, you were nothing. Your family members were poor and we always had to support them. I am fed up with your family members and this is the third time that you have gone against the culture and tradition that we follow in this house. It is you who have instigated Sisum to question these things. How does a girl of her age learn how to talk like this? ... In this house, you all are supposed to do what I say. I am the head of the family. Without me, you would not have proper shelter or even meals to eat. How dare you complain and question why women have to eat after men. It is up to us whether we want you to eat after men or not eat at all.

Sisum's brother had to step in during their father's furious eruption to prevent her mother from being beaten in front of the family and servants.

Sisum, now age 26, comes from a wealthy family, but Samtse's 500 or so residents are mostly illiterate and poor. Her education and exposure to new norms in rapidly urbanizing Thimphu have clashed with her father's expectation of keeping traditional village practices. In one world, Sisum was raised to conform to strict gender codes of subordination and respect for her father's authority; yet, simultaneously in the city, her other world, she was exposed to changing expectations about the proper roles and conduct for a girl and her father. Sisum will shortly complete her engineering degree and is determined to find a way to help change the traditions in her village. She knows about organizations that work on women's and children's rights in Thimphu, but they have yet to reach places like Samtse.

In some respects, Sisum's life straddles the 97 communities in our dataset. Overall, the communities in our study closely adhere to norms prescribing what women and men are expected to do, particularly when it comes to the division of domestic and breadwinner roles in the household. And these productive and reproductive gender role differences are mirrored and replicated at the wider community level. Change is happening, but at a very slow pace. The data show incremental and uneven changes in gender roles and norms, and a diversity of forces driving these transitions. On one hand, norms are being modified by negotiation and adaptation by men and women in response to new, emerging views on gender equality (box PI.1). Wider forces are also driving change, including new legislation, education achievement, communications technology, and many others. On the other hand, change is resisted in both discourses and practices. As discussed in chapter 2, domestic violence, in many cases seen as a man's right over his wife, occurs as a reaction to challenges to the norm; but widely held beliefs and everyday practices like dinner rules also change.

If young Sisum is confused by certain traditions in her family or how she ought to behave with her father, she is not alone. Sometimes uncertainty can be an advantage for flouting traditions that no longer make sense. And sometimes uncertainty about acceptable conduct creates space for disagreement and violent enforcement of the norm.

Ridgeway and Correll (2004) note that beliefs in gender stereotypes are so resilient that descriptive attributes of the "typical" man or woman have remained stable since the 1970s.[2] Chapter 1 reveals a similar finding: the focus groups' reports of the traits associated with the ideal "good wives," "good husbands," "good girls," and "good boys" are remarkably constant across countries and locations, and have remained largely unchanged, compared to previous generations. However, as shown throughout this report (particularly chapter 2), in everyday practices, there is more margin for negotiation, despite adherence to the ideal, and change is inescapable as more women participate in labor markets and more husbands help out at home.

By definition, social norms are accompanied by surveillance and sanctioning practices to ensure compliance, ranging from community pressure for expected behaviors to explicit enforcement by violence. Women's and men's constant accountability to conform to norms has implications for their agency and ability to take action.

Box PI.1 What Is Gender Equality? Views from the Ground

When we asked the adult focus groups about the desirability of gender equality, their views differed strongly (figure BPI.1.1). Below is a flavor of the perceptions, ranging from the large majority who were favorably disposed to the notion of gender equality to those with decidedly mixed views.

Mutual respect, understanding, consultation, harmony, freedom, less stress and violence

- "Equality between men and women means that they have a happy relationship and are comfortable talking to each other about their problems." (Adult man, Labasa, Fiji)
- "They should be able to do whatever they really want to do." (Adult woman, Hyderabad, Andhra Pradesh, India)

Sharing of work and household responsibilities

- "Equality for me means that all of us should work and should enjoy the fruit of our work. I should not work alone while the man is just sitting there." (Adult woman, urban Nsenene village, Tanzania)
- "Happiness and equality are related. If the husband understands that happiness is supporting and helping his wife in housework and in taking care of children, the happiness of the family will be reinforced." (Adult man, Ba Dinh District, Hanoi, Vietnam)
- "Before a woman had no opportunity to work, and now she does. If a woman cooks, the man should wash and change a child's diapers." (Adult woman, Santiago de los Caballeros, the Dominican Republic)

Figure BPI.1.1 Equality between a Woman and a Man?

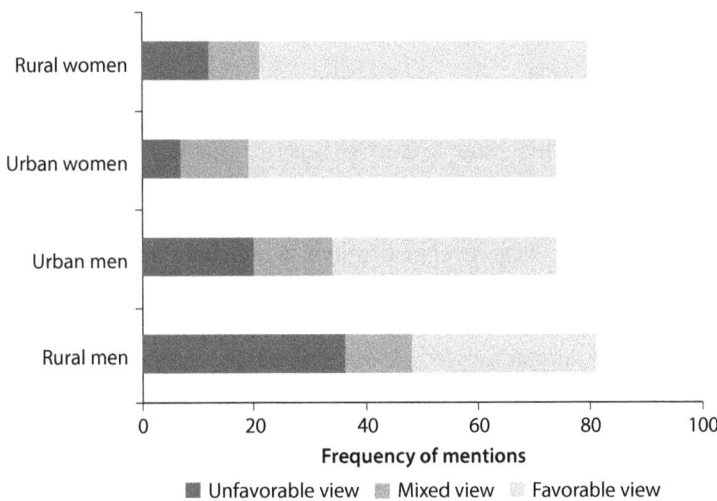

Frequency of mentions

■ Unfavorable view ▦ Mixed view ▢ Favorable view

Note: Data from 194 adult focus groups.

box continues next page

On Norms and Agency • http://dx.doi.org/10.1596/978-0-8213-9862-3

Box PI.1 What Is Gender Equality? Views from the Ground *(continued)*

Equal rights and nondiscrimination

– "Equality between a man and a woman means there should not be gender discrimination and there should be equal opportunities for both." (Urban woman Nellore, Andhra Pradesh, India)

About half of the rural men either qualified or flatly rejected gender equality as a goal for their society (see figure BPI.1.1). In the village of Levuka, Fiji, a man insisted, "There cannot be any equality between a man and a woman because men make all the decisions." A village man from Malangachilima, Tanzania, declared, "I do not think it means a lot to me. [Women] go to the office or into politics, but look at how our families are dying. They [women] do everything, but do you see the immoralities around? … That is equality. It is a disaster."

In the interviews in the Roma community in Serbia, the defense of highly unequal gender relations and the institutions that support these relations was very strong. The young Roma men did not appear to be open to questioning their privileges or to seeing any value in more equal relations: "A wife does not matter the least bit in making decisions, it is my good will"; "who even asks a woman about anything"; and "it all depends on what the husband wants. If he wants to get rid of his wife and children, it will be as he wishes. If he wants to get rid of her, but keep the children, it will again be as he wishes." A mixture of dominant cultural views about gender roles and the need to protect a permanently threatened culture seem to lurk behind these voices.

In the Muslim communities sampled, women and men sometimes quoted religious scripture and defined equality in relation to "rights and duties": men and women have responsibilities that accord with the gender-ascribed roles of male breadwinners and female caretakers. In rural Shirabad Ulya, Afghanistan, the men disagreed with "the present policy of the government and other non-Muslim people [that] women [of Afghanistan] should be free like the women of Europe or America. But we don't like this equality and it is not good."

The evidence from the research data strongly suggests that when households and communities find ways to relax and change inequitable gender norms, men's and women's individual and collective agency increase and reinforce one another. The analysis indicates that the interplay between more equitable gender norms and more widely shared voice and power is often accompanied by more inclusive and effective local-level institutions, which are embedded in and reproduce existing normative frameworks. In particular, greater gender equality in communities makes it more likely that claims by weaker groups will be heard, deemed legitimate, and addressed—even a small, inconsequential question by a young girl who is hungry. Recognition is the first step of the process.[3]

Notes

1. Pseudonyms are used in place of particular individuals or communities named in this study. In some cases, community names have been replaced with references to districts or municipalities.

2. Ridgeway and Correll (2004, 526–28) also cite a set of studies that looks empirically at the resilience of gender beliefs: Fiske *et al.* 2002; Lueptow, Garovich-Szabo, and Lueptow 2001; and Spence and Buckner 2000.

3. This is in line with Wall's (2012) emphasis on the need for societies to strengthen their capacities to recognize and address children's needs and interests in the context of advancing deeper and more effective democratization processes.

References

Fiske, S. T., A. J. Cuddy, P. Glick, and J. Xu. 2002. "A Model of (Often Mixed) Stereotype Content: Competence and Warmth Respectively Follow from Perceived Status and Competence." *Journal of Personality and Social Psychology* 82: 878–902.

Lueptow, L. B., L. Garovich-Szabo, and M. B. Lueptow. 2001. "Social Change and the Persistence of Sex Typing: 1974–1997." *Social Forces* 80: 1–36.

Ridgeway, C. L., and S. J. Correll. 2004. "Unpacking the Gender System: A Theoretical Perspective on Gender Beliefs and Social Relations." *Gender and Society* 18 (4): 510–31.

Spence, J. T., and C. E. Buckner. 2000. "Instrumental and Expressive Traits, Trait Stereotypes, and Sexist Attitudes: What Do They Signify?" *Psychology of Women Quarterly* 24: 44–62.

Wall, J. 2012. "Can Democracy Represent Children? Toward a Politics of Difference." *Childhood* 19 (1): 86–100.

The Rules We Live By: Gender Norms and Ideal Images

Drawing on the nearly 4,000 voices of the people who participated in the qualitative assessment, chapter 1 explores the prevalent gender norms surrounding women's and men's lives in the communities where the focus groups were held.[1] As key components of a society's culture, norms and roles allow people to organize their lives in consistent, predictable ways. But sometimes normative role behavior becomes rigidly defined and curtails freedom of action and agency.

To capture the ideal views of gender roles in a household, we look first at how the focus group participants defined a "good wife" and a "good husband" in their communities. Masculinity and femininity are more than sex-appropriate behaviors. They are also defined by a power relationship, and it is in the domestic sphere where subordination and domination are more clearly revealed. Chapter 1 shows how little the core practices that define the identities of wives and husbands have changed.[2]

The focus groups of adolescents (conducted in nine countries) held conversations about what traits characterized a "good girl" and a "good boy," and a "bad boy" or "bad girl." Like the adults, the adolescents' views on what makes the girls good and turns them into good wives, and what makes the boys good so they become good husbands, were very consistent across countries and communities. Chapter 1 shows how their views on the behaviors expected of both sexes in a household context are translated into and reinforced by community-level (collective) expectations of individual behavior as much as by collective behaviors (as Bicchieri [2006] notes).

Normative Frameworks for Household Gender Inequalities

Gender norms and roles are reproduced in the private and public spheres and all other areas of life. Understanding how this framework operates at the household level is important because it provides a sort of mental map of the acceptable roles, responsibilities, and behaviors for each household member. The codes that govern men's and women's relations in the household are strict and

Frankly speaking, women here are very miserable. They suffer from a lot of pressures. Pigs scream, kids cry, and husbands ask for sex.

—Village man, Hung Yeng District, Vietnam

gender-specific. They have varied a little, but when changes have occurred, they have not always remained stable over time.

How much is the traditional intrahousehold normative framework changing today? Are norms relaxing and changing as gender equality increases around the world? To answer these questions, all the adult focus groups explored stereotyped notions of a good wife and good husband. The depictions below of a good wife and good husband reflect the participants' most idealized views of gender roles and norms. They do not necessarily reflect the composition of their households, the realities of their daily lives, or their aspirations for their lives (see box PI.1). They do, however, describe the normative framework that binds both women and men.

We find that the normative frameworks governing the roles within the household have remained largely unchanged. Consistently across both men's and women's focus groups, and across the urban and rural contexts, and across different economic, political, and social circumstances of the 20 countries, men and women hold similar views of the wife's and husband's roles. Strict gender norms may be relaxing some, but they still retain a tight grip over women's and men's idealized roles and behaviors as husbands and wives. Almost every participant described a good husband as the highest household authority and responsible for being a benevolent decision-maker and a good provider for the household. The focus group accounts of a good wife depicted her first and foremost as an obedient, caring, and respectful mate to the good husband. She is responsible for all the housework and the care of all members of the household, and is held strictly accountable for her domestic responsibilities day in and day out.

The wife's and husband's roles are quite stable across the focus groups, but we also see signs of flexibility around these norms. In some places, the norms are relaxing, and some of the factors that are driving this relaxation seem to be associated with increased education levels, women's participation in the labor force, and urbanization. But we cannot affirm that there is a direct relationship with these drivers. Men, however, appear to have more leniency within their prescribed norms. In the aggregate, urban communities are ahead of rural communities in norm relaxation and negotiation.

Figure 1.1 lists the four most-mentioned topics in the focus group discussions of a good wife and good husband. The frequencies in the figure show the number of times a topic was brought up in the 194 adult focus group discussions. The figure does not specifically assess favorable or unfavorable perceptions associated with these attributes.[3]

Figure 1.1 Characteristics of a Good Wife and a Good Husband

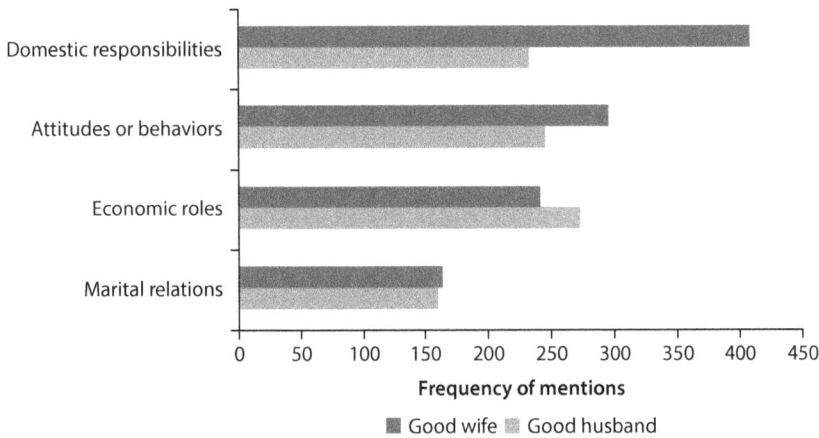

Note: Data from 194 adult focus groups (men and women).

As observed in figure 1.1, domestic responsibilities receive, by quite a remarkable amount, the greatest emphasis in discussions about the definition of a good wife. Opinions of this overriding role for women outnumber all other descriptions, whether we asked urban men and women or rural men and women. For a good husband, his economic role is mentioned the most, but in comparison with the domestic role of the good wife, this received less stress.

The Good Wife

The strong emphasis on women's domestic work and care is all the more striking because focus groups were specifically prompted about the income-earning roles of both the good wife and the good husband, and how they each balance work and family life. Domestic responsibilities are clearly the dominant tasks assigned to women.

Domestic responsibilities for women cover a broad range of activities, mostly associated with home care. In a village in the Sumadija District, Serbia, a woman described a good wife as a "housewife, obedient, loyal, good mother, good cook, cleans the house." To a women's focus group in Nellore (Andhra Pradesh), India, a good wife "looks after the family well, gives all her time to the family, and understands the family problems." Similarly, in Hato Mayor, the Dominican Republic, men portrayed a good wife as "the one who cares for the house, the children, and the husband." And in a semi-rural community of the Ngonyameni area outside Durban, South Africa, men said a good wife "makes sure that everything runs smoothly in her household, she takes care of her husband and children." Indeed, almost every focus group elaborated on a good wife's paramount role of caring for her family.

Focus groups also attached the highest ethical attitudes and behaviors to a good wife (see table 1.1). Women from urban National Capital District, Papua New Guinea, imagined her to be "honest, friendly, smart, sharing,

A good wife stays home, takes care of the house and children, cooks, feeds livestock. The important thing is that the woman should do this by goodwill.

—Village men's group, Floresti District, Moldova

[A good wife] looks after the children, does all housework, keeps her husband happy by doing everything, contributes to household income somehow, and thinks about husband and children first.

—Village woman, Naitasiri Province, Fiji

If the husband is not good, the impact on the family is lighter because the mother is the foundation of the family. If she is not good, it affects the family more.

—Village woman, Dirbas, West Bank and Gaza

Table 1.1 Characteristics of a Good Wife and Good Husband Described by Adult Men and Women in Ba Dinh District, Vietnam

A good wife		A good husband	
Women	*Men*	*Women*	*Men*
• Takes good care of her house • Takes good care of her family and children • Cares for kinship/relatives • Contributes to the family income (not necessary)	• Is faithful • Educates children well • Takes good care of the family • Is a good cook • Earns money • Has social status	• Is responsible for family, kinship, and society • Contributes to family income • Should be a good breadwinner • Takes care of his children	• Is faithful • Is a good earner • Has sympathy and helps wife and children • Has social status • Is hardworking • Does not drink or gamble heavily • Does not come home late • Is not adulterous; does not associate with sex workers

caring, helpful, submissive, loving, understanding, faithful, [have] the heart of a servant, hardworking, respectful, responsible, and wise [with budgeting]." Many focus groups stressed that a good wife respects her husband and is faithful, supportive, and submissive. In Peru, wives must have a "good character, love their husband, help their husband, and be a homemaker." In Levuka, Fiji, a good wife is "a good listener and obedient to the husband ... [and] a good advisor." In Rafah, West Bank and Gaza, a good wife is "obedient, polite, behaves well."

In most contexts in the communities sampled, women who have children and husbands who provide well for the family generally do not work.

In Bhubaneswar (Odisha), India, the women said that a good wife does not have to take a job, but "men whose wives contribute are happy because they feel a little relieved from their economic responsibility." Urban men were generally more likely than rural men to voice appreciation for wives who earn income and contribute to a household's prosperity and happiness. Nevertheless, the overall picture from the focus groups of a good wife's economic role is quite mixed. Simple urban and rural differences in whether women work for pay or do not work cannot capture the complex realities of women's lives. Often their quite-active economic participation may go unrecognized or even be hidden because of the status their communities attach to being "just a housewife."

Still, in many communities, a good wife may mean she earns income. The urban focus groups, more often than rural groups, mentioned the economic participation of good wives. (Chapter 5 looks specifically at working mothers and women's economic participation.) Their discourse about working women, however, may just be glib, reinforcing expectations that women's traditional domestic role remains the more important one. This synthesis of a good wife from men in a neighborhood of Hoang Mai District in Hanoi, Vietnam, is typical:

> A good wife should make her husband proud of her. A good wife is not necessarily a high income earner, but she has to have a stable and decent work. She has to be a good daughter in-law. Most important, she must be a good mother who knows how to raise her children to be healthy and smart.

In a similar vein, the men's group in Nsenene village, Tanzania, highlighted how their town's expectations of an urban good wife have become more relaxed and now include a provider role and activities beyond the household—*in addition* to traditional care duties:

> She does all the cleaning. She prepares breakfast. She works on the plantation in the morning. She prepares lunch. She goes to work on the plantation in the afternoon. She attends association meetings in the late afternoon. She comes back to make sure supper is ready. She serves supper. She goes to bed and should have sex with her husband.

Despite the economic role of the urban good wife, her principal priorities remain domestic and her authority is clearly subordinate to her husband's. A good wife today, noted by men in Balti, Moldova, is likely to work for pay; she "may contribute to the family budget, but if the husband is a good provider, then she should not. Her role is to create appropriate conditions for her husband to earn money." In urban Mongar District, Bhutan, a good wife "stays home, looks after the children, listens to her husband, and does not roam around. … During her free time, she works to earn extra income for the family. [She can] weave, raise vegetables or poultry." An urban good wife's provider role is also second to her reproductive roles. She will likely not work (earn income) if she has many children or her children are very young.

On Norms and Agency • http://dx.doi.org/10.1596/978-0-8213-9862-3

When we compare our urban and rural communities, we find that rural settings more often stick close to the traditional prescribed norms. Particularly with the productive role, we see some dissent among focus group participants. In rural Afghanistan and the Republic of Yemen, for instance, where it is not customary for women to work for pay, the women declared that "income is not our responsibility." In a semi-rural community of Ngonyameni, South Africa, the women indicated that good wives can work, but there was disagreement in the men's group. One man from this community suggested that a working woman can even contribute more income than her spouse, while another insisted that "good wives do not work; they stay at home and care for the children." Many rural women work on family plots and tend their own gardens and small livestock, but these farm or household activities are often perceived as extensions of their household roles. However, focus groups noted that a good wife earning outside income also announces that the household is experiencing undesirable circumstances. For instance, poor widows may have little choice but to seek jobs outside their households that provide some cash income (see box 1.1).

When asked how a good wife balances her many responsibilities, from work to family life, a common response from both urban and rural groups was that a

---

Box 1.1 Nontraditional Households

Focus groups most often discussed good wives and good husbands in relation to a monogamous couple in a nuclear family. On the rare occasions when they mentioned other types of households, women living in such arrangements were often portrayed as more vulnerable and powerless than when attached to a mate. If a woman in a village in (Odisha) India separated from her partner, she had to forfeit custody of her children; she could not expect alimony or a share of household property; she would "feel helpless even in her parents' home"; and she might be forced to remarry an elderly man. In communities in the sample where polygamy is practiced, monogamy was named by both women and men as a quality of a good husband. Sharing husbands and resources with multiple wives or living with in-laws, parents, or other relatives can be disempowering for women. In Tangerang, Indonesia, a 38-year-old widow lamented, "At present I live with my kids and parents, and still rent a house. I used to be happy because I had a husband." Sudanese focus groups talked about the great stigma and gossip that widows face because villagers assume they are "having relations with men."

In a few communities, family laws are making separations somewhat easier for women and men. A single woman, whether a mother or not, may in some contexts enjoy greater freedom of action, status, and control of assets than a married woman. A women's focus group in Liberia explained that better-off widows can get on with their lives, "but if the deceased husband was poor and her kids are still young, then she would suffer a lot unless relatives stand beside her." Similarly, in rural Papua New Guinea, better-off widows are the only women who can own land in the village. And in Afghanistan, focus groups explained that elderly widows enjoy a lot of independence and can travel in public because they are too old to shame family honor and are perceived to be the "mothers of society."

---

good wife can do everything skillfully and with ease. Whether she works for pay or not seems to be secondary to household obligations. In rural Velugodu (Andhra Pradesh), India, a good wife, according to the women's group, "always chooses to work from home." In Olsztyn, a large city in Poland where women have been out in the workforce for decades, a good wife "copes perfectly with her obligations." However, another woman retorted, "She lives 26 hours a day." In urban Bukoba, Tanzania, the men's attributes of a good wife included that "she must do business as well," but when asked how a good wife finds time for all this, one of them offered, "I think that, if she is employed, it is her fault. Let her do all her work also."

Discussion groups also compared today's and the previous generation's good wife. Many recalled that, in their mother's time, a good wife was more submissive, patient, quiet, and tolerant of being ill-treated. And a good wife in the past typically did not earn income, which was often viewed as undesirable. In rural Chiclayo, Peru, men said that a good wife in the previous generation was "dedicated to the home … scared of her husband, and hard working." Women in Umlazi township A (near Durban), South Africa, maintained that a good wife "would have stayed in the marriage even if the husband was beating her." In Olsztyn, Poland, one women's group did not mention problems of violence, but they felt that a good wife of their mother's generation was treated like a servant or "kind of slave."

In a semi-rural community of Ngonyameni, South Africa, men voiced nostalgia for earlier times when wives were more obedient: "They respected their husbands. They did not argue with them. What is happening today is just a shame." Similarly, a woman from University Quarter, West Bank and Gaza, recalled, "[The good wife from my mother's generation] used to remain quiet and not argue with the man."

Most focus groups of both sexes concurred that today's good wives are less obedient, less respectful, and less patient, and more likely to talk back and argue with their husbands. While there are exceptions, most women viewed these changes in a good wife—and in gender relations generally—favorably and described their families as now closer and friendlier. According to a village woman in Velugodu (Andhra Pradesh), India, "a good wife then was more accommodating and patient, and today's good wife is smart and ambitious."

This perception of change is crucial. For women to become empowered in the domestic sphere, they must use their agency to negotiate the nature of gender relations in the household, which in turn may influence the decisions made within it. Women's public roles may have changed in recent decades, but the limited changes in gender relations within the private sphere allow unequal gender relations to persist.[4]

The Good Husband

Set against the many ideal qualities of a good wife, focus groups depicted a good husband as the "real head of household," "a worker," "employed," and "always working hard for his family." In addition, women in rural Sumadija District,

---

A man who just stays home and has little responsibility around the house is good enough, because most men drink and hardly stay home.

—Village women's focus group, Samtse, Bhutan

There is a difference. In the past, the men didn't want to help in the kitchen. Now, men are more willing to help in the kitchen. In the past, boys weren't even allowed to go into the kitchen; now boys are told to help in the kitchen.

—Village women's focus group, Nagari Bukik Batabuah, Indonesia

---

Serbia, said he should be "handsome, open to compromise, capable, responsible, reasonable, mature, smart, permissive, and realistic." In Chiclayo, Peru, the women believed that a good husband should work with his wife "as a team" to make decisions and raise their children. He is also described as a loving and engaged father.

Yet, relative to a good wife, both women's and men's focus groups were much more likely to qualify a good husband by what he should *not* do. They often listed undesirable behaviors that a husband needs to avoid instead of affirming positive characteristics or mentioning the prescriptions of the husband's role. A good husband does not "cheat," "drink [alcohol]," "gamble," "scold and beat his wife or children," or "stay out late." According to a men's group from Ba Dinh District, Vietnam, their view of a good wife is a woman seemingly "perfect in all aspects," and her partner is expected "to be faithful," and to cease the drinking, gambling, adultery, and late nights (table 1.1).

Focus groups across all countries agreed that men's role as main provider and responsible for the economic security of the household is central. Reflecting on the strong hold that this specific aspect of the male role has, participants voiced concerns about a good husband's adequacy with breadwinning. In communities with a weak local economy, it was often enough if the good husband earned something and, ideally, stayed out of trouble. In a village outside Paro, Bhutan, women viewed a good husband as "one who is very understanding, supportive, hardworking, who does not have extramarital affairs, who does not resort to physical (domestic) violence, and who brings in steady income and provides for the whole family." The women also indicated that a good husband does not necessarily have to make a good income, but "he can contribute in a lot of other ways, such as spending time with his family and doing jobs that require physical strength." In this village, conditions were difficult, jobs scarce, and domestic violence common.

Compared to rural men, urban good husbands shoulder more parenting and housework obligations. In Aden, the Republic of Yemen, women said that a good husband "helps the mother raise the children... [and is] loving and attentive to his children." Likewise, in Hyderabad (Andhra Pradesh), India, a woman noted that a good husband "nowadays even takes care of the children if it is necessary." In rural Tanzania, where gender norms remain quite traditional, a good husband is involved in few household tasks and is appreciated if he only visits with friends "until early evening and then comes home for supper."

The focus groups also reflected on the good husband of the previous generation. They generally reported him as being a good provider and hardworking, but more strict and less affectionate toward his wife and children than today's good husband. Groups disagreed about whether a good husband of the past was more violent toward his wife or more likely to have affairs than today; however, most conveyed that good husbands used to drink less. The women's focus groups were much less likely than men's to look favorably upon the good husband of the past who "hardly listened to his wife." In contrast to the women's views of favorable trends, the men often expressed nostalgia for the days when husbands enjoyed more respect and knew better "how to keep his family under control." A man from University Quarter, West Bank and Gaza, mentioned a time when a good wife "helped her husband and did not make him feel that he is lacking anything."

In sum, men almost everywhere continue to be the dominant household authority figures and breadwinners. For their part, women continue to be held to strict account for the large majority of household work and care, no matter what other roles they may play beyond the household. Depending on the neighborhood or village, the relaxation of gender norms was portrayed as either incremental or a somewhat faster blurring of women's and men's roles and responsibilities. But these changes are generally happening more quickly in urban contexts.

Finally, the focus groups conveyed idealized notions about good wives and good husbands who enjoy harmonious and cooperative relations, but their ensuing discussions of how marital relations have changed over the generations suggested a more stressful picture. The men expressed a particular concern that the good husband is losing control over his life and his family, and their testimonies seem to question their present roles in society. Their frustrations cannot be taken lightly. In general, the discussions about a good wife and good husband display the same patterns that we find elsewhere in the dataset: women perceive that they are gaining more independence and freedom, while men often expressed a growing sense of powerlessness.

The Good Girl, the Good Boy

Girls and boys learn at an early age how they are expected to behave according to their sex. Gender norms are passed on by parents, school teachers, and peers. Furthermore, when they reach adolescence, any flexibility that the girls and boys may have had while growing up tends to disappear, and compliance with gender norms is tightly enforced. In adolescence, at the same time that the physical changes of puberty appear, gender role definition intensifies. Girls move from childhood to adult roles, such as wife, mother, and worker; and boys become workers, providers, and fathers.[5]

On Norms and Agency • http://dx.doi.org/10.1596/978-0-8213-9862-3

[The traits of a good boy are the] same as girls, but [the good boy] also does house-work like raking ... plus his own laundry, like washing his school uniform.

—Urban girls' focus group, Suva, Fiji

Figure 1.2 Characteristics of a Good Girl

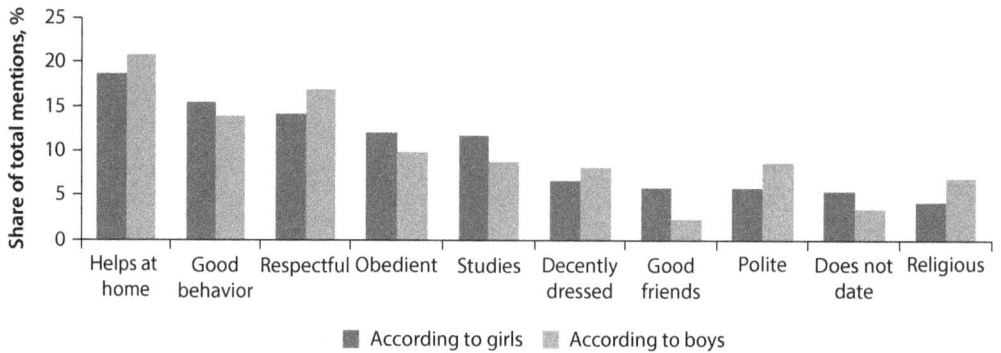

Note: Data from 82 focus groups.

Figure 1.3 Characteristics of a Good Boy

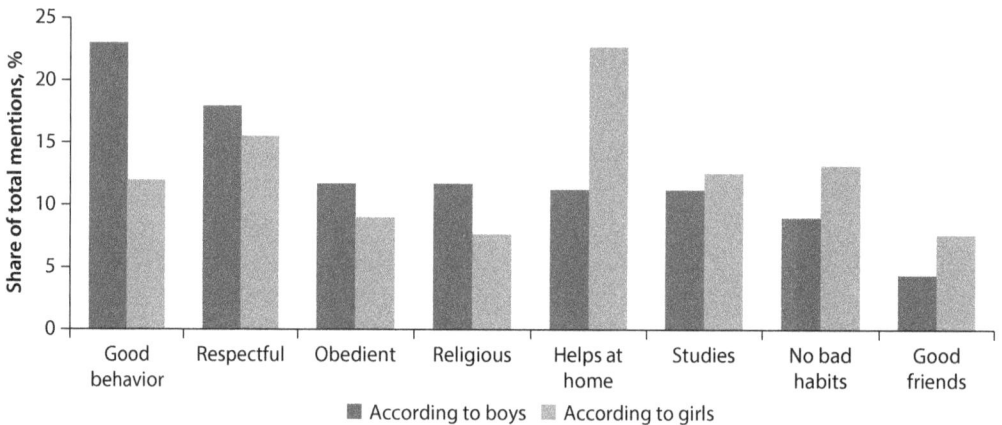

Note: Data from 82 focus groups.

When imagining a good girl, the focus groups of adolescent girls and boys provided remarkably consistent responses (figure 1.2).[6] Most often, they mentioned that a good girl models expected gender behaviors for a woman inside the household: she helps around the house and is well-behaved, obedient, and respectful. A good girl also goes to school. Likewise, a good boy goes to school, but like a good man, he is also described by certain things that he is expected not to do (figure 1.3). Girls see a good boy as helping around the house—much like a good girl—but boys tend to think this is less important than being respectful or doing other things. These patterns suggest that girls perceived fewer gender differences between the sexes in household roles and identified with more modern gender norms than did boys.

In Thimphu, Bhutan, girls depicted their good girl as "a very reliable daughter; she can take care of the house and at the same time behave well outside too." These girls required that both good girls and good boys "take care of parents." In rural Velugodu (Andhra Pradesh), India, boys said, "A good girl is religious, soft spoken, and obedient; she does all the domestic chores under the supervision of her mother. A good boy is religious, respectful to elders, and helpful." In many contexts, boys do help around the house, but more often with discrete tasks and not the time-consuming, constant daily chores expected of girls. In the Republic of Yemen and the Dominican Republic, none of the boys' focus groups associated their good boy with being helpful to their family. In Suva, Fiji, as the opening quote to this chapter attests, the girls imagined a good boy as useful around the house, while the boys offered no such indication in their list of traits for a good boy and imagined that a good girl "stays home, cooks, and washes dishes."

Other markers of a good girl and boy, as with a good wife and husband, include many desirable behavioral traits, such as honesty, good morals, and respectful and decent treatment of others. And good children (boys and girls) are expected to be obedient, deferential to adult authority, and good students. Yet, a good girl also should dress decently, act politely, and not date, which were not included in a good boy's attributes. (If anything, a good boy should not date too many girls.) And, unlike good girls, good boys were cautioned by many focus groups not to smoke, drink, use drugs, or steal. Focus groups were also more permissive of a good boy's behaviors and interactions with the opposite sex than with those of a good girl. In Ouagadougou, Burkina Faso, the boys said that a good boy does not "run often with girls," while girls indicated that a good boy "does not force the girls," but in Lautoka, Fiji, the good boy "might have a girlfriend."

In the descriptions of a bad girl and a bad boy, the focus groups specified stronger gender differences in their defining traits (figures 1.4 and 1.5). Nearly one-quarter of all the comments by boys about a bad girl identified her as promiscuous (e.g., many boyfriends, a prostitute); however, less than 10 percent of girls' comments mentioned promiscuity for a bad girl. Next in frequency were references, by both girls' and boys' focus groups, to bad girls' bad behavior: gossipy, dishonest, low morals, disobedient, and disrespectful (talks back, does not obey parents, swears). Boys were more likely than girls to think that a bad girl shirks her domestic responsibilities. In rural Koudipally Mandal (Andhra Pradesh), India, the boys said that a bad girl "won't help her mother with the household chores."

If boys expressed more concern about a bad girl's promiscuity, the girls' focus groups significantly stressed a bad boy's vices—smoking, drinking, and drugs. Boys saw this as a problem, too, but not nearly as important. Next in frequency for a bad boy are deeply aggressive behaviors, such as killing, gang fighting, and

On Norms and Agency • http://dx.doi.org/10.1596/978-0-8213-9862-3

Figure 1.4 Characteristics of a Bad Girl

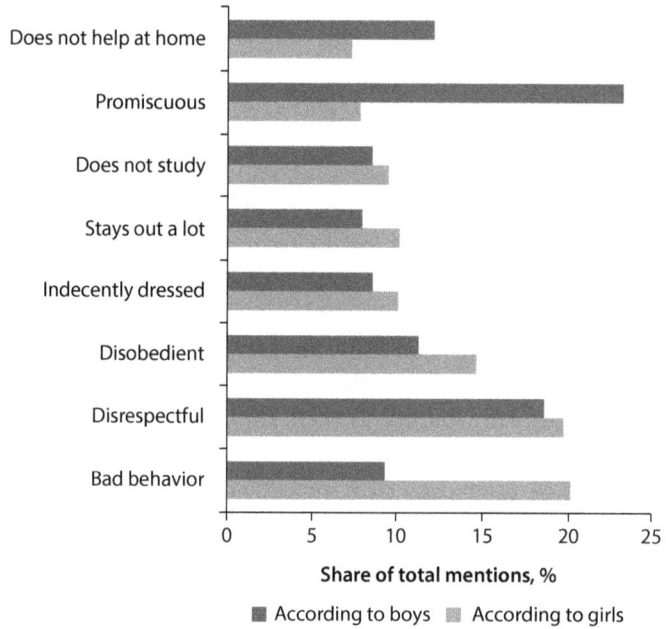

Note: Data from 82 focus groups.

Figure 1.5 Characteristics of a Bad Boy

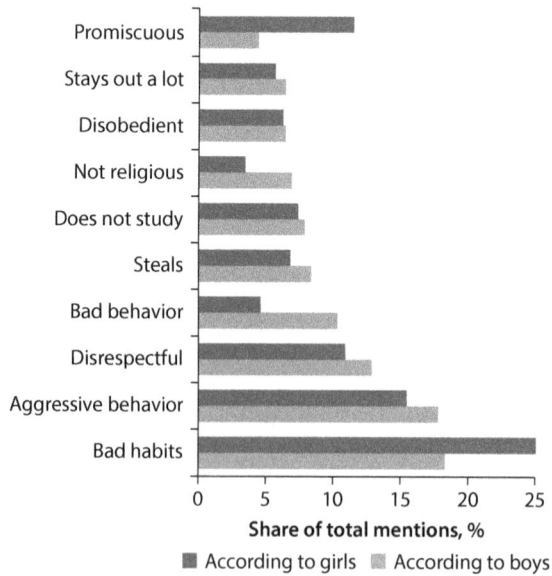

Note: Data from 82 focus groups.

rape. Both boys' and girls' focus groups attributed violence to a bad boy, but only rarely was it mentioned about a bad girl. In urban Lautoka, Fiji, for instance, the boys described a bad girl as "wearing a mini skirt, being too outgoing, going to nightclubs, and being a discipline problem," but these characteristics were much less severe than those portraying a bad boy: "smoking, drinking alcohol, sniffing glue, roaming around, having a future in jail or a future of poverty and crime."

Norms of good and bad femininity and masculinity take root at very young ages and help explain the persistence of gender differences in attitudes and behaviors from one generation to the next. The different normative yardsticks that are applied to girls and boys set the stage for stressful gender relations as adolescents head into adult years and need to manage relationships with the opposite sex. Girls and boys are both under pressure to conform to similar desirable expectations. Yet, for girls, expectations of gender-defining household roles are changing. In their testimonies, the girls themselves redefined housework as a practice that ideally should be normative for both boys and girls, and their good boy reflects that ideal. Boys are not as eager to include domestic responsibilities in their concept of a good boy. Also, both adolescent groups felt that good and bad boys are at risk for the same risky and violent behaviors that burden their fathers.

Community-Level Views of Gender Norms

What constitutes ideal gender-appropriate behavior in the household does not stop when individuals leave the domestic sphere. As the girls' and boys' focus groups discussed, their behavior outside their home marks them as being good as much as their domestic responsibilities do. Prevailing views on gender-appropriate behavior, when reproduced at the community level, can open or close opportunities for women.

In this section, we explore two areas where community sanctioning is more likely to have an impact on women's agency: (a) the ability to combine their productive and reproductive tasks, and (b) freedom of movement. As shown in *World Development Report 2012*, women's ability to use their time to work is central to their economic empowerment, while freedom of movement is one of the dimensions of their agency.[7]

Views on Working Mothers

Given how norms affect women's roles, we examine the qualities that young adults and adults find desirable and undesirable in a mother, and their opinions of mothers who balance family and work (if any). In many communities, the desirable qualities of a mother are the traditional ones of care, affection, and household management. But the younger groups in our study overwhelmingly highlighted as noteworthy women's (mothers') desire and ability to earn an income and contribute to household wellbeing together with caring for the family life.

On Norms and Agency • http://dx.doi.org/10.1596/978-0-8213-9862-3

Figure 1.6 Perceptions of What Women's Role Should Be

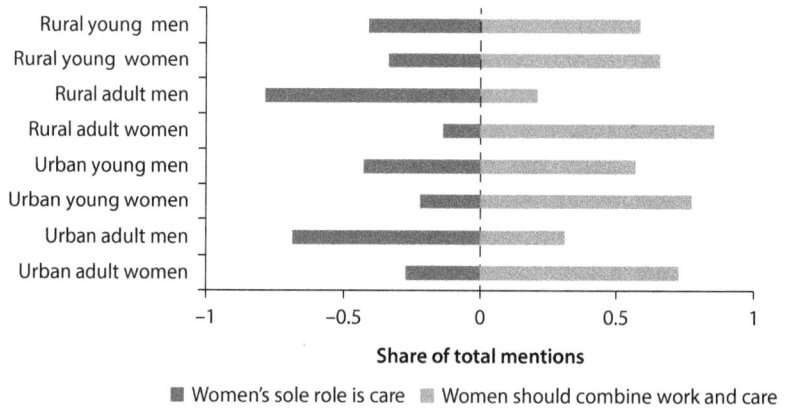

Note: Data from 370 focus groups.

While opinions split over defining the primary role for women, the participants clearly preferred that women accomplish both work and care tasks (figure 1.6). For adult men, however, the overwhelming majority (regardless of location) considered care to be women's major and only role. Little was said about the conciliation of roles between men and women.

The choices that women and men make regarding work are informed as much by their definitions of masculinity, femininity, and views of care responsibilities at home as by market opportunities. Leaving the economic context in the background for now—and how it constrains or facilitates work choices for women—we probe deeper into the justifications men and women give for choosing to work or stay home, and the normative (traditional) gender limitations imposed upon women in job searches and actual employment.

In many communities, women approach the prospect of work through the lens of norms that restrict their initiative, mobility, and autonomy. Examples of these restrictions appeared throughout focus group conversations in all communities and included taboos on commercial or social exchanges between women and unrelated men,[8] concerns for safety that prevent movement, and concerns over women's honor being tarnished in public. Other traditions or established practices regarding women's economic participation are equally powerful. For example, in Hung Yen District, Vietnam, where women's participation in the labor force is almost 70 percent, the range of women's productive activities is limited because "according to long-standing social norms and prejudices, women are supposed to take care of the family and breed chicken or pigs at home. They can only do small things." As a consequence, women in these contexts usually opt to work from home or in jobs that do not contravene the severe norms of their households and communities.

Where no such restrictions are present, acceptable professional jobs for women are often just extensions of their caretaker roles at home: teacher, nurse, and cook. Moreover, women's household (gender) duties are as powerful as any religious belief in limiting women's movements and ability to work for pay. Women negotiate work choices from the options that meet their communities' requirements for appropriate work and accountability for household duties.

When women do find employment, they face a new challenge. Can they perform well in their dual roles of workers and mothers? Women sometimes fail in their attempts to do both equally well. Whether or not women fulfill their role as mother and wife often is the deciding factor for accepting working mothers as a positive development. Taking on outside and household work simultaneously can exact a high cost from women. A young woman from the University Quarter, West Bank and Gaza, saw no problem with a mother who decides to start working, but she noted that there are trade-offs one way or another: "No woman is a superwoman [and] no woman who works will be able to balance that with another role. One has to happen at the expense of the other. For example, my mom's work as a teacher happened at the expense of her health."

The weight of a double workload, hard as it is, has even more burdens, including what it means for women to step out into the public space. Working mothers must keep their (and their family's) reputations intact. Even in urban contexts, working women and mothers must behave with decorum and politeness, pass up after-work recreational activities, and return home at an appropriate hour; otherwise, they face being stigmatized as negligent, materialistic, hedonistic, and even sexually promiscuous.

The contents and the consequences of the stigma attached to working mothers vary between communities, but they tend to center on the effects on children. In many cases, the widespread view holds that a working mother has abandoned her children. In Jaipur (Odisha), India, young women described the attitudes of their community as "friends and neighbors who don't have high opinions of [working mothers] who think money is more important than children and don't have the maternal feelings for children that mothers had 20 or 30 years ago." Some sample communities expressed concern that the children of working mothers will be negatively affected by their absence. They turned working mothers' own worries about the well-being of their children against them in the form of social criticism: their children may end up spending too much time in the street, engage in criminal behavior, and in general deviate from the right path because their mother is not present. These negative perceptions and pressures have serious impacts on women's self-esteem and behavior, as well as their agency.

In our sample communities where normative change around gender seems to be unfolding, accounts show a mismatch between personal, household, and community norms, and between generations. For young women, in particular, the decisions women make to work are not in sync with their community's normative framework. But it does not deter them, especially when they need an income or are determined to challenge the norms and affirm their independence. Young women see themselves as not needing or wanting to depend on men; they believe

a woman should provide for herself first. And although they know older generations oppose this way of thinking and believe that women should only be housewives, many young women feel it is important to be able to provide everything
needed for a home. More and more, younger women support the right of women
to get a job and earn a salary; younger generations do not condemn such behavior
as vehemently as older generations do.

Young urban women's views reveal that they are experiencing—by
themselves—the changes in the normative frameworks of their societies. Their
male counterparts are increasingly aware of notions of equality and are slowly
showing willingness to share in the responsibilities of household and child care.
Not only do some men (especially younger men) agree that women should work,
but they also think that giving women access to areas where they have been
excluded (such as certain types of jobs) benefits everyone. Even among young
rural men, the extent of approval for working mothers is higher than with older
generations, and they are willing to voice their support even in the face of community opposition or criticism. This generational change signals a trend in the
direction of greater gender equality. While partly driven by a shift in norms,
a large part of the changes in opinions about working mothers is stimulated or
facilitated by economic conditions.

From Poland to Vietnam, there is evidence that young women expect men to
take on as much housework as women do if they both are working:

> [It is a] partnership. He cooks dinner for me; he washes, clears up, dusts. I would
> not choose to marry him, if we did not share these responsibilities. (Adult woman,
> Martynice, Poland)
> [Husbands and wives] should do everything together. Everyone is tired when they
> get home after work, so they share the work. They can help each other with many
> things. (Adult woman, Hung Yen District, Vietnam)

Younger generations are embracing change. When asked what they think about
working mothers, the responses of young adults in the focus groups were unequiv-
ocally positive. From Bhutan to Fiji, from Sudan to the Republic of Yemen, young
women are seeing and demanding change. While it is still common practice for
women to stay home and take care of household chores, this is changing as more
and more women question the strict gender divisions in responsibility for the
household, become more educated, and work in more diverse occupations—
especially those considered inappropriate for women in the past.

The Good Woman (Not) in Public

A bad girl goes out a lot and a bad wife spends more time away from home than
inside the house; men and boys, on the other hand, routinely have enjoyed more
freedom in their ability to move. Women's limited mobility has long affected
their social connections, enjoyment of free time, economic options, and possibilities for civic engagement. Diverse, interlocking factors tie women to their homes,
including local traditions governing women's and girl's roles, religious practices,
limited public safety, lack of time, and poor transportation infrastructure.

As long as boys are everywhere, we can't move freely. They say that you are walking around and showing yourself off.

—Young urban woman, Aden, the Republic of Yemen

Women go out less. They go out only if we take them.

—Village man, Comendador, the Dominican Republic

She [wife] stays at home and does the house chores. She does not move around the community gossiping.

—Village man in a semi-rural community of Ngonyameni, South Africa

Gender norms surrounding concerns for women's and girl's reputations and family honor also curtail their freedoms. These barriers are easing, however. From comments heard in the focus groups, women and girls are able to leave the house more than previous generations. Yet, the difficult reality is that they have much less freedom than men and boys to go out in public.

Many of the focus groups with younger and older adult village women reported that they face heavy pressures not to move around their communities independently. "The men can move freely in and out of the village and even travel far away from their homes, too. Women cannot go anywhere, much less alone, because of tradition and culture," said a young village woman in Boyina Bagh, Afghanistan. In Koudipally Mandal (Andhra Pradesh), India, young women explained that the school is too far away from the village for girls to attend and "in our Reddy community,[9] even if we are poor, they don't allow us to go out and work. Men care [too] much about the social status." As a result, women have developed alternative strategies: "Some of the women like me have started to learn tailoring and are doing the work at home." In a semi-rural community of Ngonyameni, South Africa, women were asked what it means to have little freedom, and one replied, "It means she is controlled by her husband and cannot visit her friends."

In urban areas, women are also pressured to stay home or nearby in their neighborhoods. Young women in the focus group in Jaipur (Odisha), India, said they are free to move about their neighborhood during the day, but "if [a woman] comes back late at night, then neighbors talk bad about her, and parents and other family members get pushed [to make her behave]." Young women in Dirbas, West Bank and Gaza, agreed that women were restricted as if they were small children by "social circumstances … customs, traditions, and public opinion." In this community and many others in the sample, seclusion practices require that women be accompanied by a male guardian when in public, although educated women with good jobs and poor or widowed women who need to work enjoy more mobility. Still, young men in Dirbas warned that it is better for a woman to "stay at home" instead of "tiring herself" and bringing "problems to the family from her work."

In diverse contexts, women indicated that they may face harsh discipline for leaving housework and children for short periods. They may be openly shamed and mocked for speaking with strangers, wearing insufficiently modest attire, or making the slightest missteps that may be deemed sexually provocative or a sign of loose character. "I may have freedom as a woman, but if I want to go and dance, my husband will give me a black eye," said a woman from the National Capital District, Papua New Guinea. Aside from household obligations, concerns for women's reputations and family honor give rise to strong normative pressures on women to refrain from working or socializing outside the home.

Even in communities in the sample where large numbers of women have been part of the workforce for decades, the extent of some women's mobility is still very constrained. "Some women cannot leave the house or even talk to or hang out with neighbors. We call them 'kuper' (lacking a social network)," explained a woman from East Jakarta, Indonesia. In this same women's focus group, three women volunteered that they are largely secluded in their homes, but for three different reasons. One woman saw herself as having no freedom because of her husband's views: "I can't attend gatherings at the mosque or go sightseeing. My husband doesn't let me. I obey him because he is my husband." The second woman's limited mobility was due to time constraints of meeting her responsibilities at home: "I don't really have freedom because I always have to do the laundry." The third participant was mostly concerned about community perceptions: "If I go out by myself, the neighbors will talk. So now I sell stuff or wash clothes [from home]."

Problems of safety also disproportionately affect women. "By six o'clock in the evening, you should be indoors if you are female," warned a woman from Umlazi township B (near Durban), South Africa. And in Lautoka, Fiji, "A man can travel alone at night, but not a woman because of safety issues." Almost nowhere is it safe for women to move about at night, and even during the day large sections of their neighborhoods may also be off limits because they are unsafe. Given the incidence of mugging, groping, and verbal abuse, public transportation can be especially risky for women and girls. Risk of assault is reported even in communities considered safe by the focus groups, indicating how vulnerable women are to harassment and violence, which are often acceptable.

Although a minority, focus groups with young adults sometimes indicated that young women are flouting the norms that limit their freedom. Although not as much as men, more women are driving cars in Moldova, Poland, and Serbia, for example, and more villages are providing electricity, water, and transportation services that free women from the worst drudgeries and give them more time to venture beyond their households.

Yet, in most places sampled in this study, getting out the front door remains a daily struggle for women. And men, as well as women, acknowledged that women's restricted physical mobility in public is a manifestation of much wider gender power struggles. According to a 39-year-old man from Dirbas, West Bank and Gaza,

> a man can go anywhere to work … [yet he] gets jealous of his sister if she goes to a nearby place to work. So how do you think it will happen that she can go to a faraway place? … But the man's responsibilities are different. He has to work; otherwise, he will never build his home or get married. But for the girl it is different.

Similarly, a man from another urban neighborhood in the West Bank and Gaza argued that the lack of public safety for women is a troubling consequence of the transition underway in gender norms: "Women have just started entering society, so the man is still trying to maintain his control."

Whether in their homes or out in public, deeply embedded gender norms continue to guide the preferences and behaviors of girls and boys, women and men, in the communities visited by the research teams. But around these norms, we also see diverse manifestations of change along with tension over these changes. Young women, in particular, harbor ideals for a world where they too can enjoy whatever opportunities present themselves. Men, on the other hand— across generations and especially in rural areas—appear less willing to accept women's changing roles and aspirations.

Notes

1. The title of chapter 1 is adapted from Bicchieri (2006).

2. In fact, the exploration of what makes a good or bad wife, husband, girl, or boy was conducted within the context of the current community, the previous generation, and the future (of the adolescents). Focus group facilitators launched discussions in all focus groups with this question: "For a woman to be seen as a good wife in your community, what is she like? What does she do? Why?" All adult groups were asked how things had changed compared with the previous generation. Adolescents were asked how they saw themselves in the future at age 25 and what they thought of their parent's lives.

3. It is important to note that the frequencies (or numbers) of mention are not statistically representative data. The samples were not randomly selected and the frequencies show only how often certain themes appeared in focus group conversations. We present the coded frequencies at different junctures to help convey the pattern of findings that emerged from systematic work with the narrative data in the field reports.

4. Rowlands (1997) shows this in Honduras, and Das (2008) in Bangladesh.

5. Bruce, Mensch, and Greene (1998) note that, during this period, health and social behaviors are established that have a lifetime of consequences. Puberty triggers a marked divergence in gender-based trajectories.

6. The field work with adolescents was conducted in eight economies: Burkina Faso, the Dominican Republic, India, Fiji, Bhutan, Sudan, the Republic of Yemen, and West Bank and Gaza. Facilitators asked the children to imagine: "what is a good girl like?; what makes her a good girl?; what is a bad girl like?; and how would you describe them?" The same questions were asked about a good and bad boy.

7. See *World Development Report 2012* chapter 4 for further discussion of women's freedom of movement and chapter 5 for time use and work.

8. The consequences of such "inappropriate" exchanges range from refusing permission for women to work outside the home to insisting on segregated jobs.

9. A higher caste predominantly found in Andhra Pradesh.

References

Bicchieri, C. 2006. *The Grammar of Society*. Cambridge, U.K.: Cambridge University Press.

Bruce, J., B. S. Mensch, and M. E. Greene. 1998. *The Uncharted Passage: Girls' Adolescence in the Developing World*. New York: The Population Council.

Das, M. 2008. "Whispers to Voices: Gender and Social Transformation in Bangladesh." Bangladesh Development Series Paper 22, South Asia Sustainable Development Department, World Bank, Washington, DC.

Rowlands, J. 1997. *Questioning Empowerment: Working with Women in Honduras*. Oxford, U.K.: Oxfam.

CHAPTER 2

Negotiating the Norms That Bind: A Winding Road

Negotiations—explicit or not—have been happening over gender norms over the last generation in our sample communities, as this chapter details. Significant shifts are taking place in these norms and, more importantly, are not generally the result of conflict between couples. Instead of abrupt and conflict-ridden changes, we find that norms are relaxing slowly and sometimes inadvertently, and are creeping into the everyday lives of the people throughout our sample. But people do not always notice the subtly shifting forces, so often the process goes unrecognized.[1]

The evidence collected from the many focus group conversations on intra-household and gender relations reveals a widespread tendency toward greater acceptance of more equitable gender relations and modification of gender-ascribed responsibilities. Members of almost every group testified to the presence of these changes when asked to reflect upon generational changes in the definitions of gender roles and aspirations for the future. The large majority of the adults and young adult participants expressly wanted more cooperation and discussion between men and women. Moreover, as discussed in chapter 1, men's involvement in domestic work and childrearing is increasingly valued, as is the women's right to work and pursue productive activities.

Yet, despite encouraging signs of norms bending toward greater gender equality, this chapter also addresses countervailing forces that impede faster change. The comments from the focus groups make clear that new practices emerge and exist with ease alongside traditional inequitable practices in the same households and communities. Within most every group, participants raised discordant perspectives and opinions about how much change is perceived or desired. To the progressive voices driving change, normative ideals and aspirations may be well ahead of actual behaviors. Focus groups from diverse contexts also elaborated on how slowly changing norms that still sanction male dominance and aggression were significant triggers for marital conflict, particularly under conditions of economic stress.

Men in the past were very strict about tradition and that everything they do be done the traditional way. ... Nowadays, parents—including fathers—let their daughters have more freedom, [for example] if they want to dress a certain way. ... Because life in general is changing, it's hard to keep the traditional way of raising children.

—Adult woman, Fiji

To explore these dynamics, we first discuss how we distinguish a relaxation from a change in gender norms in the dataset, and then present focus group accounts of local trends in daily time use, household roles, marital relations, and parental aspirations for their children. We then explore the participants' perceptions of norm change and how uneven they are. We close by synthesizing accounts about the persistence of domestic violence against women (in nearly one-third of the study communities), which is perhaps the starkest evidence of gender inequality and lack of agency in the case of women. The chapter highlights forces at play that press both for and against norm change in the lives of the study communities.

The Quiet Relaxing and Changing of Norms

We asked focus groups to consider gender norms from many angles and how they are changing, as discussed in the introduction to part I. By comparing responses by the younger and older generations, we can assess how these norms may be evolving in the study communities. In this report, we also look at the focus groups' responses to questions about differences between current and past generations and about their aspirations for themselves and their children. (The recall period for these questions ranges from a decade to one generation, depending on the question.) The sampling frame in each country includes 1–2 communities chosen by the researchers for specific attributes (e.g., girls' school enrollment was high in the country or the local economy was dynamic). We hypothesized that these select communities may likely provide more incentives or opportunities for individuals (of both sexes) to challenge the boundaries of stifling norms. For comparative purposes, the country-level sampling frames also contain urban and rural communities that have the opposite experience, i.e. with fewer educational and economic opportunities.

When investigating norms, it is important to differentiate acts of compliance with the norm from resistance because they imply different levels of agency. For example, a woman who limits her fertility in a community where having many children is the norm necessarily pushes against the expected choices and behaviors for local women. She is demonstrating a different level of agency or of empowerment (if successful) than a woman who limits her fertility in an environment where small families are the norm (Kabeer 1999). It is important to

If she [the wife] is hardworking, goes to work early, comes back home late, and cares for her family, surely people would understand and sympathize with her.

—23-year-old urban woman, Ba Dinh District, Hanoi, Vietnam

recognize that men have an advantage in initiatives that uphold or challenge the norms: as the dominant gender, they can more easily flout or champion norms to suit their interests as long as that challenge does not aim at breaking the basis of their own male identity.[2] By contrast, gender power relations put women at a decided disadvantage if their interests require breaking a gender norm or holding their partner to account.[3]

In addition to the differences between norm compliance and resistance, it is important to distinguish *relaxation* from *change* of a gender norm. By relaxation, we mean that women and men are challenging and perhaps crossing the boundaries of traditional gender roles or conduct, although their actions are not recognized as a legitimate and acceptable norm. They are assuming new roles or responsibilities, but are not setting a new standard. For instance, in Zabibu village, Tanzania, the key informant (who was interviewed to provide information about his village) reported, "Rarely do women work for pay here. They have to stay at home and take care of the household and family. But what work can these women do? They have not even gone to school." Later in his interview, however, he added, "Women are mostly involved in digging holes to plant grapes, tending vegetable gardens, and making 'vyungu' [clay pots]." Women *are* working, which is a relaxation of the norm that restricts them from breadwinning tasks—and they may even be preparing and selling goods in the market. Nevertheless, these activities have not yet been recognized as income generation, but rather as an extension of their domestic duties. Hence, it is acceptable within the traditional norms.

Across the community sample, we find signs of gender norms in transition and uncertainty. Women's pursuit of an economic role or a larger say in managing their households can have unpredictable consequences where these practices are not widely accepted. On one hand, such initiatives may be interpreted as a gender-norm violation and thus subject to sanctions that can damage a woman's reputation and status. On the other hand, if a new role or conduct becomes widely accepted, it may confer on women new status, respect, and influence (or power) in their relations with others. The day-to-day activities that quietly resist or flout norms for women's roles and behaviors may not trigger a complete change or cause an unfair practice to be discarded. These initiatives are nevertheless important because over time they can *potentially* affect power relations within a household. In many cases in our dataset, where a relaxation of gender norms is evident, men's and women's unequal authority in the household remains largely intact, even though the gender differences in their roles, responsibilities, and behaviors are narrowing and disappearing.

Although it may be a subtle difference, we are referring to a change in gender norm in contexts where *both* women's and men's focus groups reported a significant shift in a gender role or in gender power relations. For example, in some communities, husbands shop for groceries when a wife does not feel like cooking and are deeply involved in raising and educating their children. But reports of such engagement were relatively rare in our dataset. A man who admits that he prepares his own dinner may be teased rather than encouraged in many focus groups.

The processes of relaxing and changing norms of behavior, which are so central to our identities and status with others, seem to be slow and hidden. As Ridgeway and Correll (2004, 528) explain,

> to the extent that people continue to deeply hold beliefs that men and women are essentially different, separate categories of people, they will likely resist beliefs that there are absolutely no instrumental differences between men and women in the "things that count," even in the face of clear displays of competence by women. This tension between the belief that men and women are fundamentally different and the displays of similar levels of competence between men and women may facilitate some cultural redefinition in what counts at a given period of history.

The contexts where we see these rarer *changes* in norms are important. Notably, Poland and Serbia have a longer history of gender-sensitive legislation and higher levels of girls' and boys' education. There, men and women can draw from a wide range of public and private discourses and institutions that favor gender equity. We also see important movements in norms in the other countries in the sample—especially in rapidly urbanizing cities and where higher education rates are nibbling at the edges of traditional cultures. In several contexts, the data reveal the presence of other factors that can drive change, such as more egalitarian traditional practices, campaigns to introduce new norms, or decisive policy action by a government.[4]

Timing Is All: Negotiating Opportunities and Gender-Specific Responsibilities

The allocation of resources—particularly scarce ones, such as time—reflects prior normative considerations in communities and households. One area where gender differences are most conspicuous is individuals' use of their time. Time use responds to the "gender contract" obligations, reflecting dominant norms about the division of labor among family members. These obligations affect individual work choices, physical mobility, access to opportunities, and the possibility of free time. In our analysis of time use by the young adult and adolescent focus groups, we find that they have shifted their daily schedules in ways that offer more opportunities for education, work, and free time, despite the persistence of gender disparities and urban-rural differences.

We expected the adolescents and young adults in our sample to more easily articulate views about progress and change in norms because their life experiences reflect gains from previous generations. Indeed, the adolescents' accounts of how they spend their days reveal that they constantly negotiate between taking advantage of "new" opportunities and tending to "old" duties in their households. Yet, almost everywhere, girls and young women still must devote more time to household and care-giving tasks than boys and young men. This is the case whether the young women attend school or not; however, those in school who must study spend fewer hours on household tasks, particularly in urban areas.

The main message from the evidence regarding time use is simple: men have more free time because they do little or no housework. Even when men work long days, they usually end it with some form of distraction or entertainment. Women very rarely pause to enjoy some leisure time. When they are not working for pay or studying, they are tending the house and children. The very definition of free time is adapted to this gendered arrangement of the use of time. Unlike men, women use their free or spare time to work; they simply shift activities. Women are the losers in the time distribution game. Men and women readily acknowledge this fact and, while there is evidence that urban men particularly are doing more to help around the house, inequalities in free time, however, remain.

Young women have more opportunities now for education and work than previous generations, and they are aware of it. Young men likewise find themselves seeking more education than in the past, but they also realize more free time now. To some extent, their gain in free time is due to their entering the labor market at an older age and to decreasing demands on young men to supplement their household's income by working for pay or helping in family businesses and farms. Along with increased opportunities for schooling, young women in both rural and urban contexts also seem to have rid themselves of some of the burdens of being an unpaid family worker. But only urban women see themselves doing less work inside the home than the previous generation. Their circumstances have changed the most, due to living in cities, and so have their expectations. Young women in urban communities want more time to work for pay, in line with their rising aspirations and opportunities. Young women in rural communities long for paid work, but mostly they aspire to do less work inside the home, which primarily occupies their days. However all women—urban and rural—strive for free time.

Incessant Activity

In both rural and urban areas, young and adult women have no or very little free time. They switch from one activity to another and, with few exceptions, are constantly engaged. In a less dynamic rural setting, such as Floresti District, Moldova, "women don't have much spare time. They work and take care of children, their husband, and the household. Free time appears late in the evening or during the winter when there is less farm work." Women in the more dynamic city of Bhubaneswar (Odisha), India, reported being just as busy during their free

On Norms and Agency • http://dx.doi.org/10.1596/978-0-8213-9862-3

It seems like there is no end to what we women must do.

—Village woman, Sungai Puar District, Indonesia

time hours. They work for the family business, teach their children, clean and organize the house, go shopping for clothes and food, and the list continues. Only three activities the women mentioned can be associated with a traditional idea of leisure: eating snacks outside, reading magazines, and buying cosmetics. A woman from urban Dobrowice, Poland (a middling community in terms of economic opportunities and normative change), noted that while men "play ball, go fishing, sit in the front of the television, or drink a beer, we are ironing as a form of relaxation."

The different uses of time by men and women underline the prevailing gender order in the community. If men are expected to enjoy free time after their working hours, norms that insist women not forget their reproductive duties, even when engaging in productive paid jobs, will also persist. This disparity was overwhelmingly affirmed throughout the sample. For men in many communities, women's work at home sustains the right order of things and is inviolate. The normative framework and power relations that impose a double burden on women (in and out of the house) do not disappear or change when economic conditions do. Unemployed young and adult men have to find ways to employ their extra time when they have less income-generating work, but housework is not a viable option. When job and business opportunities for men diminish or unemployment strikes, and women must take on the role of provider and work to support their households, the norms shaping the allocation of time and men's duties do not change.

Men have more alternatives to "kill time," a valuable resource that is under their control. Women never speak in terms of killing time, most likely because their job description as homemaker or caregiver, for example, does not end after eight hours or at twilight. The prescription means that if women wish or need to work outside the home, they may not abandon their "base line" household duties and must factor in the time to accomplish them. This female responsibility is ingrained to the point that it has become "naturalized"; women's incessant activity is not seen as an unequal burden but as part of the female nature. "Women are different. Women like working. Women often keep themselves busy because they feel the need to. They do not care about themselves. They may just go out to have a chat in their free time. In rural areas like ours, women often keep themselves busy all the time, which makes them different from men," noted a woman from rural Vietnam. It is beyond nature—"God has given women the art of multi-tasking, so we won't find anything difficult"—was the view of women in Nellore (Andhra Pradesh), India.

The naturalization or customariness of household work as women-only work also arises from the normative refusal by men to engage in home production.

This belief (and practice) has been reproduced and solidified over time, producing a pattern that is transmitted to the next generations with little change. Younger women are accustomed early to household work and stepping into the older woman's place: "When mother is absent, I am there to take care of everything. Women take care of everything. The man is the household head, but the woman takes care of everything" (young woman, Serbia).

While education and work opportunities can bring positive chances for female autonomy, at the same time, however, they imply a trap that increases women's time burden. The current generation of girls can study and have been freed from part of the burden of housework, but not of its totality. Indeed, looking at the perceptions of what it means to be a good girl (chapter 1), helping at home is still one of the main attributes of a good girl. The appeal of the world beyond the confines of the household beckons women, but such aspirations have to take into account the need to earn income to support themselves and their families, form a family, and run a household, plus manage the expectations of time associated with each of them.

The Rise of the Swedish Husband: An Emerging Male Double-Burden?

If, in previous generations, the primary defining characteristic of a good husband was that he provided for his family, today's younger generations of men and women demand more of the husband, along the lines of the example of the Swedish husband.[5] Although still essential, bringing home the money is no longer enough. Good husbands not only must secure their families' economic well-being but in addition must be sensitive to their wives' and children's emotional needs, spend time with them at home (instead of out with friends, drinking, gambling, or cheating), share domestic chores, and devote time to help the children with their homework. If and when men actually do all these things, we may see the emergence of a masculine double burden. The difference with women's double burden is a matter of emphasis and time allocation. While women may or may not work, they must in any circumstance look after the household; men have little flexibility in the imperative that they must provide for the family, but they have more scope in how much time they spend nurturing the family. The novelty is the expectation that a man spends any time or resources at all in the domestic sphere and that he shares in its management with the wife.

Notice that we are deliberately moving this discussion away from the prevalent patterns of time use and household roles in order to learn from contexts that feature significant relaxation of or incipient changes in gender norms. Adult women and men in Poland and Serbia, especially in urban locations, provided eloquent accounts of changes in the norms that define gender roles in their communities. Compared with their fathers, whose role as provider was sufficient to qualify them as good husbands, the partners of the new generation of women are expected to "understand the woman's needs," "sympathize that I have a stomach ache due to my period," "recognize that we [wife and children] need his help," "realize that I do not feel like cooking and prefer to go to a restaurant,"

On Norms and Agency • http://dx.doi.org/10.1596/978-0-8213-9862-3

I am sensitive to my wife's affairs. I don't wake her up in the morning just so she can prepare my morning coffee. I wake up to make tea and breakfast, and bring it to her because I know that she likes to sleep in the morning and it is the best time to sleep. I take care of all the house affairs in the morning because she has a right to expect me to do so. When I get home in the evening, she does everything to make me happy, so I try to do the same.

—Urban man, University Quarter, West Bank and Gaza

"remember the children's birthdays," and "remember our anniversary [celebrate it] and know how to make the pleasure" (adult women, Dobrowice, Poland).

In addition to being sensitive, the good husband engages in essential house chores. "He cleans the flat, does the basic shopping, cooks" and participates actively in the education of the children. Not only "is [he] willing to spend the time with the child," and "participates in family life and helps with the children's homework," but he has to be good at it. He needs to be "creative while playing with children, like a football game," added the Dobrowice group of Polish women. Women in urban Olsztyn, Poland, reported that "now he distinguishes the cabbage from the lettuce." The same definitions of the good husband appear in Belgrade, Serbia, where women claimed that, apart from having a "secure income … he divides the household chores with his wife, goes shopping, and is resourceful (can take care of himself) and tolerant. He must not be an idiot who is not capable of cooking a meal or ironing his clothes."

Crucially, these notions are shared by men and reinforce the assumption that the bending of norms occurs in a relatively non-conflictive manner in everyday interaction. A man from Justynowo, Poland, explained that sometimes "[when] my wife comes back from work, her female friends come to visit and she tells me to cook dinner by myself." He sees this as fair and does not think his wife is behaving as a bad wife. The fact that women and men expressed similar views testifies to a shift in what is consensually considered desirable, probably as a result of the interactions between education, economic opportunities, and messages in the media and other public spaces, where discourses about gender circulate. As a quite forward-looking adult male in urban Sjenica, Serbia, remarked, "[the good husband must be willing] to serve his wife, to be obedient, to make pies, and to wash the dishes." Simply making this statement constitutes a massive shift in the status quo of a community where the good husband of the past was "the chief income earner" and "did not help his wife in the household." A strong push for normative change has risen due to the high levels of male unemployment in the community and the emergence of opportunities for women. Men are no longer the sole breadwinners and they have had to adapt.

In Belgrade, Serbia, adult men claimed that a good husband "does not divide male and female chores. [A husband and wife] should complement each other and find mutually beneficial solutions." "He cannot just sit and watch television if the child needs to change clothes and the wife is cooking dinner." Their good husband is a "good parent, caring, thoughtful." In Pomoravlje District, Serbia, the good husband of the past "used to be undisputed in decision-making: his word was final. The wife was to obey, love, even wash his feet." Now, however, these men insisted that the good husband today "washes, irons, helps his wife, even vacuums, and usually does the hard physical labor."

In a radical departure from tradition, one man from Pomoravlje District argued that "if your wife is at home, you have to contribute something. You can't expect her to do everything and you do nothing. You can't spend your time in a pub, you have to help her." The good husband also "has to have time for the children. And this does not mean simply hanging out with them every once in a while." "He has to know what to do to get the children prepared for school, even cooking lunch if necessary, if he wants to have children who love and respect him. He has to be dedicated to them, not just let them see him once in five days." Other men in the group agreed that household cooperation is the ideal.

While men do not question these additional responsibilities as diminishing their masculinity, they have some concern that the balance of power may shift in women's favor in the future: "Men are slightly more dominant now, but women may become more dominant soon" (adult man, Pomoravlje District, Serbia). For the moment, the extra duties taken on by men do not alter the core of their role as breadwinners. As another man in the same group explained, although men are expected to do more at home, the "husband still has to provide most of the household income. His income is the biggest and the most important for the functioning of the household. It gives him self-respect." When men do not feel threatened in their main role as providers, they are more willing to accept changes in their secondary, domestic roles.

In nearby Moldova, we also find evidence of norm relaxation, but it is more incipient and appears only in urban contexts. Women in Balti see their good husband as someone who "participates actively in his children's education" and "balances his work and family in the same way as a woman does. After work he goes home and spends his leisure time with the family." Men in the same city agreed that a good husband "manages to balance work with home responsibilities and support his wife"; however, he does so only as long as the traditional association between income and self-respect that are central to his idea of masculinity remains intact.

But again in Sjenica, Serbia, increased domestic work by men is a direct result of their unemployment and men expressed their frustration. In contrast to husbands in the past, "today we are not working and we are unable to provide for and make our families happy." These circumstances may trigger violence, as explored more below, but may also produce peaceful accommodation. The apparent ease with which these new changes fit into male identity in some households and communities indicates the potential for future behavior change. The more mainstream these ideas become, the easier it is for young men and boys to follow their fathers as role models and be socialized in more egalitarian gender norms.

The relaxation and change of norms that shape gender roles is also evident in the focus groups in communities where women's education took off later and where cultural views of women are more traditional. In some sample communities in India, for example, changes in the economy and educational opportunities have spurred new awareness of the need to share responsibilities, particularly in urban areas. In urban Bhubaneswar (Odisha), India, adult women's changed expectations for their partners are evident in that they define the good husband as someone who "takes responsibility of house," "takes responsibility of children," "does household work when wife is sick," and "should work, but also should spend quality time with wife and children." Similarly, in urban Jaipur (Odisha), India, men agreed that the good husband must "take out some time from the day to day activity to help the children in studies." By comparison, in the rural groups from India, we find more modest signs of change. But even though small, women perceived a difference at the margins of the strict norms that regulate their actions:

> There is a difference [from the previous generation]. In those days, the husband was treated like a god. The wife in my mother's generation would wait for her husband to come home and she would eat her food only after her husband had his dinner. These days, the wife doesn't wait for her husband, but after he wakes her up, she serves dinner to him. (Village women, Koudipally Mandal, Andhra Pradesh, India)

Sisum's story, which opens chapter 1, makes clear the differences between urban Thimphu and rural Samtse. In the countryside, the central characteristic of the husband as the provider of the family remains, but men now seem more open-minded about the restrictions that some traditional norms impose on women. Radical change in gender roles across all countries and communities is still far away, but the emergence of more progressive views of men's contribution to housework mean, at least, greater visibility of the double demands upon women. Men are also challenging the dictate of staying removed from reproductive tasks demanded by traditional masculinity. Becoming more involved in the lives of their children arises, one assumes, not only from a sense of duty but from the pleasures and rewards associated with it. Still, men are "helping," rather than taking responsibility for household chores or children's education.

Open Dialogue and Emergence of Household Power Sharing

The notion of cooperation in household discussions—open dialogue—is requisite to the success of a couple, and central in the view of a Vietnamese man from Hung Yen District, who said, "Husband and wife should discuss [an issue] and come to the same decision. The spousal relationship should be equal. For instance, they have to discuss and agree on buying a television or not. A decision made without their [mutual] agreement is seldom successful." In Kim Dong

District, Vietnam, an adult woman described her belief about domestic balance of power:

> In my opinion, balance of power means each partner is free to share their ideas in the couple's discussion before a decision is made. It is similar to a couple [reaching] consensus. If, for example, the husband takes the lead of the family and his wife and children have to ask him for money to buy everything, his wife and children have no share of the power.

Although not abundant, evidence in this study of peaceful routine negotiations, daily conversations, and transactions between spouses or partners offers glimpses of groundbreaking changes in household cooperation, open dialogue, and even power sharing. Dialogue and harmonious relations have an instrumental, beneficial value, not only for family life but also for economic decision-making within the household (see, for example, Aizer 2010; Panda and Agarwal 2005; Pronyk *et al.* 2006; Swaminathan, Walker, and Rugadya 2008; and World Bank 2012). From Fiji to Moldova to India, the possibility of partners being able to express different opinions without conflict—open dialogue—is significant progress as gender norms bend and change. Its presence is mnemonic for contemporary visions of a "good" couple and the emerging equality between women and men.

Notably, the task of initiating more open dialogue is placed on men. It is both seemingly contradictory and expected, given that men are the main power holders and traditional leaders of the household. For example, women in rural Kalahandi District (Andhra Pradesh), India, felt that it is a good husband's *duty* to "consult his wife for decisions made in the family and discuss household issues with women." Numerous examples in the data show that women observed positive changes in their husbands and new spaces opened up for negotiation and dialogue—where husbands consulted their wives, permitted conversations to take place around family decisions, did not make decisions alone, and were open to dissenting views. Given that men are the main power holders and expected household leaders, *the creation of more space for dialogue is in their hands*.

A comment from a man in rural Zabibu Village, Tanzania, underlines this shift—by men—in domestic power relations as a result of more open dialogue between men and women: "For me, I think that if you want to remain powerful, you must collaborate with people. You must also listen a lot, especially to your wife, because sometimes women have good ideas." His further comment is even more revealing: "Look at 'H.' He was educated and had money, but he quarreled with his wife. And what happened? When he abandoned his wife, he married another one who simply ate his money, so where is he now? At the bottom [of the power ladder]."

Dialogue has an important normative component to it—meaning that both men and women adhere to it as a matter of principle. But it is illuminating if one also considers that, when women have their own income,[6] their capacity to engage men in negotiation greatly increases. Income gives women bargaining power, as the younger women in the study particularly are discovering and exploring. In addition, due to their gains in education and public engagement, the young women have also become more aware of their rights and are developing different expectations of their relationships with men. Informed, connected, and aspiring women with some income of their own are likely to demand more open dialogue in their households, but they also have more resources to prevail in some decisions or reach agreement with their husbands or partners. However, as we discuss later in chapter 5, norms do not always change with women's economic independence.

Intergenerational Transmission of the Possibility of Change

Perhaps the final quiet mechanism that ensures movement toward more equal gender norms is the infusion of this aspiration into the next generation's ideals. The "capacity to aspire" is the first step toward change (Appadurai 2004). When prompted about their hopes for their children's futures, the parents in the sample agreed that they wished for them a good education and work opportunities. Both are tools that increase their agency, fuel their drive to seek a better life, and teach them to make sound choices. Education and economic well-being dominated the discussions on aspirations for sons and daughters alike.

The parents' narratives display a diverse set of aspirations, ranging from specific changes in gender norms (daughters do not have to obey their husbands unquestioningly or will not be abused), gender relationships (open dialogue and more equality), and the traditional practices that are detrimental to women, to positive character traits (be more decisive and stronger). We find these in urban and rural communities, but significantly, they appear mostly in adult women's aspirations for girls and younger women. This is crucial, given the central role of women in the socialization of children in family norms and their potential roles as agents of change.

The hope of women that their daughters can develop stronger personalities, learn from their mothers' mistakes, and take better charge of their lives appears across the sample. Notably, in countries like Burkina Faso, the very suggestion that young girls be more alert and seek different life paths from their mothers constitutes a significant departure from tradition and a shift in the norms that link good life choices today with those of the previous generations. Mothers in Burkina Faso described the development of more courageous, less passive personalities and a reflective or critical attitude as a desire for their daughters: "They must fight more for themselves and be more daring." In East Sepik Province, Papua New Guinea, women wanted to teach their daughters from their own experiences and help their daughters avoid making the same mistakes that limited their own life choices, "[like] those girls who got pregnant early and missed out on opportunities."

Mothers' hopes for positive character traits in their daughters applied to their sons as well, although they typically spoke of sons avoiding bad behavior. For instance, an adult woman in Chiclayo, Peru, wished her son would "continue working, be as responsible at home as he is with his two sons, and not fall into alcoholism or a life of vice." If her aspirations for her son are successful,

[A woman] knows the traditions and picks what is important and tries to transmit what she thinks is good for kids now.

—Village woman, Malangachilima village, Tanzania

this mother will have bucked a set of attitudes that in Peru, as in many other countries, have defined masculinity for a long time.

In Thimphu, Bhutan, mothers' aspirations for their sons include a more direct reference to gender equality: "Equality for both would make the biggest difference in the lives of our daughters and would imbue our sons with the understanding that all humans of opposite gender are same." These women "would love to see their girl and boy children take equal stand in all sectors, where girls will not be the underprivileged gender." Just as with their daughters, mothers socialize their sons and can also be key agents for change in their son's attitudes and behaviors. The willingness of mothers and fathers to embrace gender equality in their children's education may bring massive change and make gender relations in the next generation more equitable and harmonious.

As gender norms loosen, today's young women are less content to recreate the family dynamics of their mothers. When the young adult women in the sample were asked if they wished to lead lives similar to their mothers, they responded consistently that they wanted to be more proactive, less tolerant of abuse, and more informed. For example, in an urban area of Hato Mayor Province, the Dominican Republic, one young woman asserted that she did not want to be "passive in her life" like her mother. Another urban young woman, in Nsenene village, Tanzania, disapproved of her mother's tolerance of her father's violent behavior: "She does not say anything to my father who beats her up." In Bhubaneswar (Odisha), India, young women rejected their mother's "innocence" and ignorance: "[The women] never came out of their houses, so they did not even know what was happening outside."

Further signs of change are appearing in the norms that surround marriage. A group of mothers, also in Bhubaneswar, had revolutionary hopes for their daughters: "[We wish] them to find a good life partner. If they marry by their own choice, then the boy can be of a caste lower than theirs." This aspiration that their daughters have a choice in marriage not only significantly challenges a powerful traditional gender norm but also breaks a status-related norm.

Mothers also pass along traditions to their daughters in order to safeguard their reputations, ensure proper marriages, and preserve family honor in compliance with gender norms. When asked about her desires for her child's future, a mother from Sumadija District, Serbia, declared, "She should be able to go out during the day, but not during the night. And she must get an education, otherwise she will have no chance of finding a good job." Like any mother, she wanted what is best for her children, even if some of her wishes still limit her daughter's freedoms and reinforce gender inequalities.[7]

Mothers in our study also wanted to spare their daughters from physically harmful traditional practices. For example, rural women in Burkina Faso and Tanzania opposed having their daughters undergo the traditional ritual of female genital cutting.[8] These mothers expressly talked about the harm to their daughters and that they did not want them "circumcised, so they can give birth more easily." One mother in Malangachilima village, Tanzania, was particularly eloquent about the negative impact of the practice and the need for change:

> I hope one thing happens to this community. We used to have a reality of circumcising girls. Many organizations came and sensitized the society about how bad it was and the situation seemed to improve. I have one request for my fellow women: let us be honest with ourselves and our daughters if we love them. There are still some women who are still doing this to their daughters when they are very young and it cannot be noticed easily. We take our children to visit their aunties, but that [genital cutting] is what we go to do. Let us try to convince each other to completely stop it. We are not telling anybody lies, except ourselves; our daughter will blame us and we shall feel ashamed at some point.

Gender Norms in Transition

In order to learn more about processes of norm change, we cast a spotlight above on evidence in the dataset where this is more pronounced. The transition to new and more equitable gender roles and relations is not linear: old and new co-exist. Advances toward more equitable norms on some fronts may not be matched by progress on others. Gains may sometimes be reversed. Actual behaviors may deviate from changing ideals and aspirations. And, perhaps to be expected, focus group members often disagreed among themselves about the nature of normative changes occurring in their households and communities. This muddled story on norm changes, moreover, emerges in almost every context we sampled. On balance, change is surely happening, but at the local level it is often patchy, gradual, and difficult to discern. (Also see box 2.1.)

For example, an earlier quotation by the women of Koudipally Mandal (Andhra Pradesh),[9] India, described how a new dinner rule has taken root, which no longer requires them to wait to eat until after the men have finished. This is also a community, however, where female seclusion is practiced and violence against women remains high and generally acceptable. Women there "should not go out, even if the husband scolds or beats her. She should adjust." Over and over again, the data show that, although some norms do relax, other significantly inequitable norms persist. Also, it is not only in more traditional contexts that overtly coercive forces uphold gender hierarchies. Urban Dobrowice, Poland, is another community (quoted earlier) where husbands are engaging meaningfully in household work and family care.[10] Yet, the Koudipally Mandal and Dobrowice focus groups reported that domestic violence occurs there regularly. (Koudipally Mandal and Dobrowice are outliers on the continuum of domestic violence of all focus groups, with greater levels than most.) The point here is simply that,

In the past, everyone knew which roles belonged to men and which roles belonged to women. Today you do not know which role belongs to whom.

—Urban woman, Belgrade, Serbia

Box 2.1 Co-Existence of Norms and Support for Women's Work Outside the Home in Islamic Communities

No causal connection has been shown between low numbers of women in the labor force and Islam's religious beliefs and ideals. Islam is, arguably, no more gender biased[a] than Judaism and Christianity. Other factors, such as geography, culture, and history—more so than religion—are more responsible for fewer women working, for example, in the Middle East and North Africa (Rauch and Kostyshak 2009; World Bank 2012). In fact, female labor varies widely across the Arab world, from lower levels in the West Bank and Gaza to much higher ones in Indonesia. Indeed, in Offenhauer's (2005) extensive review, these different labor rates for women reflect variations in national economic structures and strategies or in local pre-existing cultural values.

The evidence from the countries in our sample is similar, which shows no single standard or norm for women's domestic and breadwinner roles or for working mothers.[b] For example, normative restrictions are more intense in Afghanistan, Sudan, and the Republic of Yemen, although there are signs of normative change in West Bank and Gaza and open support for women's work autonomy in Indonesia, especially among young adults. While the communities in these five countries adhere to women's "natural" role as the guardian of domestic order (or "original duty,"[c] as pointed out by a Sudanese Muslim man), these views do not differ from other sample countries where different religions are practiced.

The norms, which underlie whether women can work, frame women's decisions about jobs in terms of compatibility with household duties and supplemental income to what the man earns. "They [men] deal with women's work as a necessity, but if their living conditions improve, then women should stay home and not do any kind of work" (young man, Sudan). In the Republic of Yemen, Muslim men generally felt the same way, given that "most of the available jobs for women interfere with their family care obligations. Women's work for pay gets in the way of their original (traditional) duties" (young man, Aden, the Republic of Yemen). But the economic struggles faced by Yemeni households are forcing gender norms to slacken to the point that men now *expect* their wives to contribute to the family income.

Notably, these views co-exist with other attitudes that see no problem with women working. These positive views may develop from exposure to other realities, more education, or economic hardship. In a rural village in Afghanistan, adult men explained that "before, mothers could not work out of home, but now they can because they have more education and are exposed to the opinions of other women—who immigrated when war erupted—that women can work." Urban young women in Afghanistan also sought to work as a logical

box continues next page

Box 2.1 Co-Existence of Norms and Support for Women's Work Outside the Home in Islamic Communities (continued)

consequence of their education: "It is better for women to go out to work, but if her family does not agree, it is better to stay at home. … But if the family sends the girls to school, then they must accept that the girls will work and earn an income."

In Indonesia, although the adult women were more compliant with traditional norms that dictate that they must consult their husbands before working outside the home, educated young Muslim women living in cities expressed strong opinions about their right to work and to be independent. This does not mean, however, that they do not face the same normative limitations as their mothers, but that they are willing to fight them. "In the past, the girls were not allowed to go out or even go to school, but the current situation has changed. I have a sister who is studying and will work for sure," pointed out a young man from Dirbas, West Bank and Gaza.

Overall, the situation in Islamic countries is not substantially different from other countries. Changes in views and practices are slower and uneven, but the normative frameworks in Muslim communities are clearly adapting to the new aspirations and realities of the women and men living there.

a. The positions on women held by very conservative or extreme proponents of Islam (whose aggressive actions have dominated media headlines in recent years) do not reflect what Islam actually says about women and their roles and activities.
b. Similar variation in norms is reported for Bangladesh in World Bank (2008). This study finds, for example, more support for gender equality in education, but it does not translate into views that husbands and wives should have equal education.
c. "Original duty" is the view in Islam.

under diverse conditions, new and old norms can exist together in the same households and communities. (Also see box PI.1.)

In many rural men's focus groups, particularly, it was not uncommon for members to express open dissatisfaction that women are gaining a stronger and more independent voice. The men of Hung Yen District, Vietnam, as noted earlier, mostly lauded consultative decision-making processes between couples as key to making better choices. Still, others in this group cautioned against women gaining too much power and freedom because "you can kill yourself" or "living that way, you are considered self-indulgent." One man added,

> Local women are supposed to meet four attributes of an ideal woman: industry, appearance, respectful speech, and proper behavior. Therefore, it is not good for wives or mothers to have much freedom. The image of a man who gambles and drinks alcohol has been around for ages. A woman should enjoy freedom only within a certain scope.

The women's group from Hung Yen District disagreed among themselves whether it is good for women to have extensive freedom, although they too valued more open dialogue among couples, now generally accepted. Gender differences in status and acceptable behaviors are narrowing, but views can vary greatly, even among peers of the same sex and same generation, over how much normative change is taking hold and is even desirable.

Moreover, although we often heard reports of better communication among couples, the discourse described as beneficial by both men and women did not necessarily involve a full and fair consideration of one another's views. As is evident from the data, women frequently tended to concede or compromise in order to avoid disrupting family harmony or to protect the husband's feelings, or out of concern for the welfare of the children and their own physical well-being. So, in many cases, there is dialogue, but often women pull out of the conversation before it even starts.

For example, one woman from Sungai Puar District, Indonesia, explained that "generally, the wife is more patient due to family considerations. Maybe, because the children are still little, she will let things be for a while." In Zabibu Village, Tanzania, where there is plenty of evidence of increases in women's autonomy, one adult woman thought that "good couples simply have wives who are submissive to the husbands. Couples where women are emancipated have family problems because the husband and the wife will always be in endless discussions and quarrels." One way for a wife to avoid these quarrels, according to women in Kalahandi District (Andhra Pradesh), India, is when "consulted by her husband … she agrees to what he says."

Consideration for the husband's feelings or reputation continues to be a prominent factor that prevents women in the study from pursuing their ideas or projects. As discussed in the next chapter on key decision-making processes, women do not always succeed in negotiations or in bringing about dialogue. This situation may be changing in the new generation for whom the norms are no longer sacred. An intergenerational dialogue between two women in Levuka, Fiji, made this evident. The older woman (in her 50s) asserted that "a good wife will not try to outdo her husband. Even if she is working, and he is not, she will still treat him as if he were the head of the household. She will not belittle him." The younger woman (in her 20s) argued that "maybe in the past it was like that, but my husband helps me wash clothes and cook food, so I think it is all right to be a good wife and ask your husband to help in the house."

Even one of the most progressive communities in the sample, urban Olztsyn, Poland, produced diverging views on the qualities of a good wife. One woman opined that a good wife should be very attentive to her husband's needs: "She doesn't sleep at night" if required to manage her work load, and "doesn't talk back." But other women in her group disagreed, arguing for a more give-and-take relationship and that a woman needs to "motivate her husband to help her." Mixed signs of progress were also evident in other exchanges in this group. As one woman indicated, her son-in-law "creates partnership in his marriage: he and his wife go shopping together, he always makes the bed, and he cleans up after himself. My husband doesn't." Another woman countered, "My son-in-law just does the opposite: he does not help my daughter, like my husband. He claims that he works very hard and deserves to rest—he has been brought up this way."

If some women in the study seemingly gave up in the process of negotiation, others adopted strategic responses to unequal power distributions and pretended to comply with the norm. They either included the husband perfunctorily: "You see, if you are not careful with men, you can lose it all. So you need to make sure that you involve them, so they feel involved, and then you can continue with the business" (woman in Tanzania)—or they simply acted as if they followed the rules, but then did what they wanted when their husbands were not present or did not notice.

In a few cases, focus groups reported trends that suggested backsliding on normative gender conduct. In some sample communities in Liberia, women perceived they had made significant strides in gender equality. They felt that they are clearly gaining more powerful public roles, but they also expressed frustration that their partners are becoming less cooperative. "The men refuse to cut palm nuts and brush on the farm, so we now have to do it," complained a woman from Greenville District. Throughout Liberia, men are simultaneously struggling to adapt to women's new roles and dealing with the slow recovery of the economy after the end of the civil conflict in 2003. Unfortunately, in some cases, women's economic participation can fuel violence by men against them. Women's empowerment and gender norm change do not always move amicably together.

"A Woman Should Be Beaten if She Deserves Punishment"

In this section, we present men's and women's accounts of domestic conflict and violence in their communities. Facilitators introduced the topic by asking the focus groups to reflect on what typically happens in their communities when a wife is not a good wife or a husband is not a good husband. Their responses make evident that domestic violence is all too common, albeit at varying levels across the sample. Economic factors are perceived to be a principal trigger, but focus group narratives revealed that slowly changing norms for acceptable roles and conduct also contribute to violence and the forms that it takes. The focus groups' narratives consistently reported that men who are unable to fulfill their provider role often act out their frustrations with violence, and that it remains acceptable in many communities to sanction women harshly for minor infractions that are perceived as challenging male authority or norms of feminine conduct.

In general, private interviews rather than group discussions are preferable when investigating questions of intimate partner stress and violence. (We included both in the study.) Nevertheless, the focus group discussions still painted a rough picture of what is deemed "normal" or perhaps "acceptable" in conversation about this sensitive topic among friends and neighbors. A large majority of the adult focus groups spoke in some detail on this difficult subject.[11]

The gender literature varies in its emphasis on more- versus less-coercive mechanisms that make gender norms difficult to dislodge. Actual or credible threats of violence are the most extreme, costly, and risky of the mechanisms that sustain gender inequalities and enforce gender norm compliance. Much more potent and effective, however, are the everyday routine interactions and internalized psychological processes that sustain gender hierarchies, as well as other social inequalities, with less disruption.[12] As discussed in the introduction, norms

---

Does a good husband have to be good provider? (Facilitator)

Yes, that is the main reason why he is the head of the family. You know, if he doesn't do that people will make jokes about him.

—Village man, Blue Nile State, Sudan

If she is nagging me and I tell her to stop, and she continues nagging, then it is her fault and she deserves to be beaten.

—Urban man, Belgrade, Serbia

---

carry with them a set of socially acceptable sanctions that may be invoked in instances of deviation from the norm. These acts of sanction are part and parcel of the common, acceptable conduct of household members. In addition, norms are held in place by deeply internalized beliefs about men's greater authority and competency (Ridgeway and Correll 2004). Foucault (1995), for example, argues that social control most often works through internalization, self-discipline, and vigilance rather than external coercive mechanisms that inflict pain.

In their rethinking of the notion of "hegemonic masculinity," Connell and Messerschmidt (2005, 842) stress the less-passive ways in which men use language to meet their "interactional needs" and favorably "position themselves through discursive practices."[13] They also reflect on ways that "boys and men choose those discursive positions that help them ward off anxiety and avoid feelings of powerlessness." These discursive acts to reaffirm men's dominant position are widely evident in the focus group accounts about marital strife. Their narratives pointed to causes of domestic violence as men's affirmation of their dominant role and response when it appears to be challenged. Other studies also suggest that men's peers play important roles in upholding gender norms of masculinity, dominance, and aggressive behavior: peer pressure on men pushes them to earn respect and demonstrate their competency by subordinating woman (see, for instance, Holland, Ramazanoglu, and Sharpe 1998). These demands on men to secure and display control greatly complicate women's agency and pursuit of goals that require resisting or relaxing the gender norms that govern their roles and responsibilities. They also complicate women's power to compel their partners to uphold their prescribed roles and responsibilities— for example, to insist that their husbands behave respectfully, be good decision-makers, and provide for their families.

Extent and Forms of Domestic Violence

Sisum's questioning, in the opening of part I, of a dinner rule that sparked a wild tirade by her father, was not at all unusual in our focus groups' accounts of the normative behaviors that surround marital stress. While for some participants— mostly women—the outburst itself could qualify as an act of violence, this view was not shared by most men. The men's focus group from Samtse, Bhutan

(Sisum's village), reported domestic violence as a rare event in their community, although the women rated it as occurring regularly. This discrepancy may arise because these men do not perceive displays of rage or overt threats of violence toward women as domestic violence, while the women register the physical intimidation or the knowledge that such rage often precedes violence.

Both women and men in the study often pointed out, in very different contexts, that seemingly minor actions by the female could spark explosive reactions from the male authority figure, which were wholly disproportionate to the immediate circumstances. Many focus groups indicated that a wife may be harshly scolded, or even beaten, should she "not be pleasant," talk about "small matters," "gossip," or serve a meal that is "not tasty" or "late." Men in diverse communities mentioned chiding or sternly reprimanding women for triggering conflict with their "useless talking and interference." In Pomoravlje District, Serbia, a man referred to women as "sharp-tongued; they are masters of mental abuse, they nag, they harass, they badger." In Ceadîr-Lunga, Moldova, another man warned,

> for example, if a friend of mine comes to visit me—not the family—then my wife should pour the wine into our glasses. She may also drink a glass, but immediately after she has to leave the room. God save her if she starts chatting, making comments, or judging someone or something.

Yet, in the study, for women to punish or belittle a man for these same "misbehaviors" is generally unthinkable and unacceptable. In addition, a woman is expected to discipline herself, and if she fails—for example, by not holding her tongue—then she may be harmed or abused as a consequence. Focus groups reported that a woman who is a victim of abuse may be advised by her parents, friends, in-laws, and neighbors of her duty to accept the shame and mistreatment for provoking her husband. In Ba Dinh District, Vietnam, for instance, the men's group noted, "Neighbors will give advice to the wife, something like 'your husband has a hot temper, so you should find a better time to talk with him. Try not to complain too much.'" Such are the stark realities of the unfair sanctioning practices that govern daily life and the unlevel playing field of marital conflict.

Figure 2.1 reveals that on average focus groups perceived domestic violence to be occasional events in their communities, although significantly 31 percent of women's groups thought domestic violence was a regular or frequent occurrence in their communities versus 19 percent of men's groups. Rural men acknowledged the least amount of domestic violence. Focus groups on balance indicated, however, that such violence is ebbing, compared to a decade ago. While these perceptions of how much domestic violence occurs are not derived from representative samples, they do signal that violence remains a serious threat and challenge.[14] And given the shame and stigma associated with family conflict, the discourse among focus group members likely understates the extent and severity of marital stress and domestic violence.

The averages in figure 2.1 hide significant variations. At one extreme are the sample communities that both women and men deem to be very safe and,

Figure 2.1 Perceptions of the Prevalence of Domestic Violence against Women in the Study Communities

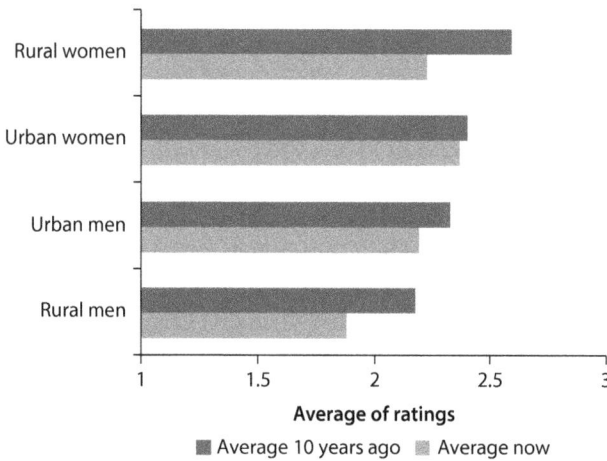

Note: The figure shows the average of ratings by focus group members in 194 adult focus groups. The ratings were done privately by individuals during the focus groups, and then the general pattern of response was discussed. Happens: 1 = almost never; 2 = occasionally; 3 = regularly; 4 = frequently.

Figure 2.2 Reports of Forms of Domestic Abuse against Women

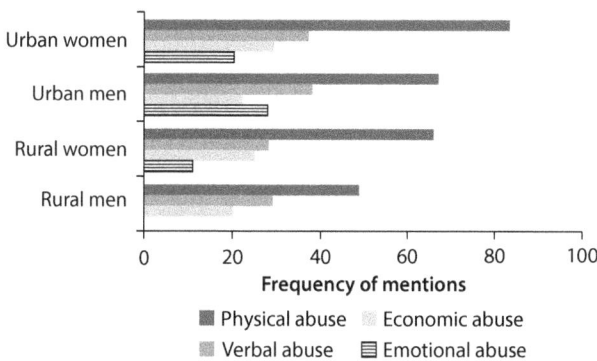

Note: Data from 194 adult focus groups.

at the other, are those where the respondents' reports echoed this man from Koudipally Mandal (Andhra Pradesh), India: "The women are not physically abused as frequently as they used to be. Of course, around 40 percent are still being abused physically. The reasons are mainly related to earnings." The large variation in local levels of violence is consistent with the findings of randomized surveys of domestic violence (Heise 2011).

Figure 2.2 presents a snapshot of the most common abuses mentioned in the focus groups' descriptions of marital conflict. Most often, and by quite a large margin, their comments centered on men's acts of physical violence against women, which was mentioned more than other types of abuse. This pattern emerged despite the facilitators' explanations to the groups of our interest in learning about all forms of violence common among couples in the community, whether verbal, emotional, economic (deprivation), or physical. Still, male-on-female physical abuse dominated the discussions, usually reported with single-word descriptions of violence, such as slapping, punching, hitting, bashing, or raping. Sometimes the participants were more specific: hitting with a broom, pulling hair, breaking arms and legs, being denied food, forcing sex, using knives, or being left outside at night.

Facilitators had the option of aiding the discussions about marital conflict by drawing a cause-impact diagram and jotting down the main comments from the group about the different causes, forms, and impacts of abuse. Figure 2.3 displays the diagram from a women's focus group in a densely populated neighborhood of Ba Dinh District in Hanoi. The diagram shows more detail in the forms of abuse, but otherwise is typical of other diagrams generated by the focus groups. Both men's and women's groups from the Hanoi neighborhood reported declining levels of violence, although the women's diagram indicates quite diverse forms of violence. The diagram also highlights how expected behaviors and gender roles are at the center of the causes, as well as in the types, of violence. For example, such practices as making all the decisions or not allowing a wife to go out are nothing but a tightening of some norms already in existence. The Hanoi women also listed many good reasons why a woman would hide being abused, including neighborhood gossip, public shame, the stigma attached to herself and her family, and high risk of further beatings.

Figure 2.3 Causes and Consequences of Violence, Women's Focus Group in Ba Dinh District of Hanoi, Vietnam

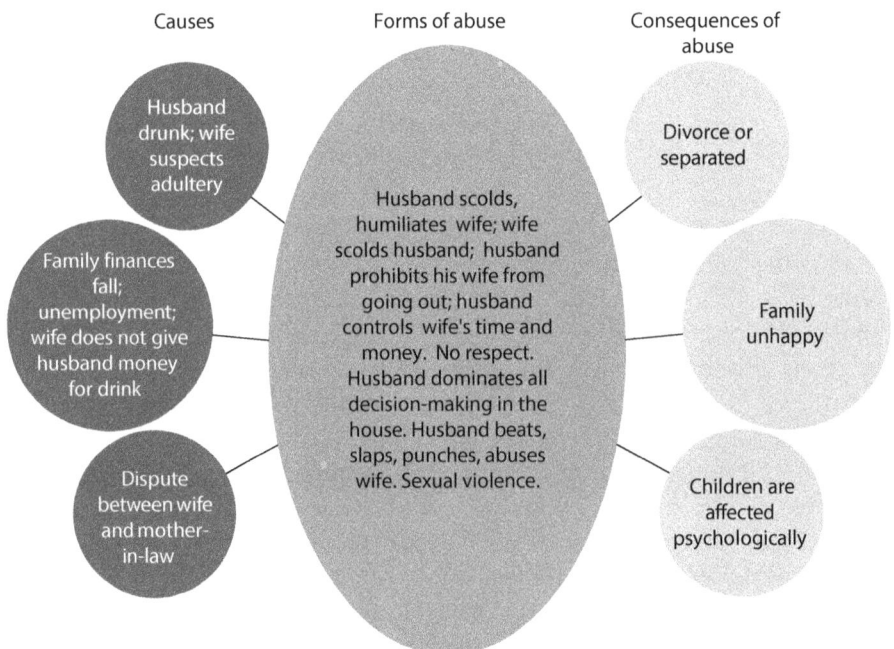

Women from this neighborhood of Hanoi conceded that they "scolded their husbands," and many focus groups of both sexes reported that women also can be emotionally and verbally abusive. Yet, the greatest preponderance of violence described was men's physical abuse of women. This passage from a 37-year-old man from the neighborhood captured this pattern:

> In our district, there are cases where men beat women and women mentally terror-ize men. Because they have different points of view on some problem, men and women argue with each other. Men do not talk about rights because men and women are equal. Men are stronger and in a dispute, when a man finds it difficult to control his anger, he may use his hand to punch or slap his woman. For the woman, because of the pressure to care for the family, it is easy for her to get angry. Women tend to have this habit of complaining to the husband when he comes back home late. It is meant to terrorize men psychologically.

Well beyond Hanoi, other men's groups viewed a wife's "banter," "sulking," "grumbling," or "complaining" as "mental torture" that merited the harshest discipline. In Hato Mayor, the Dominican Republic, the men listed one reason for violence as "women at times put a lot of pressure on them." In Balti, Moldova, urban men said that violence can happen "because the wife couldn't stop from making caustic comments about some mistakes her husband made." Clearly, deeper stresses are driving these processes.

Causes and Consequences of Domestic Violence

Perhaps to be expected, economic factors, such as poverty, joblessness, hunger, and financial problems and mismanagement, emerged most often as causes of domestic violence (figure 2.4). The narratives revealed, moreover, that many times these fights are not just about economic hardship. Men may also become belligerent because they feel they need to reassert or maintain their dominance, because they have lost the provider status or ability that underpins their power in the home, or because their partners are gaining economic independence.[15]

Figure 2.4 Perceptions of Reasons for Domestic Violence

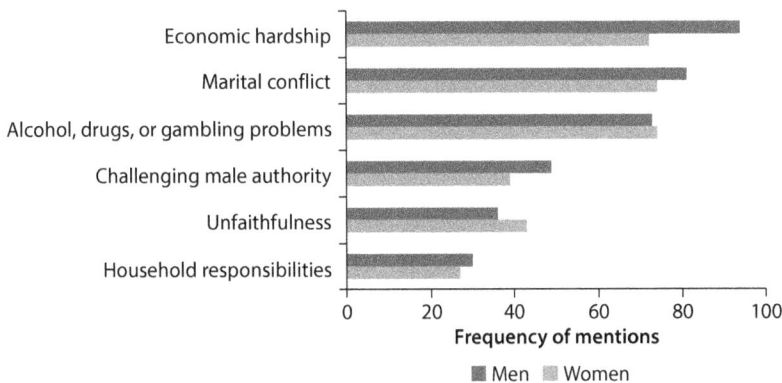

Note: Data from 194 adult focus groups.

On Norms and Agency • http://dx.doi.org/10.1596/978-0-8213-9862-3

This interchange from a men's group in Martynice, Poland, displays the tight links between money and power:

> Women are more often smart alecks [about money].
> The money issue is not settled. Most of the disagreements [in a marriage] are connected to money.
> The wife asks, "Why are you earning so and so? Couldn't you find a better job? How am I supposed to live on this money?" And if she's making more, that's even worse. She says, "What do I need you for?"
> If the wife is making more than the husband, it's over. She asks, "How come I can make such and such amount and you can't?"

In many of the contexts of economic stress on couples in this sample, men are struggling with joblessness and underemployment. Some women also reported that violent abuse by husbands may stem from the women taking out loans, being unable to repay debts, or refusing to get additional loans on behalf of their husbands. Men's acute frustration in their inability to provide is well recognized as fueling anti-social behaviors. Both women's and men's groups gave numerous accounts of men suffering emotionally (when under- or unemployed) and either withdrawing or lashing out in violence, while at the same time they may be squandering scarce assets on drinking, gambling, or other women. Yet, it is the woman—the traditional household and budget manager—who may be terribly scolded or even beaten for raising questions about running the household "on air." A woman from Velugodu (Andhra Pradesh), India, explained,

> if the husband comes home drunk, then the wife bursts out at him because she is suffering equally, or more than he is, due to their financial problems. Then the husband becomes angry and beats her. It is very common for him to beat the wife. The wife and the children watching start crying and finally after some time they sleep.

Rather than poverty alone, which certainly complicates a good wife's household role, men's insecurity in their ability to lead or provide, for whatever reasons, underlie many domestic clashes.

Marital conflict (understood as disagreements in the way the marital relationship is being conducted) is another major trigger in figure 2.4 and is perceived variously to be a cause, form, and effect of violence. Focus groups described marital conflict with terms such as disrespect, jealousy, lack of trust, miscommunication, misunderstanding, personal differences, and too much stress. Among the four adult groups, urban men had by far the most to say about the triggers of violence in general, mentioning poor marital relations the most.

Current theories of domestic violence attribute it to an "interplay among personal, situational, and socio-cultural factors" (Crowell and Burgess [1996] in Heise [2011], 7), rather than just one factor. Men resort to violent behavior as a tactic for asserting and demonstrating their manhood and their power and control over women when they feel their position is threatened (Connell and Messerschmidt 2005). In the urban focus groups, in particular, both men and women marked the stressful conditions for households and communities brought on by higher costs of city living and more unemployed or underemployed men. In response, women are stepping up their economic role and, as a result, may be expecting more authority and cooperation.

Focus groups from a bustling peri-urban neighborhood of Hyderabad (Andhra Pradesh), India, perceived that domestic violence was intensifying due to these forces. The women from Hyderabad reported that, although tension between couples often has economic roots, any trifling reason—real or imagined—that men perceived as defying their authority (or altering women's prescribed conduct) may ignite violence:

> Even if the husband is not drunk, there may be quarrels at home for different reasons. When the household faces financial crisis, he thinks that any talk about finances points to his failure. The wife cannot avoid talking about the lack of money because basic needs, like food, school fees, rent, or medicines cannot be ignored. She becomes an "irritant" when she lists what they must have, so he starts fighting. He may take anything as a pretext to show his anger and then he beats her. Sometimes he starts a fight over whether the food is not tasty or is too salty.

The Hyderabad men's accounts of violence were surprisingly similar to the women's. They concurred that "lack of money" was a principal factor, that "men abuse women at the slightest pretext," and that "when abuses fly thick and fast, the man storms out to have a drink." Men expressed awareness of women's rights, but they clearly felt that women invited the violence and, hence, it was implicitly justified: "The fights carry on for a longer time and sometimes the women succumb to pressure and agree that they were wrong."

Although norms for gender roles are clearly relaxing in this Hyderabad neighborhood, the process seems to be fraught with stress for many households. Domestic life is changing and many women now work for pay, but the community continues to value and award prestige to couples who play their traditional roles. Earlier in the focus group discussion, before the topic of marital conflict was introduced, a man lamented about the change in local women's attitudes and behaviors: "They want power. They want jewelry. They always want more and they are highly demanding. ... They always want more." The men also expressed exasperation with women who get together "to compare jewelry and tales of beatings." The men favorably recalled the wives of their father's generations who were "good" and "sacrificing," unlike today's wives who "[c]ould not give time to children and family," made "no sacrifices," and "asked for rights." For their part, women were happier with the changes in gender roles and reported that men are better now at showing their love for their children. The women cautioned, however, that a good wife should not pick fights with her husband for "silly reasons."

Indeed, women in many communities conceded they also played a part in marital conflict. Women in a neighborhood of Rafa Governorate in Gaza said they were less submissive than in the past and that violence sometimes happened because "often she just doesn't obey him as a way of abusing him." Scott (1985) usefully classifies tactics that involve resisting submission as the "weapons of the weak," and draws on the wider literature to show how acts of insubordination and evasion of responsibilities are common strategies among powerless groups struggling for recognition and influence, and how powerful groups will frequently go to great lengths to keep these behaviors in check in order to prevent them escalating to more costly cycles of resistance and reaction. Agarwal (1997, 18) similarly argues that "persistent complaining, pleading ill-health … withdrawing into silence, and withholding sex are all means by which women are known to bargain within the family." The women's group in Ba'adan center, the Republic of Yemen, for instance, agreed that "lack of money and the husband's income are some of the most important causes of fights between a couple, as much as when the husband is jobless and sitting at home. … [In this case, when] his wife and children make lots of requests [for money], the wife does not respect him."

When a marital relationship becomes locked into tense and abusive interactions, the focus groups consistently described how deep stress and mistrust can then take hold and become impossible to reverse. In a neighborhood of Moldova, the men stated bluntly: "Besides, no matter if the wife is good or bad, the husband will cheat on her anyway." In the focus groups, women sometimes argued that the specific reasons for marital discord are not only arbitrary, but generally boring or unimportant. Men more often associated ongoing stress and discipline (of the woman) with somehow failing to demonstrate adequately their competence and authority as household head. Some testimonies from men suggested they felt they need to redouble their efforts and regain control, while others just give up on the relationship, as women do. This quote from an urban men's group in Al Fashir, Sudan, is disquieting: "Disputes are something normal. Spouses may disagree over any of the daily life details and this may lead to conflict. In such cases, men have the right to beat their wives. This is normal."

The testimonies make clear that domestic violence is neither hidden nor mysterious. Men and women displayed plenty of awareness and understanding. A village man of Sumadija District, Serbia, commented, "It's a known fact in the village who behaves like this, but nobody interferes in other people's business." Similarly, an urban women's group in Pomoravlje District, Serbia, remarked, "There are women who pretend. They go out. They laugh. And they were just beaten." Focus groups also provided eloquent explanations of its causes and the logic of the cruelty. In rural Ba Dinh District, Vietnam, the men explained that "men often use their strength to abuse their wives. They do so because they are stronger and they are patriarchal and they want to satisfy their ego." Or in Milne Bay Province, Papua New Guinea, the men's group warned what underpins ongoing conflict: "When husbands and wives don't trust each other, then there is always misunderstanding between them."

In short, findings on marital strife reveal a world where intensely coercive behaviors against women are widely acknowledged. The violence is perceived to be easing, but still persists at varying levels. "Now women are becoming [more] powerful than men and men get furious," observed a woman from National

Capital District, Papua New Guinea. Because the abusive tactics that characterize marital strife have strong roots in everyday initiatives that uphold *and* resist gender norms, violence against women is likely to have a dampening effect on gender norm change. Given the risks of overt challenges to gender norms, quieter everyday negotiations and a gradual relaxation of norms may provide a safer route for many, but certainly not all.

Empowering women and increasing their agency, as much as finding exit options for women who are in a threatening situation, remain central challenges. Initiatives that address the stressful and costly consequences of male gender issues require stronger policy attention and research. A young woman in urban Emputa village, Tanzania, urged, "There is huge need for education that addresses men and their problems as men. I think drinking too much and womanizing is their disease and needs a cure in order to have a better community. Men should stop beating their wives. There is too much of that here in this community."

Notes

1. For discussion and other cases of how normative change can ensue over time through processes that imply both more and less hidden forms of resistance, see Rao and Walton (2004, 23–26) and Scott (1985).

2. For a more detailed analysis see, for example, Coston and Kimmel (2012) and Connell and Messerschmidt (2005).

3. Gender relations are power relations, even if they are not recognized as such and are willingly entered into. For example, Rich (1976, 57–58) defines patriarchy as "the power of the fathers: a familial-social, ideological, political system in which men—by force, direct pressure, or through ritual, tradition, law, and language, customs, etiquette, education, and the division of labor—determine what part women shall or shall not play, and in which the female is everywhere subsumed under the male." Men often do not realize that they benefit from patriarchy and women do not question such male privilege.

4. As Jensen and Oster (2009) document in the case of the introduction of cable television in some communities in India. Also Fogli and Veldkamp (2011) report how in the United States the expansion of women's participation in the labor force responded to access to information and peer examples.

5. Sweden has consistently been ranked as one of the most gender-equal societies in the world. It regularly appears as one of the top five countries for gender equality in the World Economic Forum's *Global Gender Gap Report 2012* (Hausmann, Tyson, and Zahidi 2012) and UNDP's Gender Inequality Index (2011). Gender equality in the household and domestic responsibilities sharing between men and women has been attributed to family-supportive legislation and gender-sensitive social policies (for more details see Nyberg 2011).

6. Changes in bargaining power within the household have been widely documented by Lundberg and Pollack (1993), Stevenson (2008), and Aizer (2010), among others.

7. There is a large literature on intergenerational transmission of norms. For thoughtful discussions, see Farré (2013), Quisumbing (1994), Inglehart and Norris (2003), Bisin and Verdier (2001), and Farré and Vella (2007).

8. Despite active campaigns in these countries to raise awareness about health and other risks of female genital mutilation, norms in some quarters persist in shunning "uncircumcised" girls, which leaves them severely disadvantaged in marriage markets (see Mackie 1996, 2000). Note that the World Bank does not use the term "female circumcision," preferring the more accurate term, female genital cutting.

9. In chapter 2, section titled "The Rise of the Swedish Husband: An Emerging Male Double Burden."

10. Also in chapter 2, section titled "The Rise of the Swedish Husband: An Emerging Male Double Burden."

11. A small number of groups dismissed domestic violence as a problem for their community and had little to say on the topic.

12. For an economic perspective on these processes, Hoff and Stiglitz (2010) show how power historically has constructed social categories and identities that can reproduce status differences long after opportunities across groups are made equal.

13. The concept of hegemonic masculinity was developed as a reference framework encompassing the different traits of the normative ideal of male behavior. It refers to the dominant way to be and act like a man.

14. Focus group participants were asked individually in private to estimate the incidence of domestic violence in their communities before any detailed discussions took place on this subject with the group.

15. Generally, survey research is mixed on the association between domestic violence and women's economic independence (Heise 2011). Two recent studies finding a significant link, however, include Hjort and Villanger (2011) and Heath (2012) on Bangladesh. See Chin (2011), who shows that reduction in domestic violence to rural women is associated with less exposure to their abusive husbands (reacting to their wives working for pay outside the household) rather than with their (wives') increased negotiating power.

References

Agarwal, B. 1997. "'Bargaining' and Gender Relations: Within and beyond the Household." *Feminist Economics* 3(1): 1–51.

Agarwal, A. 2003. "Gender and Land Rights Revisited: Exploring New Prospects via the State, Family, and Market." *Journal of Agrarian Change* 3 (1–2): 184–224.

Aizer, A. 2010. "The Gender Wage Gap and Domestic Violence." *American Economic Review* 100 (4): 1847–59.

Appadurai, A. 2004. "The Capacity to Aspire: Culture and Terms of Recognition." In *Culture and Public Action*, edited by V. Rao and M. Walton, 59–84. Stanford, CA: Stanford University Press.

Bisin, A., and T. Verdier. 2001. "The Economics of Cultural Transmission and the Dynamics of Preferences." *Journal of Economic Theory* 97 (2): 298–319.

Chin, Y. 2011. "Male Backlash, Bargaining, or Exposure Reduction? Women's Working Status and Physical Spousal Violence in India." *Journal of Population Economics* 25 (1): 175–200.

Connell, R. W., and J. W. Messerschmidt. 2005. "Hegemonic Masculinity: Rethinking the Concept." *Gender and Society* 19 (6): 829–59.

Coston, B. M., and M. Kimmel. 2012. "Seeing Privilege Where It Isn't: Marginalized Masculinities and the Intersectionality of Privilege." *Journal of Social Issues* 68: 97–111.

Crowell, N. A., and A. W. Burgess. 1996. *Understanding Violence against Women*. Washington, DC: National Academy Press.

Farré, L. 2013. "The Role of Men in the Economic and Social Development of Women— Implications for Gender Equality." *World Bank Research Observer* 28 (1): 22–51.

Farré, L., and F. Vella. 2007. "The Intergenerational Transmission of Gender Role Attitudes and Its Implications for Female Labor Force Participation." Discussion Paper 2802, IZA, Bonn, Germany.

Fogli, A., and L. Veldkamp. 2011. "Nature or Nurture? Learning and the Geography of Female Labor Force Participation." *Econometrica* 79 (4): 1103–38.

Foucault, M. 1995. *Discipline and Punish: The Birth of the Prison*. 2nd ed. New York: Vintage Books.

Hausmann, R., L. D. Tyson, and S. Zahidi, eds. 2012. *The Global Gender Gap Report 2012*. Geneva, Switzerland: World Economic Forum.

Heath, R. 2012. "Women's Access to Labor Market Opportunities, Control of Household Resources, and Domestic Violence." Policy Research Working Paper 6149, World Bank, Washington, DC.

Heise, Lori L. 2011. *What Works to Prevent Partner Violence: An Evidence Overview*. London: STRIVE Research Consortium, London School of Hygiene and Tropical Medicine.

Hjort, J., and E. Villanger. 2011. "Backlash: Female Employment and Domestic Violence." Preliminary working paper, Department of Economics, University of California, Berkeley, CA.

Hoff, K., and J. E. Stiglitz. 2010. "Equilibrium Fictions: A Cognitive Approach to Societal Rigidity." *American Economic Review* 100 (2): 141–46.

Holland, J., C. Ramazanoglu, and S. Sharpe. 1998. *The Male in the Head: Young People, Heterosexuality and Power*. London: Tufnell Press.

Inglehart, R., and P. Norris. 2003. *Rising Tide: Gender Equality and Cultural Change around the World*. Cambridge, U.K: Cambridge University Press.

Jensen, R., and E. Oster. 2009. "The Power of TV: Cable Television and Women's Status in India." *Quarterly Journal of Economics* 24 (3): 1057–94.

Kabeer, N. 1999. "Resources, Agency, Achievements: Reflections on the Measurement of Women's Empowerment." *Development and Change* 30: 435–64.

Lundberg, S., and R. A. Pollack. 1993. "Separate Spheres: Bargaining and the Marriage Market." *Journal of Political Economy* 101 (6): 988–1010.

Mackie, G. 1996. "Ending Footbinding and Infibulation: A Convention Account." *American Sociological Review* 61: 999–1017.

———. 2000. "Female Genital Cutting: The Beginning of the End." In *Female Circumcision: Multidisciplinary Perspectives*, edited by B. Shell-Duncan and Y. Hernlund, 245–82. Boulder, CO: Lynne Reinner.

Nyberg, A. 2011. "Sweden Country Case Study." Background paper for *World Development Report 2012: Gender Equality and Development*, World Bank, Washington, DC.

Offenhauer, P. 2005. *Women in Islamic Societies: A Selected Review of Social Scientific Literature*. Washington, DC: Library of Congress.

Panda, P., and B. Agarwal. 2005. "Marital Violence, Human Development and Women's Property Status in India." *World Development* 33 (5): 823–50.

Pronyk, P. M., J. R. Hargreaves, J. C. Kim, L. A. Morison, G. Phetla, C. Watts, J. Busza, and J. D. H. Porter. 2006. "Effect of a Structural Intervention for the Prevention of Intimate-Partner Violence and HIV in Rural South Africa: A Cluster Randomized Trial." *Lancet* 368 (9551): 1973–83.

Quisumbing, A. R. 1994. "Intergenerational Transfers in Philippine Rice Villages: Gender Differences in Traditional Inheritance Customs." *Journal of Development Economics* 43 (2): 167–95.

Rao, V., and M. Walton. 2004. "Culture and Public Action: Relationality, Equality of Agency, and Development." In *Culture and Public Action*, edited by V. Rao and M. Walton, 3–36. Stanford, CA: Stanford University Press.

Rauch, J., and S. Kostyshak. 2009. "The Three Arab Worlds." *Journal of Economic Perspectives* 23: 165–88.

Rich, A. 1976 (1995). *Of Woman Born: Motherhood as Experience and Institution.* New York: W.W. Norton.

Ridgeway, C. L., and S. J. Correl. 2004. "Unpacking the Gender System: A Theoretical Perspective on Gender Beliefs and Social Relations." *Gender and Society* 18 (4): 510–31.

Scott, J. C. 1985. *Weapons of the Weak: Everyday Forms of Resistance.* New Haven, CT: Yale University Press.

Stevenson, B. 2008. "Divorce Law and Women's Labor Supply." *Journal of Empirical Legal Studies* 5 (4): 853–73. doi: 10.1111/j.1740-1461.2008.00143.x.

Swaminathan, H., C. Walker, and M. A. Rugadya, eds. 2008. *Women's Property Rights, HIV and AIDS, and Domestic Violence: Research Findings from Two Rural Districts in South Africa and Uganda.* Cape Town, South Africa: HSRC Press.

UNDP (United Nations Development Programme). 2011. *Human Development Report 2011: Sustainability and Equity: A Better Future for All.* New York.

World Bank. 2008. *Whispers to Voices: Gender and Social Transformation in Bangladesh* Washington, DC: South Asia Sustainable Development Department, World Bank.

———. 2012. *World Development Report 2012: Gender Equality and Development.* Washington, DC: World Bank.

PART II

Having and Making Choices

The power and ability to have choices and make decisions, and especially to have a say at crucial junctures of one's life, are arguably the elements most frequently associated with agency. Together with having control over assets, including income from earnings, they are also the measures of agency most often used in the literature.[1] As Ibrahim and Alkire (2007) note, while asset and income control are more preconditions to agency than actual reflections of it, together with decision-making these measures allow for international comparisons, which are central to a study like this. The power to choose largely arises in household decision-making because there "individuals confront basic livelihood concerns, norms, values, power, and privilege" (Narayan *et al.* 2000, 219), including gender roles, as discussed in chapter 1. Women's participation in decision-making at the household level is essential to their well-being and sense of self-efficacy. But this is not true for all domestic decisions. In the next chapter, we look at intra-household decisions linked to agency, such as those related to family formation and education of children.

Women's life trajectories are dependent on certain choices that they may (or may not) be able to make. While women and men make decisions every day, not all carry the same weight. Certain decisions have a greater impact on women's and men's lives' paths, particularly whether and when to work, when and whom to marry, and how many children to have and when—which Kabeer (1999, 436) calls strategic life choices, or those choices "which are critical for people to live the lives they want." Women participate in many routine decisions appropriate to their traditional role and the gender division of labor in a household. But these decisions are unlikely to be "strategic" and translate into empowerment or improve gender equality as a consequence. Women's gains in power to decide or negotiate more significant issues are more evident in strategic life choices, where they perceptibly affect the course of women's lives or influence desired outcomes.

Strategic decisions include how much to invest—or whether to invest at all—in the human capital of children (girls' and boys' education) and how to allocate different responsibilities, assets, duties, and rights inside and outside the household (e.g., who works, who does the caretaking, and who makes major spending decisions and on which expenditures). They are influenced by prevailing gender roles and norms, and by the relative voice and bargaining power of the adult members of the household. In a continuous feedback loop, as described in *World Development Report 2012*, the endowments that individuals have accumulated, the opportunities available to them, and their control over resources give individuals increased decision-making power and greater agency. Jointly with the relaxation or change of gender norms, such agency allows women to take advantage of opportunities to accumulate assets, challenge disadvantages arising from gender inequalities, and gain more control over their lives.

The choices in crucial household decisions are subjective, reflecting individual preferences and interests, but are also influenced by specific contexts and constraints. Partly dependent on the opportunity structure around a decision—for example, the presence of schools, the state of the local market economy, or availability of reproductive health services—choices are also subject to norms and how they shape women's and men's preferences. Here, "culturally produced dispositions, beliefs, and behaviors" are likely to operate as "constraining preferences" (Rao and Walton 2004, 15). They reflect both the internalization of the possibility of success or failure, given the dominant norms regulating a man's or woman's position in the broader social structure, and the ability to take advantage of the structure of opportunities. The slow pace of change in the "terms of recognition," as Appadurai (2004, 64) notes, emphasizes the conditions and constraints under which women (and men) negotiate the gender norms that frame their lives. These terms of recognition are present in different forms, from rituals to cultural practices to public discourses and internalized beliefs—including whether a woman or man is recognized as entitled to be the decision-maker. They are central to having a voice and they affect the outcomes of decisions at all levels.

What is evident, according to many of the focus group participants, is that a window to aspire to a different life, to more education, or to have a choice in important matters (such as family formation) has opened up. Whether or not these aspirations materialize depends on the structure of opportunities and available resources, but the existence of such aspirations drive women (or men) to achieve them. The focus groups made clear that changing aspirations regarding children's education lead to greater-than-average achievement by adolescents and youth in the community and encourage girls and boys to dream more ambitiously. What focus groups recounted about educational achievements in their communities tends to fall midway between norms and desires, due both to the presence of more schools and to the change of view regarding the value of education for children in general and girls in particular. A similar situation can be seen in other cases such as age of marriage or childbearing. Young women's and men's aspirations are not yet achieved, but they see the most likely materialization in their lives to be somewhere in between what has been the prevalent norm in their communities and what they aspire to for their own lives.

Note

1. For a review of agency, see Jejeebhoy, Presser, and Sen (2000); Ibrahim and Alkire (2007); Kabeer (2001); Samman and Santos (2009); and World Bank (2012).

References

Appadurai, A. 2004. "The Capacity to Aspire: Culture and Terms of Recognition." In *Culture and Public Action*, edited by V. Rao and M. Walton, 59–84. Stanford, CA: Stanford University Press.

Ibrahim, S., and S. Alkire. 2007. "Agency and Empowerment: A Proposal for Internationally Comparable Indicators." OPHI Working Paper 4, Oxford Poverty and Human Development Initiative, Oxford, U.K.

Jejeebhoy, S. J., H. B. Presser, and G. Sen. 2000. "Women's Autonomy in Rural India: Its Dimensions, Determinants, and the Influence of Context." In *Women's Empowerment and Demographic Processes: Moving Beyond Cairo*, 204–38, edited by H. B. Presser and G. Sen. New York: Oxford University Press.

Kabeer, N. 1999. "Resources, Agency, Achievements: Reflections on the Measurement of Women's Empowerment." *Development and Change* 30 (3): 435–64.

———. 2001. "Reflections on the Measurement of Women's Empowerment." In *Discussing Women's Empowerment: Theory and Practice*. Sida*studies* 3. Stockholm: Novum Grafiska AB and Sida.

Narayan, D., R. Chambers, M. K. Shah, and P. Petesch. 2000. *Voices of the Poor: Crying Out for Change*. New York: Oxford University Press for the World Bank.

Rao, V., and M. Walton, eds. 2004. *Culture and Public Action*. Stanford, CA: Stanford University Press.

Samman, E., and M. E. Santos. 2009. "Agency and Empowerment: A Review of Concepts, Indicators, and Empirical Evidence." OPHI Research Paper 10A, Oxford Poverty and Human Development Initiative, Oxford, U.K.

World Bank. 2012. *World Development Report 2012: Gender Equality and Development*. Washington, DC: World Bank.

CHAPTER 3

Strategic Life Decisions: Who Has the Final Say?

The women—and men—participating in this study make or influence their life choices via a process set within a non-egalitarian gender system that constrains their agency. In this chapter, we look at several specific strategic life choices (Kabeer 1999), which can be critical in determining the life men and women actually live and the life they want to live.[1] We do not ignore the relevance of making small decisions or "empowerment in small matters" (Schuler and Rottach 2010, 381) or its potential link to the ability to make large decisions. As Malhotra, Schuler, and Boender (2002) note, being able to decide what to cook—while not equivalent to having the power to make decisions about children's schooling, health, or marriage—when aggregated with other small decisions may provide useful insights on intrahousehold decision-making processes. We asked the focus groups how much freedom women and men, young and old, have to make decisions about their own lives. Could they identify constraints? Did different social and gender norms affect their decision-making processes?

The chapter begins by looking at education decisions. Here we assume that parents make the decisions rather than children. Deciding whether a girl or a boy goes to school, continues in school, and completes school has more to do with the parents' decision-making authority and their views on education. As revealed by the "good student" attribute of both good girls and good boys (see figures 1.2 and 1.3 in chapter 1) and parents' general aspiration of education for their children (as well as by young women and men for themselves), we can assume that, across the sample countries, focus groups so valued education as an investment in future well-being that it prevailed over traditional gender norms and roles. The second set of decisions the chapter looks at pertains to the first job. This decision sometimes remains in the hands of the parents, who may push children into the labor market to get an early return on the investment in their education or to acquire extra income to help deal with economic need. In other cases, the adolescents or young adults themselves make the decision to start working for pay.

The most visible of all strategic decisions for women center on family forma-tion. Women's control over their own bodies is a strong marker of their agency, although it has been—and remains—highly contested. In traditional settings, where early marriage and childbearing for girls is common, parents usually decide when (what age) and whom a girl will marry. Also, mothers-in-law and other family members often have significant influence over a young wife's childbearing, specifically when she should start having children, how many, and what desired sex. Sen ([1993] cited in Kabeer [1999, 458]) notes that reproduc-tive choice can be about agency, but it also may be a trade-off for other sources of power: "Bearing the approved number of children will grant a woman the rights and privileges accorded to a fertile woman, but does not necessarily give her greater autonomy in decision-making."

Similarly, decisions to wed may bring both new freedoms and new constraints for women. A woman may decide for herself when, who, and under what condi-tions to marry, but she may also "choose" under family and social pressures to comply with expected norms. Marital practices usually reflect cultural norms and are a sure sign of how gender relations and social relations are generally organized within a society (Malhotra 1997). As Kabeer (2005) observes, little agency exists when there is little choice or just a passive form of it. Agency that conforms to traditional gender norms may help women be effective in their gender-assigned tasks and roles, but it does not challenge the gender system.

The chapter ends with the matter of intrahousehold decisions on use (expen-diture) of assets and household purchases. Women's ability to get a job or start a business—in other words, to earn independent income—is a strategic means of increasing their bargaining power and participation in household decisions. Independent income also gives women something to fall back on if they need to leave a difficult or violent domestic situation. Being able to accumulate some assets, and to control them, also increases women's agency and voice.[2]

Across the 20 countries in our study, some similarities in the major barriers to the exercise of agency emerged. It is not surprising that strategic life decisions are not necessarily affected by economic development. In some urban communities in the sample, we see more opportunities for women to actively exercise their agency and a greater universal value of education for both boys and girls. But in the private sphere, behind the household's front door—*regardless of location*—conformity with traditional gender norms and practices remains persistently intact. While the aspirations of the younger generation are changing, many are unable to realize their goals, but signals show that they are on the way to do so.

Investing in Education: Why Should Girls and Boys Go to School?

Despite ongoing conflict and deterioration of local economic conditions and employment opportunities, access to education in Rafah, West Bank and Gaza, has persevered and risen, like most of the sites visited for this report: both women and men are graduating from secondary school and university or voca-tional school (tertiary level) at higher rates than 10 years ago. According to

For those who have education, every single door is open.

—Urban man, Kragujevac, Serbia

the community's focus group in the study, these changes occurred due to constant negotiation and interaction with prevalent gender norms.

The adolescents' focus groups from Rafah pointed out that, in line with traditional gender roles, their fathers' voice prevails in household decisions, including who stays in school and who must drop out. While some acknowledged that both parents decide about their schooling, the decision is largely out of their (girls' or boys') hands, regardless whether the parents consider their preferences or not.

The parents participating in the Rafah focus groups gave similar reasons for pulling their children out of school that we find in other sample countries. In the case of boys, household financial problems often dictate breaking off their education: "The boy and his parents decide he should leave school in order to find a job and help provide for the family." For girls, marriage trumps education: "If the girl is pretty, then her parents stop her schooling to get her married." (This may also apply if the girl is a bad student.) If a suitable man asks for a girl's hand, she no longer needs to be educated because her future is guaranteed.

In decisions about education, gender norms are in full play—the father's authority, the good boy who works and provides for his family like a good man, the good girl who becomes a good wife and manages the household. When a girl leaves her parents' house, though, education is then negotiated with the new man in her life. One 20-year-old woman in Rafah lamented, "I was studying to be a veterinarian, but because I had to go out to the farms with men as part of the practical study, neither my husband nor his family would accept it. My only solution was to change my major." These normative constraints, however, are now pushing up against people's growing recognition of the value of an education, both as an investment for future well-being (e.g., getting a good job) and as a transformative power that opens up previously unattainable possibilities and expectations, or the capacity to aspire (Appadurai 2004). Educating children—including girls—has become a new norm and deemed necessary to ensure their future, as almost all our focus groups agreed. Yet, the results of educating girls and boys are not as straightforward as they seem: the new aspirations and opportunities for those with more schooling are not always enough to overturn longstanding social and gender norms.

The impact of education on access to future opportunities for boys and girls is undeniable. We know that the parents in our focus groups place high value on their children being good students and getting an education because they told us. But did the adolescent boys and girls agree? We asked the 670 adolescents in our study, who were 12–17 years old and lived in 41 urban or rural communities in 9 countries.[3] According to their average school enrollment, almost all of them go to school, but the girls aspire to higher levels of education than the boys (figure 3.1).

On Norms and Agency • http://dx.doi.org/10.1596/978-0-8213-9862-3

Figure 3.1 Ideal Level of Education Reported by Adolescent Boys and Girls in the Study

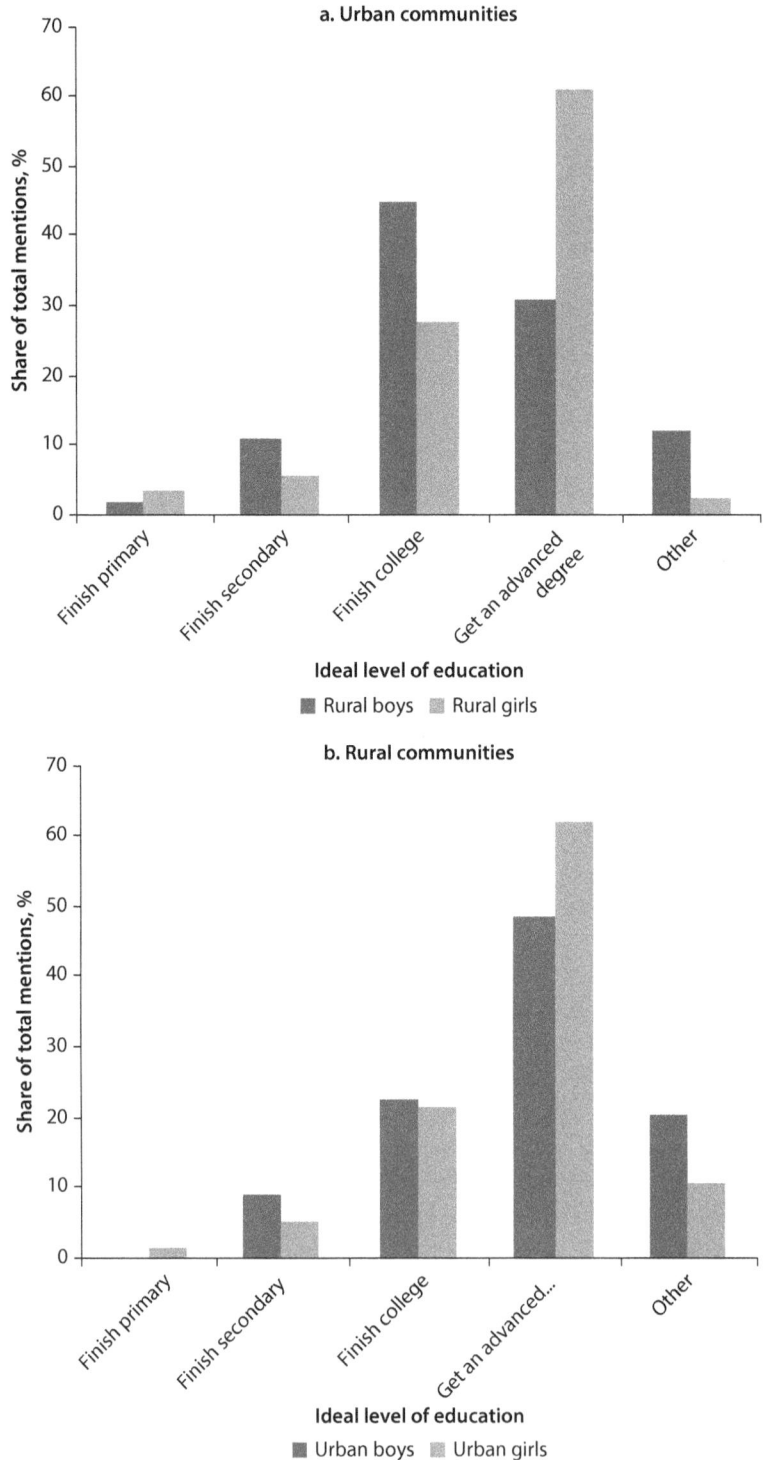

a. Urban communities

Rural boys Rural girls

b. Rural communities

Urban boys Urban girls

Note: Data from 670 students between 12 and 17 years in 8 countries.

More than 60 percent of the girls in both urban and rural areas hoped to obtain advanced degrees, but only 40 percent of the boys sought this level of education. Girls and boys both expected that getting an education would give them a better future than their parents and would permit them to fulfill their parents'—and their own—aspirations for them.

Boys, girls, and their parents invest in education because they expect to see a return on it, whether it is functional literacy or an advanced graduate degree. As Patrinos and Psacharopoulos (2004) document, education returns—expected earnings—have risen in all world regions. The increase in returns is higher for girls than boys when they go beyond primary school.[4] "Education takes us to good places; it is our road to employment and a path out of poverty," exulted an adolescent boy from Fiji. A young man from Sudan agreed, "Education lets us join the modern world and offers us better jobs now. In the past, it was not important because our people were farmers and did not pay attention to the future or look to change the present." Boys from urban Mongar District, Bhutan, explained that the gains are not only for them but for their entire families: "We can go to college, earn a salary, and help our struggling parents. It is payback time. We want to help our parents who got us educated with their hard-earned money."

But when people perceive that returns from education are low, investment in it falls off. Boys from urban West Bank and Gaza commented that staying in school longer than necessary was a waste of time and had little effect on their future economic participation: "[Higher education] is not important to us because we can learn a craft and work without a university degree." In rural Sudan (Blue Nile State), boys also did not believe that education could really help them in the future. They mentioned knowing college graduates in the area who were unemployed. Worse, when prompted to describe themselves 10 years in the future, a group of boys from urban Sudan (Khartoum) answered, "jobless."

From education's instrumental relation with income generation we can see how gender norms and expected behaviors pressure boys to contribute to the household in advance of their future role as expected provider—so much so that the opportunity to earn income takes precedence over any education opportunity: "If there is money, there is no need to learn" (young adult man, Olsztyn, Poland). The poor economic conditions of many of the communities in the research sample also contribute to the lack of confidence in the value of education: "People don't have any interest in education because they are too busy making a living" (adult man, Naw Da, Afghanistan). However, as discussed earlier in part I, boys and men both are starting to resist and contest the expectations laid on them, and are contesting the masculine ideal of being the main provider and deciding to stay in school or to combine education with working in view of future aspirations.

More education also imbues people with increased self-efficacy and confidence. For adolescent girls specifically, the added value of an education—beyond mere economic returns—is its positive impact on their agency, which is less important to boys as a reason for valuing education. Similarly, *World Development Report 2012* shows that higher levels of education reduce the grip of social norms that restricts women's autonomy. For example, in South Asia and the Middle East and North Africa, women with more education are not as likely to have to ask their husbands or family for permission to seek medical care. Education gives them more freedom than earnings (World Bank 2012).[5]

The adolescent girls in the focus groups agreed, reporting that education helps them gain more control over their lives, bolsters their self-esteem, and opens up opportunities to earn their own income—all elements of independence. A girl from Hyderabad (Andhra Pradesh), India, explained that, as part of achieving her goal to graduate from college, she tries to imagine what it takes to be self-sufficient and learns how to manage her money. Another girl from urban Lautoka, Fiji, believed that education not only provides her with knowledge but also gives her the courage to "become someone in life, to even become the head of the household."

"Education is a girl's best weapon to face the world," summarized a girl from the neighborhood of Rafah, West Bank and Gaza. And she is right. Education has started reshaping local norms that define women and changing perceptions and expectations. It is often the mothers who envision a different life for their daughters and strongly advocate for them to stay in school. In Fiji and Bhutan, both rural and urban girls told us that their mothers encourage them to study hard, so they are able to become independent and to look after themselves.

Moving up half a generation to the 18–24-year-old women in the sample, who may have at least finished secondary school, we see that they share a similar view of education. They highly value education because they expect it to help them better their own and their children's economic well-being and, more importantly, advance their personal development. Education leads to better decision making and strategic decision making requires information and education. "If you are not educated, you cannot think. When other people tell you things, you take too long to understand," said a woman from Emputa village, Tanzania. "Education brings awareness of more things so that I make better informed choices," noted a young woman from Bhubaneswar (Odisha), India.

The literature shows that women with more education tend to have more control over other life decisions, and they tend to marry later and have fewer children,[6] which was confirmed in many comments by the girls in the study about the lives they see their mothers leading: "My mum had to help look after her brothers and sisters [when she was young], so she could not complete her schooling or have the opportunity to work. She then bore six children and had to stay home and look after them. She spends all her time doing housework and looking after the family" (adolescent girl, rural Fiji). "My mother only finished 10th grade. Her life was very simple in order to raise us. That is why I certainly don't want to be like her (urban adolescent girl, Dirbas, West Bank and Gaza). Social norms and the fulfillment of traditional gender roles, again, are the main reason that the girls' mothers left school, and they remain as barriers to future opportunities for the new generation.

When we asked parents in all 20 sample countries directly about their expectations for their daughters and sons, they tended to mention education as one of the primary options that can offer their children a better future. They felt that having a school nearby or in the community was essential for their daughters, especially in difficult locales, such as the West Bank and Gaza, rural Afghanistan, or traditional communities in Burkina Faso, and among such minority communities as the Roma in Serbia and indigenous populations in Peru. Fathers and mothers alike noted that their daughters gain more equal standing and have more independence from their future husbands when they can earn their own income. Young girls will "not be so easily confined" (Burkina Faso) when they secure the freedom to look after themselves. "For my daughter, I want her to have power. I want to give her an education, so she has more opportunities, and even a degree, so she can be independent. I want my daughter to be better than me," asserted a rural woman from Peru. Neither mothers nor girls want to replicate the lives women in the past have endured, and they recognize education as their main outlet to change.

Why Should I Leave School? Not My Choice!

Who decides when it is time for a child to leave school? What factors influence this decision? Looking at our data, one-third of the young adults reported leaving school because they completed their education. Depending on the context, completion meant primary school to college level.[7] A little less than one-third of the young men said that the decision to leave school early was their own, while an additional 22 percent indicated that the decision was made jointly with an adult. For young women, 15 percent acknowledged that they did not have a say in decisions about ending their schooling, compared to about 7 percent of boys (figure 3.2). Young men were more likely to say that the decision to leave school was their own than were girls.

Figure 3.2 Who Makes the Decision for Children to Leave School?

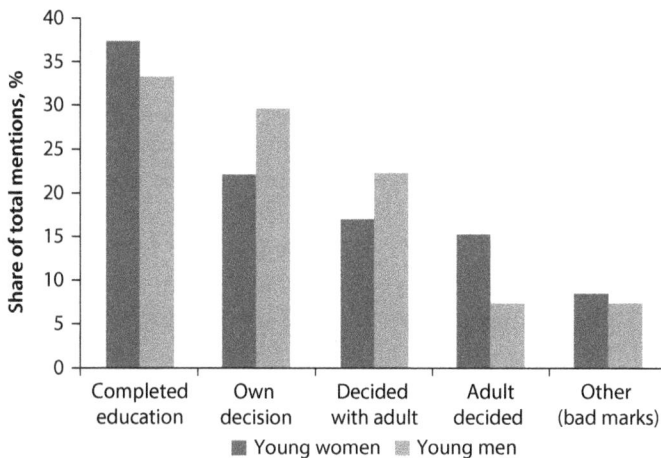

Note: Data from young women and men (18–25 years old) in 113 focus groups.

My parents wanted me to keep learning up to 8th grade. I wanted to finish high school, but my father forbade me. He said, "What do you need school for? You will get nothing out of going to school. You are just wasting your days. So I secretly went to school, but he found out and yelled at me, "I warned you about school!" I feel remorse that I listened to him. I could have continued, but you need books and other things for school, and you need a lot of money for education. My mother only does what my father tells her to do. My brother only finished 5th grade because he did not like it. I liked school, but my father would not allow it. He was afraid that I'd meet somebody there who would take advantage of me because I was a girl.

—Urban woman, Kragujevac, Serbia

Over half the young women and men in our sample dropped out of school early, which will have a significant impact on their future. Unfortunately, it means the level of education that many of them hoped to reach will remain merely an aspiration. For example, from the Republic of Yemen to Bhutan and from Burkina Faso to India, the adolescent girls wanted to get at least a college degree, and the rural girls were aware that their education will likely only go through secondary school, if they are lucky. When we asked girls from India how far they thought they were truly likely to go in school, their answers varied. Like other girls from rural communities, some guessed they would just make it to secondary school and not fulfill their dreams of becoming doctors, lawyers, or engineers.

The boys, too, aspired to get college and professional degrees, but realized that, like those in Burkina Faso and Fiji, primary school might be the end of their education. Other boys in Burkina Faso did not want to go beyond primary levels, and boys in the Dominican Republic put a low value on the promise of education to provide a better future. Indeed, parents of boys in four of the six African countries in our sample felt that their sons—not their daughters—did not take education seriously or value its potential benefits enough.[8] Young men more often reported not liking school over other reasons for dropping out, including the need to work and the absence of a school in their community.

Often, though, the adolescents' and young adults' focus groups mentioned lack of money and their parents' decision as the two main reasons they left school. The lack of power to have the final say over their education cannot be disentangled from the reasons behind a decision to leave school. Stated preferences and individual decisions do not take place in a void, but are constrained by opportunities, power imbalances in the household, gender systems, lack of information, and more. Distance and lack of infrastructure—from no roads to no nearby school—affect both boys and girls, but girls have more difficulties if there is no school in their village, if they have to travel long distances to school, and if their friends drop out (they have no peers to walk with them to school) because their mobility is more restricted than boys'. Both also leave school to help support their families (boys by earning an income, girls by working at home), to prepare for and marry early, or—as girls from Bhutan, Burkina Faso, the Republic of Yemen, India, and Sudan added—so they will be safe from violence and unapproved pregnancies.

Given the high valuation of education held by the communities in the study, it is not surprising that the participants always described the decision to pull children out of school as difficult. The same two fundamental reasons that drive families to educate their children—a better life and more income—are also the first ones parents mentioned for stopping their children's education. On one hand lies lack of economic resources for school fees, transportation, and school materials, and on the other is the desire or obligation for young people to generate income or relieve their families from the economic burden that education represents for the household budget.

Forgoing the opportunity to invest in future returns from education may, at first glance, point to a lack of agency by a young woman. Both the Bhutanese girl, who opposed her father taking out a loan to pay for her education, and the young woman from India, who decided to leave school because her family cannot afford her education, are making a deliberate choice. Financial issues and family loyalties are so intertwined, however, that it is not that clear that this is an *empowered or strategic choice*. We can mark their decision as either a sign of self-determination or a passive choice due to pressure and lack of alternatives. When we judge a boy who leaves school because of financial constraints, the same duality appears.

Especially with entrenched poverty, young people seem to have little bargaining power to state their preferences. A young man especially faces strong gender mandates calling him to be a family provider and act like a man. Young men's accounts of leaving education due to family financial straits, however, show a proactive component. "Our family condition (financially) was not so strong. We thought of supporting our families" say young men from Jaipur (Odisha), India, and like them, other young men leave school not only to reduce stress on the family budget but also to make a positive contribution. "I had to leave school because my father separated from my mother and I had to support her," noted a young man, from Lambayeque Province, Peru. The same imperative to generate an income was heard from boys in Moldova, West Bank and Gaza, and other countries. But when some boys and young adult men in the sample left school to gain economic independence, they surprisingly reported a sense of empowerment that other accounts did not have: "My parents weren't happy when I decided not to go to high school. But I already had a job and was earning my living. I couldn't focus on my studies anymore" (young man, East Jakarta, Indonesia).

Looking further into young men's accounts, we find that, even when they reported making the decision to leave school independently, they regretted it. They sometimes expressed as strong a wish to go back to school as the young men who had no say in the process. This signals that the decision was influenced more by restrictive circumstances, whether need or norm, and less by preference. It may be that the young men adapted their preferences to practical conditions and needs.[9] Again, social norms associated with a sense of duty appear to be a primary factor. One young man in Lautoka, Fiji, put it matter-of-factly, "Father got sick, so I made my own decision [to leave school]." An Indonesian young man from Tangerang presented another constrained choice: "I wanted to continue my studies, but we didn't have the money. So I decided to stop after I finished junior high school."

Overall, for young women, the traditionally instilled norms of inequality inside and outside the home raise more barriers to finishing their education. How are they able to exercise agency from their unequal bargaining position in the face of the traditional authority of fathers and husbands? A young woman in Tewor District, Liberia, justified leaving school: "[It was] my own decision because I had a husband and I had to follow his way. He said no, that I could not go to school." Her situation showcases both lack of agency and her belief in what a good wife should do. While it may seem contradictory, because more girls than boys currently attend school, social- and gender-normative restrictions are more evident in regions where education for women still lags behind men's or where general enrollment in school remains low, such as Sub-Saharan Africa and some regions of India:[10]

> – *The pressure of endless domestic tasks:* "You see, if we went to school, who would do the housework?" (Rural young women, Malangachilima village, Tanzania)

> – *Early childbearing:* "My boyfriend got in the way of my education. When I was in the 6th grade, I got pregnant. I had the child and my boyfriend left me." (Urban young woman, Greenville District, Liberia)

> – *Traditional mobility restrictions on women in order to protect their virtue, propriety, family honor, and safety:* "How can we walk on deserted and lonely jungle paths to reach school?" (Rural young women, Kalahandi District, Andhra Pradesh, India)

> – *Household preference for educating boys:* "As a girl, I had to agree with my parents to support the education of my brother. Time passed and now I am married with kids, and I have not been able to complete my education." (Rural young woman, East Sepik Province, Papua New Guinea)

We cannot claim, however, that it is more altruistic for boys to drop out of school to financially support their household than for girls to leave school to do housework or to let a male sibling attend school. Agarwal (1997) reaches a similar conclusion: girls and boys equally have no choice but to agree to these "voluntary" concessions.

A frequent justification for preferring to educate sons rather than daughters involves inheritance laws and traditional roles associated with family financial support, especially in rural areas. Because young women will join another household when they marry turns their education into a bad investment for their family. Their acquired capacity from education will not serve their family: "There is a common belief that when we [women] get married, our education benefits the husband's family, not our families. So a father feels that his family loses if he educates you" (young woman, Malangachilima village, Tanzania). Educating young men, on the other hand, has direct returns to the household. And while male power affects both girls and boys when it comes to education, only girls are bound to transition from the school to the household.

Despite diverse barriers, both boys and girls are staying in school longer than previous generations, and the overwhelming embrace of education is causing deeply engrained norms to slowly relax and bend. Signs of change are visible in narratives from the adolescents' focus groups, which related accounts of traditional, restrictive fathers who push their daughters to study and of mothers whose gains in voice may be counteracting the fathers' resistance to schooling their daughters. "I am studying because my mother insisted that girls should at least complete 10th grade, even though my father doesn't want me to study in a regular school," announced an adolescent girl from rural India. For a Bhutanese girl, it is her educated brother who is pushing for change—"My brother forced my parents to put me in school. My parents never felt that I needed to go to school"—even though her parents' views did not change in the long term. "They believed that I have to stay home and take care of the land and the main house of the family." This girl eventually was pulled out of school when her brother left the house, but her knowledge and aspirations changed in the process.

From School to Work: Getting the First Job

Strategic choices do not arise frequently in a person's lifetime, which makes their impact less visible in the short term, but their impacts are significant over a longer time frame. Starting a productive activity, such as finding a first job, is one example. As Malhotra, Schuler, and Boender (2002) recognize, getting a job can be a manifestation of women's agency as a decision-making exercise, as well as a driver to promote greater agency. Women's economic participation can be an enabling factor to predict women's increased control over other important decisions in the household and their lives. Not all women, however, are free to make (or capable of making) the decision to leave the domestic space to start working. Household circumstances, gender roles, entrenched norms, and market opportunities all play into their decisions.

In most of the communities in our survey, women have participated in the labor market for more than 10 years, but, like the 500 million women who have joined the global labor force since 1980, they have worked under disadvantaged conditions, with limited access to assets and services, and coped with the unequal gender distribution of household responsibilities.[11] Getting a job requires that women, like men, have the skills that fit the work and access to information about labor opportunities; but unlike men, they also need an enabling environment that includes options for childcare, redistribution of domestic tasks, access to transportation, and mobility.

On Norms and Agency • http://dx.doi.org/10.1596/978-0-8213-9862-3

In many developing countries in our survey, contexts of scarce opportunities drive the timeline for starting work. By age 13—some in rural areas were as young as 10 years old—the majority of the adolescent participants were already economically active (much earlier than we expected), even if not continuously; they also frequently worked while going to school. Not surprisingly, some felt that they were thrust into the job market despite their desire to learn a skill or to complete their education. In addition, although more than half the young adults in the focus groups described making an independent decision to work (figure 3.3), in most rural settings and for women (regardless of location), it was less likely to be their decision than an adult's. Urban young men appeared to have the most freedom to decide to work, as well as a larger, more diverse pool of opportunities.

Like leaving education, the decision to start working is also usually made within constraints: the need to support the family, the lack of resources to afford education, the desire to be economically self-sufficient. "It was my own decision to help my parents" is something that we heard from urban young men and women in Indonesia and in the Republic of Yemen, where almost all adolescents interviewed stopped their education, due to lack of resources, to start working or start helping at home. It was rare in the focus groups to find examples where adolescents or young adults managed to combine education and work success-fully in the long run. Going to school and holding down a job, when household finances were tight, often made continuing their education impossible, but also gave them a sense of independence from their parents' designs—a first step toward self-efficacy and the capacity to act. According to adolescents in Umlazi township A (near Durban), South Africa, working and studying helped them

Figure 3.3 Who Decides When Young Adults or Adolescents First Go to Work?

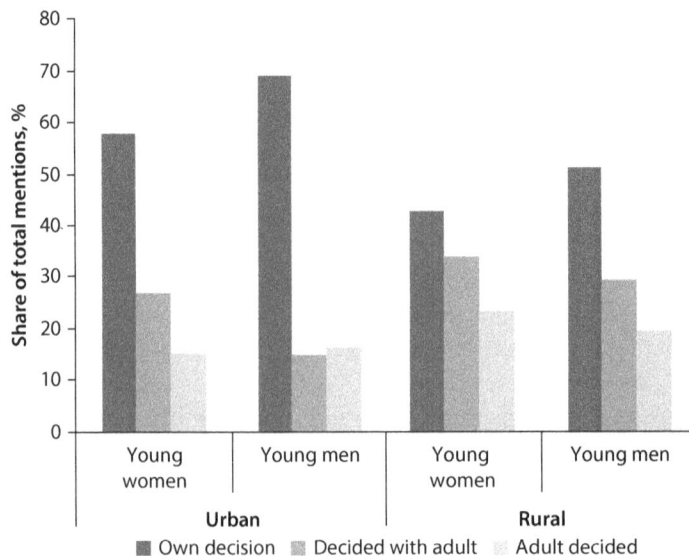

Note: Data from 194 male and female focus groups.

learn to be responsible and to manage their own money, but it is not easy, and more often than not students ended up choosing immediate returns over long-term investments. "Work is very demanding; it takes a lot of energy. If you are a student, it interferes with studying because your mind is always tired," said a young girl from Umlazi township B.

For about 20 percent of the adolescent focus groups, male and female, their first job was the first available job they could find. Education does not always guarantee more choices for economic engagement or meet all expectations—in particular for young men (Jeffrey 2008). One young man in Khartoum, Sudan, noted, "It is difficult to find a job, so we grab any that are available. You are lucky if you find a job in your profession. I studied computer science, but am working in a bank. It is a good job, but I want to be a computer programmer; I just didn't find the chance." "I think that even after completing their studies, some girls still have to stand behind a shop counter and some guys have to work at construction or something," said a young girl from Justynowo, Poland. In some cases, their education qualifications become irrelevant under changing economic circumstances that are not under their control:

> You work at what you can, at whatever is available. I know someone who finished three years of vocational school for plumbers and got a job in "Goša" paying 35,000 dinars. Now, because the company was sold, he works as a security guard for 20,000 dinars where his education credentials are not recognized. He can't find any work in his profession." (Village young man, Sumadija District, Serbia)

In a few communities, however, where job prospects appear to be improving, the narratives of boys and girls were more positive in terms of decision-making power. A group of young girls in Hyderabad (Andhra Pradesh), India, said, "mostly the boys decide where they want to work ... [but] now the girls can too because there are many job opportunities." And with more work opportunities, education becomes more valuable. "For uneducated people, there are limited choices for work, so they have to take the first one. But in the many malls and shops, there are more jobs available if you have schooling," the girls from Hyderabad explained further. A young man of Hoang Mai District of Hanoi, Vietnam, noted that "in Hanoi ... those who have little education can work as motorbike drivers or masons. It doesn't matter as long as the work brings an income." Unfortunately, these examples are the exception. Adolescents and young adults predominantly pointed out that acute economic need in the family prompted their job-seeking decisions regardless of the availability of employment choices.

You Say, I Say: The Weight of Adult Voices on Job Decisions

A young woman from Floresti District, Moldova, explained that "it is hard to say who pushes you to start making a living. When the economic situation of your family is poor, you have to make difficult decisions and, in this case, you have to ask for advice from your family." Her comment refers to three elements that impinge on the decision to start working and run throughout the narratives

> *[After leaving school] I started working as an apprentice in a store with the help of my grandmother.*
>
> —Urban young woman, Assoli Prefecture, Togo

we heard in different communities: poverty or lack of resources, a sense of responsibility toward family, and the requirement to consult the family. Relatives and parents not only enforce behaviors—what a young man or woman can and cannot do—but also (particularly in contexts of limited resources and information) act as facilitators and guides in the quest to find a job.

Parents and relatives are heavily involved in the search for the first job. On one hand, as the authorities in the family, parents must sometimes grant permission for their children to work (when they are not actively pushing them into the job market). On the other hand, young people can tap into adults' experience and knowledge of the labor markets, as well as their connections or information about job opportunities. For young women particularly, "it is important to get approval [from the adults and heads of their households]. Without parents' approval, you cannot work" (young woman, Sungai Puar District, Indonesia).

Parents fiercely protect young women's and girls' safety and take measures to compensate for the girls' lack of experience and information when it comes to decisions such as to work outside the home. For example, in Hung Yen District, Vietnam, young women think that "it is better to make a decision with an adult. Because you are inexperienced, you need your parents' direction and support. After finishing school, I did not know much about the outside world, so my parents guided me." And even young men, who rely less on adults (see figure 3.3), admitted that they seek advice from adults in their families. "I would ask my parents what they think about a particular offer or if they know the company. However, I would mostly ask my father, not my mother," said a young man from Dobrowice, Poland. But gender bias, as always, is never far away. Due to men's privileged engagement with the labor market, as household provider, they not only have better knowledge about the labor market but also have better contacts and networks to break entrance barriers. Mothers and other women may have similar experiences and information, but they are not seen as the best option, or sought out first, for counsel about getting a job.

Sufficient labor opportunities and exposure to them often drive individual expressions of agency by young people in the sample, especially when training and local market opportunities combine. They take ownership of their decision and sense they can succeed. As a young woman from Hung Yen District, Vietnam, said, "I am highly independent and make all my decisions by myself. Even if my parents give their opinions, I will still choose the job I like." Changes in her community, including a new road connecting to the large city nearby, are catalysts of such behavior. Even the norms for parent-child relations give way in the face of the autonomy of the decision to work by young men. As one young man in urban Santiago de los Caballeros, the Dominican Republic, explained, "It is difficult in Santiago de los Caballeros for a father to tell his son what job he should get."

On the other side, norms that restrict women's roles to the household can overwhelm their ability to make decisions to work in the public sphere and may increase parental involvement to the point that there is no individual choice. Young women in rural communities in India in the sample stressed over and over their complete lack of individual agency and that their only choice was total compliance with parental decisions. Young women "will do whatever work the parents assign" and if "parents tell [them] to stop going to school and support the family," they submit without a word. In Koudipally Mandal (Andhra Pradesh), girls recognized that "mostly parents decide what we should do"; in Velugodu (Andhra Pradesh), the entire focus group recounted how adults determined their first jobs; and in Kalahandi District (Andhra Pradesh), a girl's parents "refused to let me study further and insisted I look after my younger siblings. They also made me go to the jungle and collect produce, and hired me out for wage work." Nowhere did young men in the sample relate such stories. Even when pushed to take certain jobs to comply with masculine expectations or to augment the family's income, they believed they contributed to the decision and could give their opinion.

"First Comes Love, Then Comes Marriage, Then Comes Baby in a Baby Carriage"

From early in life, we face constant reminders of the relations expected between women and men. Even playground games and songs—such as the title of this section,[12] which is a song used by children to taunt boys and girls seen as getting too close or too romantic with each other—charge our lives with gender signification. Thorne (1993) refers to this process as gender play and children, as well as adults, recreate gender in everything they do, such as creating a couple when they see a boy and girl together. For most children, when they grow up, this becomes a reality. Starting a new household and having children are the most visible and significant life decisions, and are both the norm and the aspiration of most girls and boys.

This section discusses how norms and prevailing practices around marriage and childbearing are bending, although they are infrequently challenged. As women's empowerment grows, they gain more control over their bodies and fertility choices, such as contraceptive use, family size, spacing between births, and the sex composition of their children (Jejeebhoy 1995b; Malhotra, Schuler, and Boender 2002). In turn, these new reproductive behaviors and changes in family formation influence women's major life decisions.

The position of women in the household is central to their ability, or lack of it, to exercise their agency, and this position varies with age, the bearing of children, economic participation, and more. Marriage and reproduction have a different effect on men's lives and agency. For many men, family formation moves them from a subordinated position—as sons under the authority of an older male—to the position of power in their own households. But with that power come responsibilities, such as the economic support of the new family and the pressures to comply with associated norms.

One of the messages that emerged from the discussions with young adult women and men in the study is a desire to delay starting a family until they have greater control over their lives. They consider having an education and a job with a steady income, as well as physical and psychological maturity, to be preconditions for a secure adult family life. These yearnings for control, however, constantly interact with social norms and expected behaviors about how and when family formation should begin. Different views on the appropriate age for marriage may have an impact on the accumulation of endowments (e.g., education) and the capacity to take advantage of economic opportunities.

Marriage may free young women from their father's control, but it often is simply a transition into different situations of disadvantage with another male (their husband) and of decreased agency as a junior female among the women in the husband's extended family (Kabeer 2001). Arranged marriages are still customary in some of the study communities, as are financial payments, such as a bride price (*lobola* in southern Africa) or a dowry. In other sample communities, women have to yield to strong pressure from husbands and in-laws over the number of children they bear. Retrospective accounts of young women who regretted getting married and having children too early make evident the importance they attach to starting a family at the right moment. The accumulation of experiences, awareness of women's rights, gains in bargaining power, and accumulation of resources are all curtailed by early family formation, as are women's achievement of their individual aspirations and expectations for the future.

There are two main decisions that lead to family formation: childbearing and marriage (both arranged and consensual unions). What signs tell women and men when is the right time to wed and start a family, whether to have children (or not) and how many, and whether they have enough autonomy to make these decisions? Agency develops throughout life on a continuum of small gains in empowerment: gains early in life emerge later as an improved capacity to decide. Factors, such as marriage circumstances and family formation, may at times be at odds with gains in agency, especially from education or a job, and have to be negotiated with existing social norms.

For example, one of the most contentious areas of autonomous decision described by the focus groups has to do with reproduction. The arguably central position of sexuality in shaping gender relations and reproducing inequality between women and men constrain sexuality and reproduction both socially and politically.[13] In fact most gender issues, whether in work, family life, or divisions of labor, revolve around reproduction and sexuality.[14] Reproduction encompasses more than the single event of having a child. It triggers a set of other future choices that push women toward specific paths in line with norms and social and cultural ideas, and practices surrounding childcare and motherhood. The cross-cultural character of this study reveals how the beliefs, norms, and values surrounding women's reproductive behavior significantly affect all realities, in both rural to urban locations, in all countries. These norms are so entrenched, according to the focus groups, that a woman who does not opt for reproduction is seen as denying what she really wants. But a man who is not particularly involved in childrearing, does so because fatherhood is not based on the same natural drive as a woman. Among the study communities, it is still assumed that motherhood is a core marker of adult femininity and that the normal outcome of marriage is the production of children. And more often than not, motherhood exacerbates gender inequalities derived from gender roles.

So He Proposed...

Data dating back to the 1950s, from a set of non-OECD and OECD countries, show that women's age when they first marry has increased, although they are still marrying at a younger age than men, and that men's average age at marriage has remained stable.[15] The young adults in our study mirror these global averages along with rural and urban differences with marriage. Almost half the rural women's groups said that women in their communities marry by age 17. In urban settings, only 30 percent of young women marry this young (table 3.1); most young women wed between the ages of 18 and 25, around the age of majority in many countries; however, the difference between the rural and urban young women is more than 10 percentage points. Similarly, rural young men and rural young women marry earlier than their urban counterparts.

Most young women and some men in the sample, rural and urban, wished to marry when they were older, even those young women who were already married at the time of the interviews (the majority). Some communities, however, did not approve of couples marrying or having kids over a certain age and, although the appropriate window of time varied, most agreed that the ideal age was 18–20 years and not before.

Reasons for delaying marriage were similar to those for delaying reproduction: maturity and social and financial stability. One young woman from Jahran District, the Republic of Yemen, was married at 15 and explained that "getting married at a young age was a disadvantage and hard on me because a girl cannot handle all the household responsibilities and have children at that age." Marrying too early also interferes with education: "I got married at 16 years old, but it was supposed to be when I was to be 24 years old and had completed my education," lamented a young woman from River Nile State, Sudan. Marrying later leads to a better outcome for both partners: "Both of us are employed, so that we started

Table 3.1 Age of Marriage for Women and Men in Focus Group Communities
percent

		15 years or less	16–17 years	18–25 years	26+ years
Men	Rural	15	23	54	8
	Urban	14	17	57	12
Women	Rural	26	22	44	7
	Urban	13	18	48	10

Note: Average age of marriage in each community as reported by 194 young adult focus groups.

On Norms and Agency • http://dx.doi.org/10.1596/978-0-8213-9862-3

life together on a solid basis" (young woman, Sumadija District, Serbia). Indeed, research shows that women's education is a stronger determinant than men's for higher age at marriage and first child.[16]

Rural young women and girls in our sample were five times more likely than rural young men and boys to drop out of school to marry or have children. For urban young women and girls, pregnancy or marriage made no difference in school dropout rates, although girls were more likely than boys to interrupt their education to marry. Like other studies, couples where the women had more education tended to have fewer children (Iyigun and Walsh 2007), both because the women may have more agency within the household and because they have better opportunities and are more likely to participate in the labor market. And educated mothers were more likely to invest in education and better nutrition for their children's well-being (Thomas, Strauss, and Henriques 1990).

The reasons young women in the study married younger than they wanted highlight the imposition of strong social and cultural norms, namely, marriages arranged by their families or forced unions for financial reasons and pregnancy. For example, in Firestone District, Liberia, young women and girls explained that "pregnancy can force people here to live together in a Congo [makeshift structures attached to the main house to accommodate the new family]. As soon as a boy impregnates a girl, he can bring the girl to his family's home." Similarly in Peru, co-habitation was reported as the obligatory step after an unintended pregnancy. In Samtse, Bhutan, young women and girls felt strongly that arranged marriages should cease and that men and women should have the freedom to choose their partners.

The younger adult women's groups expressed discontent with current marriage practices, especially young urban women, and tended to question them, although their opinions were divided. Young men's views were also split, but urban young men were slightly less inclined to reject current marriage practices, probably because they have more freedom to choose. Young women in towns and cities seem more dissatisfied (or more able to express dissatisfaction) with marriage practices than all other groups. In some cases, the expenses associated with a formal wedding were a concern; in others, traditional practices, such as dowries and bride prices, were questioned as being unnecessary and costly.

Most of the women and men in the study felt that they freely decided their marriages, and reported seeing greater autonomy in some communities in selecting their partners, compared with their parents' generation. For example, young people in Poland generally felt free to be with whom they wanted and to decide whether to live together or get married. One young woman noted that pressures to marry in case of pregnancy, while they have not disappeared entirely, are fading away, even in rural or more traditional communities like hers. On the other hand, arranged marriages are still customary in West Bank and Gaza, the Republic of Yemen, and India. In these countries, according to our study, the bride and groom may not necessarily oppose the union, but have no say in selecting their partner. This is particularly true for young women and girls, whose roles are mostly passive. Men may indicate their wish to wed a particular girl without convening the norm, although it may or may not be approved by their families. In India and West Bank and Gaza, traditional arranged marriages are more common than freely chosen ones, even though some love marriages do occur (between 3 and 20 percent, according to focus group participants).

Frustration with current marriage norms is most evident in sample countries where traditional rituals involve economic costs for the bride's or groom's family, such as bride price (e.g., South Africa, Tanzania, Papua New Guinea, and Afghanistan) or dowry payments (e.g., Bhutan, Sudan, Liberia, India, and Serbia). While the young people did not always disagree with these cultural practices, they spoke of the difficulty in complying with them, when facing economic hardship, and the power differentials that they can create in the bride's future home.[17] For example, girls who do not have an adequate dowry have trouble getting married or are mistreated and abused by the groom's family. "If girl brings a large dowry, she will be treated well"; "girls who don't have a proper dowry are not treated well"; and "they will be treated well only for a few years," said young women from India. Another young woman in Jaipur (Odisha), India, related how her sister had been deserted by her husband and in-laws because of what was considered insufficient dowry: "She was physically tortured for a period of time to get INR[18] 50,000 more from our parents, which they did not have the resources to give." Young Indian women in Bhubaneswar (Odisha) strongly felt the dowry system should be stopped entirely: "The bride's family should decide how much they want to give to a daughter on her wedding." In cases where the bride's family receives the assets, girls in Malangachilima and Zabibu village, Tanzania, complained that they were being married off for economic gain:

> Some parents force their children to get married in order to get income from the bride price. Girls are married off at an early age; but they are young and behave like children, so they never last in marriages. Most times, these girls are poor because they have had no jobs, except farming, and their husbands mistreat them because they are dependent on them. Yes, there needs to be change. Our parents should not see us as an income-generating asset. We should be able to choose the right time to marry and which men we want to marry. (Rural young woman, Zabibu village, Tanzania)

Bride prices paid to a household represent a valuation of the woman's productive and reproductive capacities. Dowry, on the other hand, speaks to the groom's capacity to earn an income, as well as a valuation of his status in the social hierarchy.[19] Generally, young women's decision-making power in marriage choice or timing is completely nonexistent when financial gains are at stake. Young women in the study also rejected the consequences of payments in terms of male "ownership" of the wife. For example, for women in National Capital District, Papua New Guinea, a bride price renders them more vulnerable to domestic abuse since "customary marriages mean once the husband buys the lady, he can do whatever he wants to do with her. Her parents and brothers are not able to do anything to help her. A wife cannot go back to her family if problems arise in her marriage." Young women have little leeway to choose their partner and have little voice once they enter into a domestic partnership.

On Norms and Agency • http://dx.doi.org/10.1596/978-0-8213-9862-3

While, in theory, bride price can be interpreted as explicit recognition and valuation of women's potential contribution to marriage, in practice, it often limits women's control over their own lives. Similarly, in theory, dowry may endow daughters with property (or an inheritance) early in life to protect them (or give them some agency), but in practice, it transfers "their" property rights to the husband. It is worth noting that it is not just women who want to change traditional marital practices. A young man in Koudipally Mandal (Andhra Pradesh), India, explained that, although a dowry is traditional and common practice, although he took a dowry for his wife, and although he (like other men) has control over the assets taken under dowry, he still felt that "more love marriages should take place." Young men in Sudan (Red Sea State) also wanted to be able to freely choose who to marry, but they did not believe that women should have the same right.

Most focus groups indicated that formalizing a union via wedding or civil ceremony is customary, but they called less forcefully for expanding that practice. Interestingly, in Peru where informal unions are more frequent, some young women wanted legal unions because they felt that a marriage contract brought them more benefits and rights, such as financial support for childrearing and social status and respectability. They also believed that they gain *voz y voto* (voice and say) in their household. For them, a formal marriage license, by securing their status as wives, is a means of getting more equal footing with their partners.

But norms and practices are hard to change. The desires of young women to change certain practices restricting their freedom to choose do not go unchallenged. Young men in Afghanistan, the Republic of Yemen, Tanzania, Sudan, Vietnam, South Africa, and Fiji, and some adult women in South Africa, the Republic of Yemen, and Vietnam, pushed back strongly. They argued for the protection of traditional marriage customs to preserve the norm—the way things have been done in their culture as passed down by the ancestors—for the future.

How Can a Child Take Care of Another Child?

The average age of a girl or young woman when they bear their first child varied among the communities studied. As seen in table 3.2, rural focus groups reported that women start having children much earlier than their urban peers, and earlier than the average age that young men become fathers for the first time. Nearly 50 percent of rural groups said most girls were mothers by age 17, compared

Table 3.2 Age of Men and Women at Birth of First Child

percent

		15 years or less	16–17 years	18–25 years	26+ years
Men	Rural	15	23	54	8
	Urban	14	17	57	12
Women	Rural	26	22	44	7
	Urban	13	18	58	10

Note: Average age of marriage in each community as reported by 194 young adult focus groups.

On Norms and Agency • http://dx.doi.org/10.1596/978-0-8213-9862-3

with 30 percent for urban women, who started having children at the same age they married—between 18 and 25 years—much like urban men and a significant share of rural men.

Whether urban or rural, male or female, the majority of focus groups agreed that the current average age that women had their first child or pregnancy was not appropriate and should change, and that women were having children too early in life. But like the decision to marry, urban men were the only group that split between questioning current practices and trends, and not changing them; but again, they have more flexibility about when to wed and more options in choice of potential partners, as well as a larger range of opportunities to work, study, and access contraception.

The gap between the current and desired age to become a parent, described by the focus groups, is significant. Most groups preferred 20 years of age or more, and sometimes even older than 30. Their main reasons for delaying childbearing were similar: mother's physical health, parents' maturity, and parents' social situation (marital status, financial situation, and education level). A young man from Monrovia, Liberia, summed it up, saying "parenthood is not for young people."

Indeed, the discussions about delaying childbirth often raised the issue of the health (and even the life) of the mother when she is too young, but more as a general concern than a challenge to the norm that marked young age as appropriate for starting reproduction. Still, many communities consider teen pregnancies problematic. According to a young woman from Tchien District, Liberia, "[At 14] the girls' bodies are too small. They suffer too much. ... They get sick. Some of them have to go to the hospital because their bodies are so small." Another Liberian young woman from Zorzor worried that "sometimes you can die when you have a baby this early [16 years old]." In the Republic of Yemen, one young woman's 14-year-old sister died due to early pregnancy, as did the school friend of a young woman from the Dominican Republic. Even a man from Emputa village, Tanzania, noted, "In our community, women have children at the age of 12."

Both boys and girls in their focus groups mentioned pregnancy as one of the reasons girls and boys left school early. A young woman in Firestone District, Liberia, warned that, at early ages, girls are "not ready for children. When you have a child, you will not be able to go far in school. You will suffer because the boys will disown the pregnancy and will not support you when you get pregnant." Even young men agreed that women should prioritize education over childbearing. For a young South African man, a woman should have children "at the age of 23 because she has completed her tertiary education, maybe has a decent job, and is able to support her children." A young woman from Cusco Province, Peru, who had her daughter at 18, wished that if she "could do everything all over again, [she] would have had her daughter at 25 so [she] could continue studying." In Velugodu (Andhra Pradesh), India, a young woman who was married when she was 10 and had her first child at 15, asserted, "This is not the right age. ... A girl should have a child when she is able to understand what is right and what is wrong." Overall, the focus groups felt that having children too early means that the parents, especially the mothers, must give up their dreams for the future.

On Norms and Agency • http://dx.doi.org/10.1596/978-0-8213-9862-3

How Many Children Is Too Many?

Once reproduction has started, couples should be able to negotiate the number of children they want to have. As shown in figure 3.4, the discussions in most urban focus groups, and by rural men, indicated that couples jointly decide on the number of children to have. Only 20 percent, however, of the young adult women in both rural and urban areas said that the decision on how many children to have was in their hands. Rural women (40 percent), though, described it differently: what men consider a joint decision in rural communities is basically the man's decision. The husband decides the number and spacing of children because it is inherent in his role as household head; the wife agrees with his authority and accepts the outcome of the decision.[20] Some young women justified a man's right to decide because he pays the bride price or has the power to impose his will through violence. Other women indicated that, when faced with disagreement about having children, men compelled their decisions either through forced sex or by threats to leave the wife or take an additional wife.

In some cases, the decision to keep having more children is also imposed by men as a means of keeping women under control: "The decision of how many children to have comes from the man. The man tells the woman the number of children he wants. If she says she's tired, the man will beat her," explained a young woman from Zorzor, Liberia. And young men are also aware of their decision power: "Mostly the man says he will marry another wife if she doesn't have

Figure 3.4 Who Decides on Number of Children?

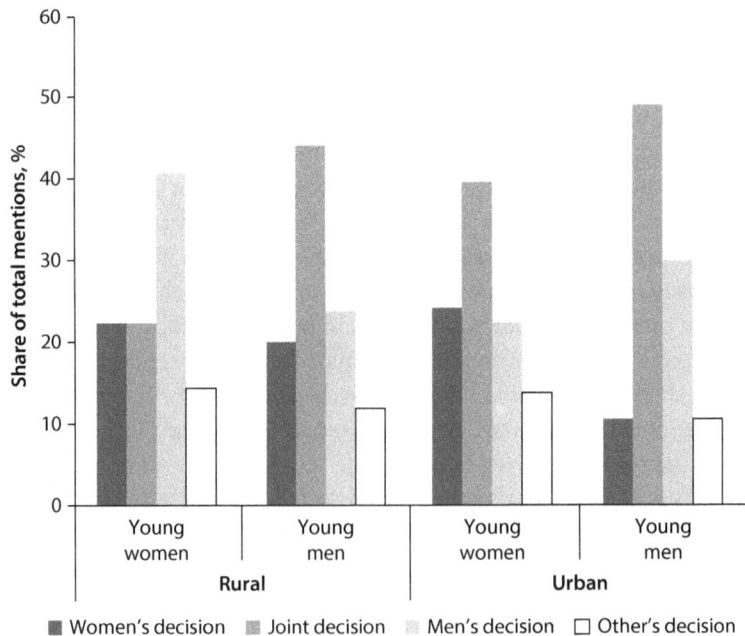

Note: Data from 194 young adult focus groups.

On Norms and Agency · http://dx.doi.org/10.1596/978-0-8213-9862-3

[a] baby" (Old City, West Bank and Gaza). In the Roma community of Kragujevac, Serbia, comments extended to the extreme of valuing women only for their reproductive capacity. "A woman exists only to give birth to a child. What does she have to do with deciding how many children to have?"

In the sample countries, the Republic of Yemen, Afghanistan, Sudan, India, West Bank and Gaza, Burkina Faso, Fiji, Liberia, and Vietnam, and among the Roma population in Serbia, young women felt that the decision to have children was forced on them, not just by their partners, but by family members (his and hers). Sometimes it is an older woman who imposes her will on a young woman. The role of mothers-in-law in determining the number of children young wives have appears unchanged in Fiji, India, and West Bank and Gaza, especially the pressure for male children. Furthermore, in many of these communities, women attributed their future reproduction to forces beyond their control, such as God's or Allah's will, fate, and more. While the exception, a few focus groups rejected any public discussion about reproduction as inappropriate, showing how little control over reproduction is talked about.[21]

More groups than we expected described childbearing as a non-decision. In Peru, the Dominican Republic, and many African communities, the adults and even younger women spoke of childbearing as accidents or as events that just occur. In the experience of young women in Chiclayo, Peru, and Tchien District, Liberia, having children "is not something you decide. It just comes and you have to look after [the baby]." In these cases, while social norms may not be binding, their lack of agency combines with lack of information about their own reproductive process.

There are indications that the grip of some social norms on family formation has started to relax (Jejeebhoy et al. 2002; Malhotra 1991). Better information and access to family planning (mainly contraception) enable women to claim agency and greater control over their bodies, even though progress may still be limited by the opinion of others—family members, community, religious groups, and others. Women's lifetime earnings and education are negatively associated with the number of children they have, particularly those who begin childbearing early, so acting to take control of their situation is an important step.[22]

In the rural areas that make up almost half of the communities in the research, we expected to find restrictions on contraception availability and use. Both rural and urban women in the study, however, can get contraception and use it frequently. Control over one's own reproduction and fertility, and use of fertility-control mechanisms are clear signs of agency, control and ownership, and self-determination by women.

We see a crucial change when we compare the generations of adult and young adult women in the sample in their access, knowledge, and acceptance of family planning services. Young adult women have far more control over their reproduction, due to the life-altering changes made possible by the availability of family planning services. For example, in Samtse, Bhutan, the young women pointed out that "before there was none ... but now around 90 percent of women use injections to limit the number of children in the family." In Comendador, the Dominican Republic, a young woman felt that "one has control because there are so many methods," and in Tewor District, Liberia, another young woman noted that "now women can decide. Now there is family planning. Before, the man used to tell the woman how many children to have." Either because of contraception's positive effect on women's empowerment or because its use is driven by the soaring costs of raising children (as mentioned by the Vietnam and Papua New Guinea participants), women are controlling their fertility more as they desire.

This increased control and attitude change is striking when we compare the average number of children their mothers had with the number of children the younger generation of women desire to have (table 3.3). An overwhelming majority of the older mothers in the study had a minimum of three children or more, with some variations. Urban women—probably due to their exposure to more relaxed norms, more certain supply of contraception, and better economic opportunities—were more likely than rural women to have fewer than three children. (These same factors hold for younger women as well.) Rural women, however, wanted more children than urban women. The picture changes when we look at young men, who aimed for a larger family size than women, particularly in rural contexts.

Like marriage, childbearing changes the status of women in some localities, which influences their ability to control when to have children (and the number). When the same women in Tchien District, Liberia—who asserted that children just happen—get married, they face heavy pressures to have a large number of children, which has become a competition among families in the community. It is no surprise that the man's status is at play: "The men decide. They tell me that they want 7, 10, many children. They make sure that their women bear that number," related a young Liberian. Having many children reinforces the husband's conformity with the prevalent norms of masculinity. "You cannot tell men to use birth control; they want children. The more they have, the more manly they appear to be" (young woman, Zabibu village, Tanzania).

In line with perceived ideal masculine behaviors, young men did not oppose the use of contraceptive methods by women, but they generally refused to use them, even where HIV/AIDS is a known risk. (Tanzania is one exception.) Young men from Umlazi townships A and B, South Africa, rejected condoms for their impact on their sexual enjoyment, preferring "skin to skin" relations because "you cannot eat a sweet with the wrapping." In Santiago de los Caballeros,

Table 3.3 Number of Children of Mother Compared with Desired Fertility for Self
percent

	Location	1 child	2–3 children	3 or more children
Mother's average number of children	Rural	0	19	81
	Urban	0	24	76
Women's expectations for number of children	Rural	9	47	44
	Urban	12	49	39
Men's expectations for number of children	Rural	8	31	61
	Urban	9	41	49

Note: Data from 194 young adult focus groups.

the Dominican Republic, young men wear condoms only when having sex with women other than their wives to avoid bearing bastard children. In the specific case of vasectomies (available in public reproductive health services in India and Bhutan), men and women feared that it affects men's physical strength, capacity to work, and sexual drive. Because it might alter their manhood, men preferred that women undergo sterilization, if that is the couple's decision.

Pink or Blue? Girl or Boy?

The preference for sons is associated with cultural custom and norms, local community characteristics, the ability of women to have a say about their reproductive preferences, and household characteristics (Astone and Pande 2007). Social norms in this context probably play the largest role, in terms of the value of women in society, the association of sons with transmission of bloodline (Das Gupta 2009), inheritance practices (Carranza 2012), and other traditions. In some countries, the quest for a son is reflected in a larger number of children when the first born is not a male, while in others—most noticeably China and India—it has led to skewed preferences and unbalanced sex ratios.[23] When asked about their preference for the sex of their children, the participants in our study indicated that the traditional preference for sons wanes in cities, especially among young women. Along with conventional arguments on the benefits of having boys emerged narratives about the advantages of raising girls. Figure 3.5 shows that all the men clearly preferred male children, particularly rural men, where 46 percent of preferences are for a son. Urban men and women show similar levels of indifference regarding their children's sex, but have opposite views when it comes to preferring a boy or a girl. More women overall, though, actually prefer girl children than having no preference for the sex of a child,

Figure 3.5 Sex Preference for Children

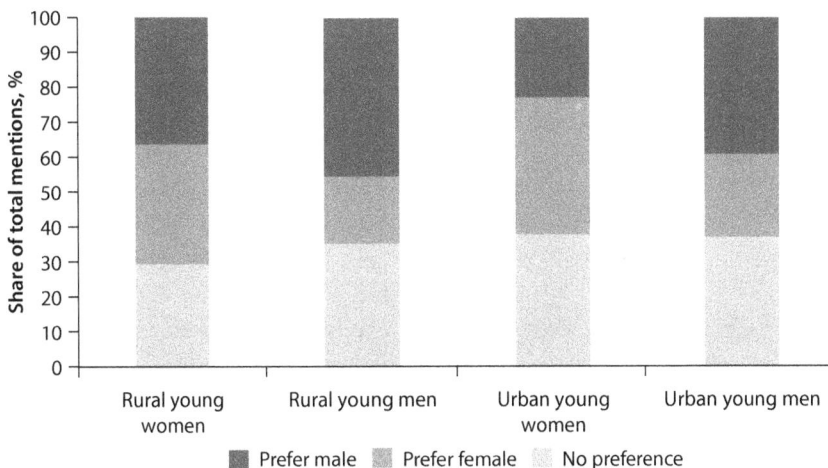

Note: Data from young adult focus groups (258 mentions).

On Norms and Agency • http://dx.doi.org/10.1596/978-0-8213-9862-3

although rural women are equally split between preferring male and female children.

A deeply ingrained set of normative views about gender distribution of responsibilities and perceptions by communities permeated the reasons for preferring sons, echoed by the participants. It is based on the consequences of inheritance laws and customs that determine what the male members of the family are entitled to, such as family property and business; having boys guarantees that assets or patrimony remain in the family:

> In our community, life is difficult for the man [and his immediate family] who does not have a son. Most of his relatives expect to get his property when he dies and his property is distributed by his relatives and not [given to his] wife or daughter. If he has a son, all his property will belong to his son. (Rural young woman, Naw Da, Afghanistan)

Males carry the family or clan name and guarantee the continuity of the lineage; the family's status increases if the son does well: "I prefer a boy. I will be socially accepted if he succeeds" (young woman, River Nile State, Sudan). Boys are expected to help support the household with their earnings and provide for elderly parents: "We have to depend on our sons to take care of us. Daughters have to care for their husband's family" (young man, Hung Yen District, Vietnam). Many participants considered sons easier to care for because they represent less risk to the family's honor: "It is more difficult to provide a good upbringing for female children. To go out to a café and drink alcohol is all right for men, but not for women. If a girl sleeps with 115 guys, everyone labels her in one way; if a man does the same, everyone sees it differently [as not so bad]" (young woman, Sumadija District, Serbia). Boys who have more freedom carry positive externalities for the father: "A father can have fun with a son or drink with him" (young man, Justynowo, Poland). And in conflict areas, such as Afghanistan and West Bank and Gaza, sons help protect the household better than daughters.

The reasons for preferring girls also reflect the normative and institutional systems underlying gender inequalities. When daughters were preferred, the focus groups desired them for their feminine qualities. Daughters take care of the parents, especially in old age: "It's different when you grow old. A daughter will more likely take care of the mother than a son (young woman, Justynowo, Poland); "[I want] my first child to be a girl so she can help me with housework" (young woman, East Sepik Province, Papua New Guinea). Girls have a better understanding of household management and its difficulties. Girls are easier to bring up because "a girl is more docile and she keeps you company" (young woman, Chiclayo, Peru). Families look at the future economic reward that girls represent when they marry: "I prefer daughters because I know that at some stage I will benefit from her [bride price]" (young man, Umlazi township B, Durban, South Africa).

These views plainly reflect the expectations attached to different life paths for male and female children. The preference for girls has increased in our sample communities, especially in urban areas, which may be due to women's greater access to education and economic opportunities, but may also point to a change in the overall position of women in society—as experienced and witnessed by the young women interviewed. The fact that preference for girls is still very much based on their roles as homemakers and caregivers, however, shows the persistence of traditional gender roles and power, and asset distribution in the hands of men.

What Is Mine Is Yours: Asset Control and Decision-Making

Control over resources—measured by women's ability to earn income, control their income, and own assets—is instrumental to women's agency and may increase their bargaining power, their position, and their ability to make decisions or gain voice in a household, as noted clearly in *World Development Report 2012*. It gives them power over their lives by allowing them to leave an unequal family situation and raises their value in society and to their families.[24] Lack of assets severely limits women's choices by rendering them powerless to negotiate better terms for themselves in their households or with a range of formal and informal institutions where control over income or assets becomes important for them to have a voice (Narayan 2002). Not having control over one's own assets basically means not having those assets at all, which diminishes one's capacity to make strategic life choices.

Women are not strangers to asset management. They tend to manage the everyday expenses required to run a household and care for dependants—the small choices we mentioned at the beginning of this chapter. Men, however, remain in charge of major expenditures, such as expensive animals, real estate or land, and (generally) education fees. The differences in asset or financial control are exacerbated in poor households where women have much less control or management of their income and assets. The rational explanations for women giving up decision-making power to men or for men taking such power from women are a matter of strong social norms that govern specialization of duties in the household.

The narratives from the communities in our research predominantly put men in charge of the family income, including any wages earned by other members of the household, especially women. Women never control men's money (or at least not all of it), and shared control (by men and women) of a man's money is rare, but common for a woman's money.

Our focus groups discussed the situation of Judith and James, a fictional couple living in their communities, who negotiate Judith's decision to start a business and the use of its profits.[25] Starting when Judith manages to get start-up capital for a small business, the focus group discussions tracked her ability to actually go ahead with her idea, how much support James would give her, her chances for success if James opposed her foray into business, and her authority to decide how to use the returns of the business. The discussions proved quite telling. Figure 3.6 shows the different opinions in the focus groups about control of income earned

When the money is mine, I spend it on my family because we share our life. ... Money is for all the family. It is mine, but my husband and I decide how to spend it.

— (Rural woman, North Darfur State, Sudan)

Figure 3.6 Who Controls Judith's Money?

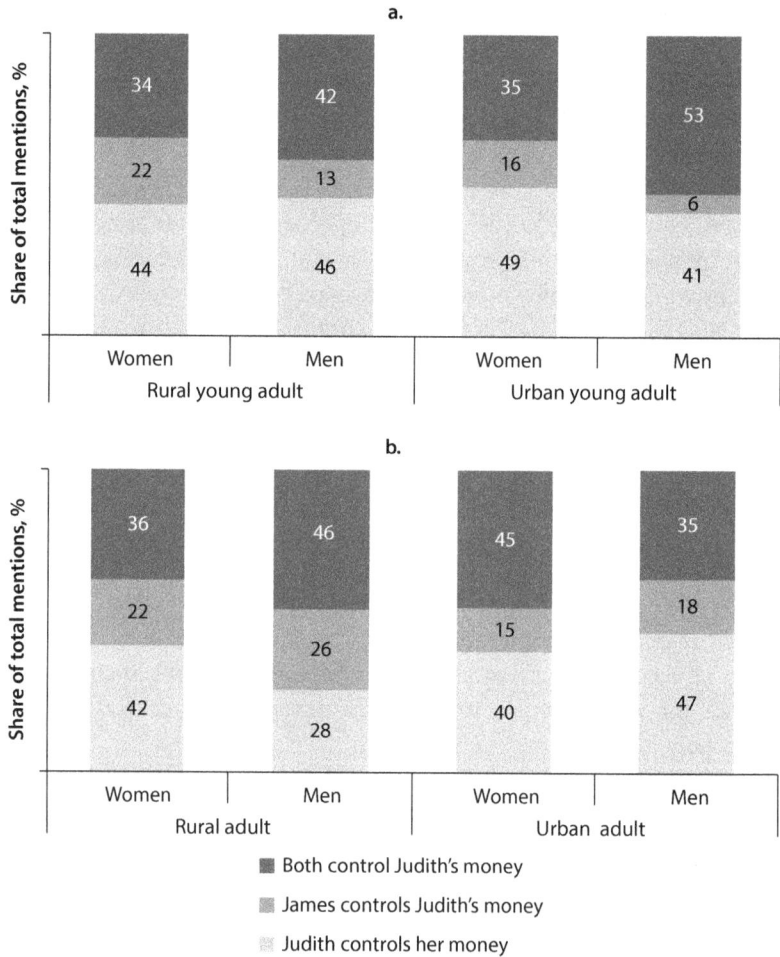

Note: Data from 388 focus groups.

by Judith. Shared control of Judith's money or Judith getting to control her income were the most common answers, across all locations and age groups.

More than 40 percent of the groups acknowledged that Judith should have a say about her money, except rural adult men—only 27.6 percent agreed that Judith should control her money (compared with 45.8 percent among rural young adult men). A significant number of participants chose shared control over Judith's business profits. A small number of groups discussed whether the couple should also make joint decisions about James's money, if he started the business. The predominant view preferred that James control his money over sharing control with Judith.

The first impression of fairness and women's control in figure 3.6 is deceiving. A little probing by the discussion facilitators into how the shared decision-making process operates revealed that men's opinions carried greater weight in most decisions about Judith's income, even when reported as shared control. And among the 64 groups that account discussing the reverse situation, where the business was owned by James, women and men both were much less likely to share control over James's money.

When it comes to major expenses, the process is similar: women in the study were almost never solely in charge of these decisions. Even when women reported that they had autonomy to decide how to use their income, they still followed the directions of a man. More often than not, women's accounts of their independent decision cited compromises reached with their husband or partner. On the whole, there is overwhelming evidence, reported by both women and by men in a number of communities (showing no specific regional or country pattern), of how little autonomy women actually exercise when it comes to their own assets and income.

Men and women participants justified male control over all earnings and assets belonging to the family or belonging to the women in the family by referring to traditional customs (some of which are religious) and equally traditional entitlements attached to the head of the household. For example, in three of the communities in Papua New Guinea, men claimed to control assets on the basis of tradition or custom: "It is the man who dominates, who owns everything." One of these communities has a matriarchal tradition, but even there men are perceived as the natural heads of households, although "women are financial controllers" and "the bosses." When it comes to making certain decisions, the women's tradition-bestowed power does not hold. Women "don't sell anything because women's place is in the house." Men from this Papuan matrilineal community asserted that the husband has a large say in the use of money earned by his wife. To them, James as head of household was endowed with the entitlements and responsibilities associated with that role, and they overrode even the traditionally recognized lead role of women in their community.

There is little distinction between being a man and having authority. A good husband has the biggest voice and the final say over any decisions for managing women's income and assets. The Judith and James scenario prompted a group of women from a village of Sumadija District, Serbia, to present these situations:

> –There would be bloodshed if she [the wife] spent the money by herself. When I received some money, 250,000 dinars, we put the money in one place because my husband said so. If my husband had received the money, he would have made the decision himself. He is my husband, he is the boss, he is the man.

On Norms and Agency • http://dx.doi.org/10.1596/978-0-8213-9862-3

–[This is] an example that is applicable to the majority of us here. Some men are cunning and manipulate their women in a nice, slick way and others pound their fists on the table to get their way, but the end result is always the same.

But this automatic authority may also be detrimental to men, who are expected to provide all necessities, buy big things for the house, and always pay because it makes them the man of the house. This expectation remains in effect, even if lost employment, poor local economic situations, or lack of skills prevent men from fulfilling this role.

Sometimes it is less about explicit dominance, despite men always having a say. A careful look at what the women in all 20 countries said reveals that many men genuinely welcome cooperation and shared opinions, but only if they do not affect household balances. In Hung Yen District, Vietnam, when asked if Judith can decide alone how to spend her money, one woman noted, "She can decide how to use her money, but she needs to consult her husband. Otherwise, her relationship with her husband will be negatively affected." Decisions about their money are, for women (unlike men), part of the primary considerations for keeping family harmony and balance. "The money can be mine, but the moment I need to do something for the family, I need to have him also decide on [how to use] my money. Sometimes we women do this, not because we think it is right, but simply because you need the family relations to keep going well," said a woman from Zabibu village, Tanzania.

Some women in the study referred to traditional norms to rationalize their lack of power: "According to our tradition, the biggest things are not controlled by women. Also, women cannot buy and sell anything in our village"; and "according to the culture of our community, women do not do business, so of course women alone cannot do business in our village" (women in Naw Da, Afghanistan). In a semi-rural community of Ngonyameni, South Africa, women described a tradition mixed with patriarchy: "This is a very patriarchal community. We believe that men are the heads of the households and they make all the decisions. This is also a traditional community, so the man has a final word in any decision regarding the household. It does not matter if Zodwa (Judith) worked for that money; she cannot decide alone how to use it." References to decision-making power and control over assets, as one of the rights of the head of household, were heard repeatedly in communities in Africa, India, and the Middle East.

In a rural community of Ngonyameni, South Africa, a mix of cultural tradition, men's reputations and respect in the eyes of the community, and a sense of marital duty combined to justify male control over assets and income. Its tradition supporting unequal control of assets was first based in magical-religious elements. The villagers defended the impossibility of women sharing ownership of the house they live in with their husbands with their belief that "his ancestors have lived in that house, so the land belongs to them." A woman cannot own a house because "she left her ancestors when she got married, so it is her husband's ancestors [in his house] that watch over the family. If she claims the house is hers,

On Norms and Agency • http://dx.doi.org/10.1596/978-0-8213-9862-3

it might bring her misfortune." Only after the death of the husband is a woman allowed to take control of the property.

In Ngonyameni everything belongs to men. Women take their husband's surname as a sign of becoming his property and their assets also get a new owner, whether they are brought into the marriage or generated after. "You may buy livestock on your own, but the purchase is in your husband's name, and that gives him respect in the community." Women are not only barred from ownership but "some women have to tell their husband about every penny they earn."

By and large, women are economically dependent for everything, including necessities, even if they bring assets to the marriage. Furthermore, in some sample communities, the institution of marriage also meant that women are transferred to the husband's family as property. A man in Liberia challenged whether a woman can own property since she is part of the household assets:

> She can get property, but she can't own property. For example, if her brother gives her a cow, it is hers. But before she sells it to someone else, she must consult the man (brother or husband) and the man must agree. Even the woman herself is your property. The only reason she is respected is because she is a human being.

Finally, community pressure to conform to expected behaviors can be the most effective method to keep a woman (or put her back) in her rightful place. In a community in Vietnam, if Hoa (Judith) makes her own decisions about spending her money, the local women's association will visit and explain to her that women are supposed to ask their husband's opinion before deciding on the spending, even though it is her money. They will remind her of the Vietnamese saying: "Couples living in harmony have strength to displace the Eastern Sea."

Pocket Money

Not everything acts as a constraint, although it may seem like it. Even under restricted conditions described by the focus groups, women are usually allowed to handle everyday expenses independently, as long as they purchase inexpensive household items for household consumption—nothing that will increase the women's bargaining power or their voice in the household and supersede men's authority. Women are often accused of bothering their husband if they ask him about minor needs.

At this level of decision-making, norms are slightly more flexible and women find ways to exercise some degree of autonomy. More than a few women in the study were able to set aside money occasionally and did not tell their husbands or refused to surrender control over it. Indeed, women were recognized as wiser money managers than men by a men's focus group from the Dominican Republic in several different discussions, echoed by a (Tchien District) Liberian man who admitted that "some men are good managers, but women are better. A man can decide to do whatever he wants with his money if he is a rich man; if he is less well off, he should consult his wife on how to spend his money because she is more likely to prioritize household expenditures." These men saw themselves at

On Norms and Agency • http://dx.doi.org/10.1596/978-0-8213-9862-3

high risk of spending the money on themselves and falling into the bad husband category.

Men's tendency to squander their income outside the home was a recurring problem and may underlie the perception by the focus groups that women are better managers. Both men and women in widely diverse countries in the study recognized that men spend too much of their earnings on alcohol, women, and gambling, while women use their (earned) money to sustain the household. Evidence of differences in expenditures has been widely documented, proving that women favor investing in children. This preference partly relates to social norms, which imbues women with greater knowledge of children's needs due to women's traditional gender roles. Women's control of income and assets is also important for their children's well-being.[26] The motives behind men's spending on alcohol have been less researched, but they appear to be related to demands to assert their masculinity in the eyes of the community, as much as an escape from living up to the hegemonic masculinity model or gender role prescriptions.[27]

The focus groups again brought up men's private consumption of income in relation to control over household finances. "Most men will spend money on mistresses and gambling, expenditures that will not be discussed with the wife" (adult man, Paro, Bhutan). "A man does not provide any money to his wife when he wastes money on drinks. He spends a lot of money on alcohol and then starts asking the wife to get money from her father" (adult woman, Velugodu [Andhra Pradesh], India). Even the fictional James was matter-of-factly described as spending the profits of his (or Judith's) entrepreneurship on partying by a man from Comendador, the Dominican Republic.

On rare occasions, women actually manage the entire family income with their partner's consent, much like this woman in Serbia: "My husband receives his salary and gives it to me. He does not carry money with him, and I pay all the bills. He never asks me how I spend the money." Other women reported some awareness of their rights that led to some level of control or that associated autonomy with effort. Women in Fiji, India, Sudan, and the Dominican Republic felt that, if Judith is the one who makes her business succeed without James's help, she has the right to decide alone how to use her money. The idea of bestowing the right to decide on women is a sign of attitudinal change challenging the norm of sole male control of financial decisions in the household. Chapters 4 and 5 present more evidence of women actually acting upon these views of their own entitlements.

Moving Up and Forward

Even when women's right to decide is recognized, women are still not always able to decide alone or may not opt for selfish consumption. When women have access to earnings or assets, they tend to include others in their decision-making more often than men. Even the women in the study cannot easily detach themselves from their household roles and responsibilities as mothers and home-makers.[28]

Justifications for how responsibilities and entitlements in households are distributed, however, appear to be changing in some of the sample communities.

On Norms and Agency • http://dx.doi.org/10.1596/978-0-8213-9862-3

While some women and most men accepted traditional customs and norms for asset control (the rights of heads of households and husbands, and rights handed down by ancestors), other men and women saw a need to alter them and referred to changes that have already taken place, such as inheritance laws that include women or the benefits of women generating and managing their own income.

Once women accumulate wealth—or their family does—they also seem both to accumulate decision-making power and to gain access to larger assets. Women in less dire economic circumstances, and certainly women with more independent economic means, have more control over their assets and earnings than poorer women, even if women's autonomy is tightly restricted in other areas of their lives. Poorer women more frequently require permission from their husbands to use their own money, as attested to by women in Boyina Bagh, Afghanistan. In Sigatoka, Fiji, as family finances ease, women often gain more control over income from agricultural products and small livestock and poultry, for example, and eventually ownership, control, and decision over land.

Women's right to self-determination is starting to be recognized by the women and men in the focus groups, even when autonomy and control of money they earn remains elusive. "I respect her and her right to start her own business," said a man from East Sepik Province, Papua New Guinea, "but apart from money for clothes, for everything else, her husband will have access to and control of her money." A Vietnamese woman from Hung Yen District saw a more positive future: "Women's roles have changed a lot. Women's social relations are the same as men's. Both daughters and sons get the inheritance. However, the sons are given larger inheritance than daughters, even though it is stipulated by the law and the court that daughters and sons should have the same inheritance."

When Does Choice Mean Agency?

In the strategic decisions covered in this chapter, women have gained some autonomy to decide about their education, jobs, marriage (who and when), and reproduction, although they still are permanently challenged not to neglect their domestic duties. Men in the study are showing more willingness to consider sharing power (if not actually share it) and to release some control over household decisions to women. Shared decision-making means men have to bend constraining norms, but it introduces a better decision-making process into their households. And as these men and women change, they transform the traditional playing field in their communities. In the domestic sphere, the women are stealthily altering traditional definitions of duties and responsibilities associated with their expected roles, which may induce change in the norms or make them more flexible.

The evidence from the different communities in our study shows that it is young women in urban areas who are more overtly acquiring a greater sense of self-determination and agency in the decisions discussed here. Within persistent constraints, they are beginning to envision a future similar to young men: education, independence, greater financial autonomy, and shared responsibility for their family. Adult men and women in rural areas, have a less positive view of the changes occurring in their societies, both given the difficulties they have faced or because of uncertainty from challenges to their traditional power roles and identities. However, perceptions and voices are changing, and they mark real movement in women's power and freedom. Whether women make more traditional or modern choices (box 3.1), the goal is to make their own decisions with fewer constraints.

Kabeer (1999) sees the ability to exercise choice in terms of three inter-related dimensions: resources, agency, and achievements or outcomes. Resources, the contexts, and conditions that the men and women in the study have to make choices vary with each decision, as they have clearly described. Women's acquisition of education, income, and jobs, and access to services—resources—act as

---

Box 3.1 Choosing Not to Change Things

Agency does not always entail making progressive choices. Conservative choices are made in at least two scenarios: (a) where options are limited or where restrictions and conservative choices increase people's status or improve their general well-being, and (b) where true commitment to the norm is not strategic.

An example of a conservative choice that has been interpreted multiple ways is the use of the veil among Muslim women. It has been argued that religious and social ideals and norms are not always (or even usually) rejected by women as oppressive, but are sometimes appropriated and creatively used to increase their agency and achieve positive goals (Mahmood 2001). Adolescent girls and young women in West Bank and Gaza refer to restrictions on their mobility in ways indicating that it constrains rather than enables their agency. But wearing the veil in public is also an apparent strategic choice to gain a degree of autonomy, even though it appears constraining.

Although the focus groups did not discuss it extensively, enough comments gave evidence that the veil is accepted both as a matter of course and as a passport to greater mobility and autonomy. Adolescent boys and girls in communities near Rafah (West Bank and Gaza) both agreed that it is easier for "veiled girls to go to school" or move around in public. In a neighborhood of Rafah Governorate, the adolescents also reported that girls work while going to school to help support their families, but it is more difficult if they do not wear the veil. Making a progressive choice (in this case, not to wear a veil) affects their ability to earn income and reduces their agency.

The evidence for a strategic use of the veil, however, does not rule out adherence to the norm from true commitment to religious or moral values. The statement by an adolescent girl from Rafah that "we have to be veiled, it is our religion" should be taken seriously and not explained away by reference to social conditions. Truly conservative choices that are not a response to restrictions were rare in our study, but this may be the result of the emphasis in the research on the conditions that enable or limit agency, rather than on values and religious ideals.

---

preconditions to exercising their agency. The actual ability to make strategic decisions, however, does not always follow immediately, but as women's horizons and options broaden, so does their ability to envision a different life and act upon it—and achieve it.

But aspirations that lead to action do not take place in a void. As Ray (2003) notes clearly, individuals still fall back on their local reference frameworks as guidance. They make comparisons with their peers and qualify their own situations relative to community references, which shape their aspirations. From their communities flows information and how to interpret it; communities identify role models and produce "others like me." Aspirations for economic mobility and power are contextual and depend on how much mobility one perceives in a local community and in society.

Notes

1. This is akin to Amartya Sen's (1985) notion of "functionings," which range from basic concerns (e.g., being healthy, having a good job, and being safe) to more complex states (e.g., being happy, having self-respect, and being calm). The freedom to achieve functionings obviously has an instrumental value, but it also has intrinsic value to a person's quality of life.

2. Chapter 4 in *World Development Report 2012* analyzes available evidence from around the world on this relationship.

3. Fiji, the Dominican Republic, Bhutan, India, Burkina Faso, Sudan, West Bank and Gaza, and the Republic of Yemen. Togo adolescents were also interviewed but the data were not included in the figures in this section.

4. The highest returns on education are recorded in low-income and middle-income countries when looking at income levels. When looking at regions, Latin America and the Caribbean region and Sub-Saharan Africa region see the highest returns. The lowest returns are in non-OECD European countries and the Middle East and North African countries.

5. See *World Development Report 2012* (World Bank 2012, 169) for estimates on the probability of women who need permission to get medical care based on demographic and health data.

6. See Field and Ambrus (2008), Goldin and Katz (2002), and Pezzini (2005), for example.

7. Our survey did not collect specific data about the education level attained by the participants, just their comments on, and their perceptions of, levels reached in their communities.

8. Participants in urban and rural communities in South Africa, Tanzania, Burkina Faso, and Togo also echoed this perception.

9. "Adaptive preferences," as described by Sen, respond to the material conditions of individuals' lives. Nussbaum argues that these choices are not real expressions of agency, but a simulacrum of choice.

10. *World Development Report 2012* refers to these groups as severely disadvantaged populations or regions.

11. *World Development Report 2012.*

12. *World Development Report 2012* (World Bank 2012, 217–19) has a section with this same title, which deals with the differences in time use between men and women and their impact on women's labor market outcomes. It notes that gender differences in time use patterns stem from the gender division of roles and responsibilities inside a household.

13. Brickell (2006) and Ginsburg and Rapp (1991) provide a good overview and summary of these issues in sociology and anthropology.

14. In feminist work, and in sociology more generally, sexuality usually refers both to the individual's practices and identities, as well as to the ideologies, discourses, and social arrangements around it (Holland *et al.* 1998; Walby 1990).

15. Diez Minguela (2011), based on United Nations' data on world marriage.

16. For example, see research by Breierova and Duflo (2004) in Indonesia; Dayioğlu, Kirdar, and Tansel (2009) in Turkey; Long and Osli (2008) in Nigeria; and Perelli-Harris (2006) in Ukraine.

17. Anderson (2007) notes that asset transfers per marriage can be as high as six times the annual household income in South Asia (Rao 1993), and four times the annual household income in Sub-Saharan Africa (Dekker and Hoogeveen 2002).

18. Indian rupees.

19. Rao (1993) shows how dowries in India increase in amount for higher-ranked castes and when the groom is more educated.

20. These opinions came from Naw Da, Afghanistan; Labasa and Sigatoka, Fiji; Koudipally Mandal and Velugodu, India; Sungai Puar District, Indonesia; Briceni District, Moldova; and Milne Bay Province, Papua New Guinea.

21. In the Boyina Bagh, Afghanistan, focus group, the young women claimed "not knowing about this question because it is a private issue between husband and wife." Participants from the Red Sea area of Sudan reacted to the question with surprise and anger, and refused to continue the conversation until the subject was changed: "No almighty but Allah, you disbelievers! This comes from God, and we have nothing to say about that."

22. A review of this evidence can be found in Buvinic, Das Gupta, and Casabonne (2009).

23. A detailed analysis of the phenomenon of "missing girls" can be found in chapter 3 of *World Development Report 2012* (World Bank 2012, 120–27).

24. See chapter 4 in *World Development Report 2012* (World Bank 2012) for a detailed review of the evidence.

25. The exercise was conducted with young adult and adult men and women.

26. In studies of countries as varied as Brazil, Côte d'Ivoire, Ghana, Mexico, South Africa, and Turkey, women's spending on goods that benefit children has prompted the introduction of social policies, such as conditional cash transfers. See Schady and Rosero (2008) and Doss (2006).

27. See Lemle and Mishkind (1989), Holland *et al.* (1998), and Barker (2005).

28. These and other accounts should be complemented by economic research on women's expenditure preferences, as well as anthropological research. Miller's (1998) study on shopping shows that housework and homemaking are strong sources of self-identity and solidify family bonds in working- and middle-class English homes. Miller argues that everyday shopping and management carry meaning, among other reasons, because they maintain crucial relationships and allow women to positively mold

family members. The assumption is that male and female members of the household adhere to and follow a moral scheme of what is good to instill in others, using provisioning and housekeeping to do it. This is not normally recognized because action in the domestic sphere is considered, by default, as inferior to action in the public sphere.

References

Agarwal, B. 1997. "'Bargaining' and Gender Relations: Within and Beyond the Household." *Feminist Economics* 3 (1): 1–51.

Anderson, S. 2007. "The Economics of Dowry and Brideprice." *Journal of Economic Perspectives* 21 (4): 151–74.

Appadurai, A. 2004. "The Capacity to Aspire: Culture and Terms of Recognition." In *Culture and Public Action*, edited by V. Rao and M. Walton, 59–84. Stanford, CA: Stanford University Press.

Astone, N. M., and R. Pande. 2007. "Explaining Son Preference in Rural India: The Independent Role of Structural versus Individual Factors." *Population Research and Policy Review* 26 (1): 1–29.

Barker, G. 2005. *Dying to Be Men: Youth, Masculinity, and Social Exclusion*. London: Routledge.

Breierova, L., and E. Duflo. 2004. "The Impact of Education on Fertility and Child Mortality: Do Fathers Really Matter Less Than Mothers?" NBER Working Paper 10513, National Bureau of Economic Research, Cambridge, MA.

Brickell, C. 2006. "The Sociological Construction of Gender and Sexuality." *Sociological Review* 54: 87–113.

Buvinic, M., M. Das Gupta, and U. Casabonne. 2009. "Gender, Poverty, and Demography: An Overview." *World Bank Economic Review* 23 (3): 347–69.

Carranza, E. 2012. "Islamic Inheritance Law, Son Preference and Fertility Behavior of Muslim Couples in Indonesia." Policy Research Working Paper 5972, World Bank, Washington, DC.

Das Gupta, M. 2009. "Family Systems, Political Systems, and Asia's 'Missing Girls': The Construction of Son Preference and Its Unraveling." Policy Research Working Paper 5148, World Bank, Washington, DC.

Dayioğlu, M., M. G. Kirdar, and A. Tansel. 2009. "Impact of Sibship, Size, Birth Order, and Sex Composition on School Enrolment in Urban Turkey." *Oxford Bulletin of Economics and Statistics* 71 (3): 399–426.

Dekker, M., and H. Hoogeveen. 2002. "Bridewealth and Household Security in Rural Zimbabwe." *Journal of African Economics* 11 (1): 114–45.

Diez Minguela, A. 2011. "Mating (Marriage) Patterns and Economic Development." *History of the Family* 16 (4): 312–30.

Doss, C. R. 2006. "The Effects of Intrahousehold Property Ownership on Expenditure Patterns in Ghana." *Journal of African Economies* 15 (1): 149–80.

Field, E., and A. Ambrus. 2008. "Early Marriage and Female Schooling in Bangladesh." *Journal of Political Economy* 116: 881–930.

Ginsburg, F., and R. Rapp. 1991. "The Politics of Reproduction." *Annual Review of Anthropology* 20: 311–43.

Goldin, C., and L. F. Katz. 2002. "The Power of the Pill: Oral Contraceptives and Women's Career and Marriage Decisions." *Journal of Political Economy* 110 (4): 730–70.

Holland, J., C. Ramazanoglu, S. Sharpe, and R. Thompson. 1998. *The Male in the Head: Young People, Heterosexuality, and Power.* London: Tufnell Press.

Iyigun, M., and R. P. Walsh. 2007. "Building the Family Nest: Premarital Investments, Marriage Markets, and Spousal Allocations." *Review of Economic Studies* 74 (2): 507–35.

———. 1995b. *Women's Education, Autonomy, and Reproductive Behaviour: Experience from Developing Countries.* Oxford, U.K.: Clarendon Press.

Jejeebhoy, S. J., S. S. Halli, C. B. Lloyd, J. R. Behrman, N. P. Stromquist, and B. Cohen. 2005. "Marriage Patterns in Rural India: Influence of Sociocultural Context." In *The Changing Transitions to Adulthood in Developing Countries: Selected Studies*, edited by C.B. Lloyd, J.R. Behrman, N.P. Stromquist, and B. Cohen. Washington, DC: National Academies Press.

Kabeer, N. 1999. "Resources, Agency, Achievements: Reflections on the Measurement of Women's Empowerment." *Development and Change* 30: 435–64.

———. 2001. "Reflections on the Measurement of Women's Empowerment." In *Discussing Women's Empowerment: Theory and Practice*, 17–57. Sida*studies* 3. Stockholm, Sweden: Novum Grafiska AB and Sida.

———. 2005. "Gender Equality and Women's Empowerment: A Critical Analysis of the Third Millennium Development Goal." *Gender and Development* 13 (1): 13–24.

Lemle, R., and M. E. Mishkind. 1989. "Alcohol and Masculinity." *Journal of Substance Abuse Treatment* 6 (4): 213–22.

Long, B., and U. Osili. 2008. "Does Female Schooling Reduce Fertility: A Nigerian Experiment." *Journal of Development Economics* 87 (1): 57–5.

Malhotra, A. 1991. "Gender and Changing Generational Relations: Spouse Choice in Indonesia." *Demography* 28 (4): 549–70. doi: 10.2307/2061422.

———. 1997. "Gender and the Timing of Marriage: Rural-Urban Differences in Java." *Journal of Marriage and Family* 59 (2): 434–50.

Malhotra, A., S. R. Schuler, and C. Boender. 2002. "Measuring Women's Empowerment as a Variable in International Development." Background paper prepared for the World Bank Workshop on Poverty and Gender: New Perspectives, Washington, DC.

Miller, D. 1998. *Theory of Shopping.* 1st ed. Ithaca, NY: Cornell University.

Narayan, D. 2002. *Empowerment and Poverty Reduction: A Sourcebook.* Washington, DC: World Bank.

Narayan, D., R. Chambers, M. K. Shah, and P. Petesch. 2000. *Voices of the Poor: Crying Out for Change.* New York: Oxford University Press for the World Bank.

Patrinos, H. A., and G. Psacharopoulos. 2004. "Returns to Investment in Education: A Further Update." *Education Economics* 12 (2): 111–34.

Perelli-Harris, B. 2006. "The Influence of Informal Work and Subjective Well-Being on Childbearing in Post-Soviet Russia." *Population and Development Review* 32 (4): 729–53.

Pezzini, S. 2005. "The Effect of Women's Rights on Women's Welfare: Evidence from a Natural Experiment." *Economic Journal* 115 (502): C208–27.

Rao, V. 1993. "The Rising Price of Husbands: A Hedonic Analysis of Dowry Increases in Rural India." *Journal of Political Economy* 101 (4): 666–77.

Ray, D. 2003. "Aspirations, Poverty, and Economic Change." Photocopy, Department of Economics, New York University.

Schady, N., and J. Rosero. 2008. "Are Cash Transfers Made to Women Spent Like Other Sources of Income?" *Economics Letters* 101 (3): 246–48.

Schuler, S. R., and E. Rottach. 2010. "Women's Empowerment across Generations in Bangladesh." *Journal of Development Studies* 46 (3): 379–96.

Sen, A. 1985. "Well-Being, Agency, and Freedom: The Dewey Lectures." *Journal of Philosophy* 82 (4): 169–221.

Sen, G. 1993. "Path to Fertility Decline: A Cross-Country Analysis." In *Development and Change: Essays in Honor of K.N. Raj*, edited by P. Bardhan, M. Dattachandhri, and T. N. Krishnan, 197–214. New Delhi: Oxford University Press.

Thomas, D., J. Strauss, and M.-H. Henriques. 1990. "Child Survival, Height for Age, and Household Characteristics in Brazil." *Journal of Development Economics* 33 (2): 197–234.

Thorne, B. 1993. *Gender Play: Girls and Boys in School*. New Brunswick, NJ: Rutgers University Press.

Walby, S. 1990. *Theorizing Patriarchy*. Oxford, U.K.: Blackwell.

World Bank. 2012. *World Development Report 2012: Gender Equality and Development*. Washington, DC: World Bank.

PART III

Empowerment

In our 97 sample communities, we invited men and women to reflect on the role of power and freedom in their lives. What does it mean to be a powerful woman or a powerful man in their community? How can a woman or man become more powerful and free? How can they lose power and freedom?

Our aim is to systematically record the factors that women and men in the study saw as helping increase their feelings of empowerment. As outlined in the introduction, agency and empowerment are contested concepts with different definitions and perspectives of their importance to processes of social change. Kabeer (2001, 19) defines empowerment as the "expansion in people's ability to make strategic life choices in a context where this ability was previously denied to them." We do not hold the focus groups to this benchmark. In fact, we set aside the academic terms of agency and empowerment and instead explore their dynamics with the focus groups by turning to local understandings of the more common terms of power and freedom.

The capacity of women and men (or groups) to pursue goals, their agency, may or may not achieve the desired outcomes. Local context also significantly influences their pursuits. "Clearly a process of empowerment is incomplete," explain Ibrahim and Alkire (2007, 9), "unless it attends to people's abilities to act, the institutional structure, and the various non-institutional changes that are instrumental to increased agency." In our exploration of the gender dimensions of exercising agency, we explicitly look at the interplay of three dynamics that may lead to a sense of greater power and freedom, or empowerment: (a) the behaviors or actions that men and women associate with exercising agency, (b) the conditions and trends in their local structure of opportunities, and (c) the change in gender norms as part of those structure of opportunities.

Social norms reproduced across institutions feed into a gender system that demands that men and women act in certain ways, although it also provides

I am free and I have some power; my partner has the same: sovereign decisions are freedom and power.

—Urban man, neighborhood of Olzstyn, Poland

a sense of identity and a position in the community structure. (Whether this is equal or favorable is a different matter.) As such, this system, and how it is changing, determines what is possible to imagine and to achieve. We also look at the enabling local conditions that make it possible to pursue and realize aspirations.

We use two tracks to assess factors and processes gleaned from the focus groups' understanding of empowerment. We first parse out women's and men's perceptions of the different factors that increase their power and freedom, and the role that gender norms play in their interpretations of what creates empowerment (chapter 4). In chapter 5, we explore the local context in more detail and how it influences the processes and outcomes of agency, especially those elements over which individuals may have no control, such as market forces, local governance, and civic action, and the norms for women's inclusion and leadership in these public spaces.

Overall, in our sample, women more often than men reported becoming more empowered and spoke of gaining more influence and freedom of action in either their domestic or public roles. Men's changes in their sense of power and freedom, however, were far more tightly tied to their role as providers and to the health of the local economy.

Our assessments of the focus groups particularly reveal that women's sense of empowerment and the factors shaping it can be very different from men's, even in the same community. This discrepancy in large measure has to do with gender norms. Although we observe many new norms slowly taking hold, when reviewing all the responses in aggregate, important gender differences still persist in aspirations and in perceptions of, and access to, opportunities. These differences were reflected in the men's and women's evaluations of their capacities to act and empowerment trends for their own gender. As Kabeer (1999) and Mahmood (2001) point out in different ways, empowerment does not always or necessarily result from deviations from the norms. While it is true that complying with norms may lead to increased status, and that this may be antithetical to autonomy, the actual outcome depends on the context of women's social relations and individual histories. Alkire (2009, 4), in a discussion of approaches to assessing agency, explains that, "people who enjoy high levels of agency are engaged in actions that are congruent with their values." A strong desire for harmony between values and behaviors is common in local understandings of what brings power and freedom, and the values often embody strong gender dimensions.

In chapter 5, we connect the men's and women's assessments of trends in empowerment for their own gender to data gathered about local markets and state and civic institutions. From this, we note that the perceived empowerment outcomes, trends in local norms, and access to opportunity structures do not necessarily move together. Changes in one domain may not be matched by changes in others, with gender norms often lagging. In general, we often observed that communities with more dynamic economies stimulated a greater sense of empowerment in men and women and greater relaxation of norms. But even in the most supportive of contexts, women and men pursued local opportunities in ways that did not conflict with their gender-prescribed roles, responsibilities, and conduct.

Given the great diversity of individual perceptions and local conditions, we aim first to identify the main pathways, or combinations of factors, that lead to increased senses of power and freedom in the sample communities.[1] In a nutshell, we find that a clearer path emerges for urban women than rural women. Urban women perceived more extensive gains in their power when *they control major assets, are free (or freer) from domestic violence,*[2] *acquire greater social capital, and have a supportive local opportunity structure.* For instance, the agency of women in the study benefited from the presence of active women's organizations that tap into partners and resources outside their localities. Urban women also benefited from residing in neighborhoods where gender norms are more relaxed, markets are stronger, and public services more accessible.

For rural women in the sample communities, identifying causal factors associated with empowerment was more difficult. This likely reflects the diverse barriers that village women confront in order to attain more autonomy for themselves. Like women in the cities, however, the model suggests that rural women do somewhat better when *they have supportive local opportunity structures, enjoy more mobility, and face less domestic violence.* These factors are more present in the sample communities marked by deeper poverty and little human development.[3] A fourth factor affecting rural women's capacity to increase their agency is *scarce labor opportunities for men* in the formal economy.

Urban and rural men's gains in power are largely dependent on *economic growth and the existence of and access to jobs.* In fact, the explanatory forces behind perceived expansions in female empowerment hold no meaning when applied to men. Male pathways are narrower and dominated by local and national economic conditions.

The identified pathways do not present a comprehensive picture, but are a starting point for chapters 4 and 5, which delve deeply into perceptions of agency and freedom, and how inequalities inherent in gender norms and gender power relations create different sets of opportunities and challenges for women and men. A woman who seeks greater power and freedom of action in her life may constantly have to negotiate norms that discourage her from taking initiative and modifying expected gender-typed behaviors. For example, norms of femininity prescribe submissive behaviors; however, women speak of the need for acting boldly and taking risks in order to pursue aspirations, such as earning an income outside the home. And if success in these initiatives means a woman faces greater possibilities of domestic violence, then it renders her gains in economic independence and assets useless. By contrast, factors that propel men upward are clearly in line with accepted definitions of masculinity and mandates for what it means to be a good man. Men's access to opportunities is less dependent on their own efforts than women's because being a good provider and being powerful and free are widely accepted traits of men. Fundamentally, women's rising empowerment in a community—and their eventual transformation of expected feminine attributes of domesticity, docility, and obedience—is a process that ushers in significant change in gender norms, power relations, and institutional inclusion.

Notes

1. In order to learn more from our dataset about women's empowerment, we invited sociologist Charles Ragin to collaborate with us in investigating causal factors. We used qualitative comparative analysis (QCA) to track each community's changes in empowerment on a "ladder of power and freedom" (explained more fully below) as a configuration of traits or aspects, rather than representing aspects as separate, independent variables, which neutralizes and thus sacrifices context. QCA ensures that it is not just single variables acting independently that drive outcomes but combinations of causal conditions (Ragin 2000, 2008). This book's appendix on the methodology has more details on this exercise.

2. These findings are consistent with broader surveys, such as Agarwal and Panda (2007), which show that women's ownership of major assets can be a protective factor.

3. As measured by the Human Development Index of each country (UNDP 2011).

References

Agarwal, B., and P. Panda. 2007. "Toward Freedom from Domestic Violence: The Neglected Obvious." *Journal of Human Development and Capabilities* 8 (3): 359–88.

Alkire, S. 2009. "Concepts and Measures of Agency." In *Ethics, Welfare, and Measurement*, Vol. 1 of *Arguments for a Better World: Essays in Honor of Amartya Sen*, edited by K. Basu and R. Kanbur, 455–74. Oxford University Press.

Ibrahim, S., and S. Alkire. 2007. "Agency and Empowerment: A Proposal for Internationally Comparable Indicators." OPHI Working Paper 4, Oxford Poverty and Human Development Initiative, Oxford, U.K.

Kabeer, N. 1999. "Resources, Agency, Achievements: Reflections on the Measurement of Women's Empowerment." *Development and Change* 30: 435–64.

———. 2001. "Reflections on the Measurement of Women's Empowerment." In *Discussing Women's Empowerment: Theory and Practice*, 17–57. Sidastudies 3. Stockholm: Novum Grafiska AB and Sida.

Mahmood, S. 2001. "Feminist Theory, Embodiment, and the Docile Agent: Some Reflections on the Egyptian Islamic Revival." *Cultural Anthropology* 16 (2): 202–36.

Ragin, C. 2000. *Fuzzy Set Social Sciences*. Chicago, IL: Chicago University Press.

———. 2008. *Redesigning Social Inquiry: Fuzzy Sets and Beyond*. Chicago, IL: Chicago University Press.

UNDP (United Nations Development Programme). 2011. *Human Development Report 2011: Sustainability and Equity: A Better Future for All*. New York: UNDP.

CHAPTER 4

What Drives Agency? What Crushes It?

Men and women in the study reported that quite similar factors fuel their empowerment. They spoke most often about how their own economic initiatives help them gain more power, followed by positive attitudes and behaviors, then education and skills. When we compare discussions by women and men from the same locality about what triggers empowerment, however, significant gender differences often emerge. Understanding how local gender norms are evolving locally is often critical for making sense of why women and men may perceive sharply different causes of and trends in empowerment.

Indeed, one of the findings from our study is that urban women perceive significantly more gains in their power and freedom over the past decade than any other group sampled. This is consistent with the rural and urban differences, noted in previous chapters, in relaxation and change in gender norms. The reports by urban women, moreover, starkly contrast with urban men's sense of loss of power and freedom over the same time period and the challenge that this presents to their compliance with expected models of masculinity. The findings also suggest that gender norms may be more important than generally recognized to understanding the capability of local-level institutions to serve the public good, and hence the pace at which communities are able to shift to more inclusive and prosperous development.

Step by Step: Climbing the "Ladder of Power and Freedom"

To guide our analysis of the complex factors and processes that underpin how and why individuals are able to gain power and freedom—become more empowered—we draw on a concept of *agency* as "the ability to define one's goals and act on them"(Kabeer 1999, 438). If successful in their pursuits, individuals may both increase their agency, or capacity to negotiate and make decisions, as well as their power and freedom to control resources and shape institutions that affect their lives (Narayan 2002). Yet, not all women's and men's initiatives to exercise agency are successful. Empowerment is conceived as a product of the interaction between, on one hand, individuals and groups seeking to exercise

The moment that you know that you can do things by yourself and not have to depend on a man is the moment you begin moving up. I see some women being beaten by their husbands every day. When you talk to them, they say they are married and cannot leave their husband. These [women] will never climb out of their situation. They will stay at the bottom.

—Urban woman, Emputa village, Tanzania

According to the tradition of our village, women cannot move about freely. But old women who are on step 2 or step 3 (the top step) can go out and about in the community to the homes of relatives, friends, and neighbors.

—Village woman, Naw Da (Parwan), Afghanistan

At the top of the ladder are people who feel confident about their lives and their future. They are well placed to realize their life's goals and ambitions.

—Urban man, Hyderabad (Andhra Pradesh), India

agency and advance their interests, and on the other, changes to their local opportunities structures.[1] In our dataset, for instance, we observe how changes in local opportunities seem to exercise strong effects on aspirations and agency, but sometimes these effects vary markedly by gender.

Before moving into the analysis of the different factors and dynamics associated with power described by the focus groups, we briefly review the data collection method, which is important for making sense of the findings that follow. The field instrument used was entitled, "ladder of power and freedom," which builds on similar instruments in other studies of poverty and economic mobility.[2] The ladder exercise was conducted only with the 194 adult focus groups (one group for each sex in the 50 urban and 47 rural communities). The focus groups initially spent some time building their ladder to establish a common understanding, or framework, for assessing the dynamics of gaining and losing power in their communities (see box 4.1).

Facilitators introduced the topic by asking participants to identify the characteristics of the most powerful and freest women or men of their neighborhood or village. (Men described men and women described women.) Similarly, they discussed qualities of the least powerful and least free women (or men) of the community. With this information, they defined the top and bottom step of a ladder, and the facilitator annotated the key traits for each rung on a large piece of paper in front of the focus group. Intermediate steps were then determined by the participants.[3] While complex and multidimensional, the ladders do not completely describe all the power structures for all the different types of women (or men) who reside in a study community. Some of

Box 4.1 Challenges with Measuring Social Change from Below

Analyzing and comparing complex processes of social change, which necessarily transpire over time and across diverse contexts, is inherently a great research challenge. We approached this by building on qualitative research traditions of learning inductively from local people's own interpretations and understandings of what power and freedom mean and how they lose or gain them in their lives. Issues of recall and context-specificity, however, are two key concerns that must be addressed in such analysis.

First, asking individuals to recall situations always introduces the risk of getting partial information or an interpretation of events that the individual has developed to make sense of their current condition (Dempsey 2010). Some of our questions about agency required study participants to identify factors and recall conditions affecting agency for their own gender a decade ago. Yet, the natural course for individuals is to remember most clearly those actions that they made happen themselves and that best explain their circumstances now. Such processes mean that our focus groups at times might tend to downplay the relevance of seemingly unimportant events (in the course of pursuing goals) or wider environmental factors (which also influenced their choices) over which they often feel they have little control, such as weather, birth caste, presence of roads, access to services, etc.

Second, this study applied a rapid and relatively standardized method of constructing a "ladder" to facilitate comparative analysis of men's and women's understandings of agency across their diverse contexts. Yet, we recognize that our method just provides a general picture; much of the nexus of agency and changing gender norms is deeply contextual to each specific location and is more clearly delineated with techniques that feature small samples, revisits, extended observation, and detailed life-story tools. Without question, dynamics of change are better captured through longitudinal techniques that involve tracing social change across generations in specific localities. Examples of insightful multigenerational investigations that provide a valuable perspective on how gender and poverty dynamics operate in specific localities or population groups include Perlman's (2010) work in the *favelas* of Rio de Janeiro, Brazil; Moser's (2009) study of a neighborhood in Quayaquil, Ecuador; Epstein, Suryanarayana, and Thimmegowda's (1998) two villages in India; Fishburne Collier's (1997) study of a Spanish village; and Lomnitz's (1977) study of a Mexican shantytown.

the information provided is more stylized than based on actual women and their characteristics.

After each group built their ladder, the discussion shifted to how someone can climb up each step to the next, and what factors may push someone down the ladder. Finally, participants were requested to identify how they would distribute 100 women (or men) on the different steps to represent the current distribution of power and freedom among community members of their own gender. The same sorting exercise was repeated, but this time the focus groups were asked to imagine where these same 100 individuals would have been found on the ladder a decade ago. A completed ladder, with steps, dynamics, and distributions of power for two points in time (2000 and 2010) produced a rough roadmap

On Norms and Agency • http://dx.doi.org/10.1596/978-0-8213-9862-3

of a community's social structure for that gender, and whether and how this structure is perceived to be changing.

Each ladder is highly influenced by local characteristics; however, commonalities can be discerned among the different ladders in the traits of the different steps and in the reasons for movement up and down. Also, the general mobility trends reported by the focus groups can be compared. For this purpose, we synthesized the numerical data from the ladder sorting exercise into a "mobility index" that equals the difference between a ladder's mean step now and the mean step 10 years ago. We will return to this index after highlighting common characteristics of the ladders.

Defining the Steps on the Ladder

To illustrate the exercise of creating a ladder of power and freedom, we turn to one created by the women's focus group from a traditional mountain town of 6,000 in Ba'adan center, the Republic of Yemen. According to the women from this community, "enjoying a lot of freedom means that women can express their views and move about freely, but only within certain limits and under the authority of men and the customs, traditions, and social norms." In this town, for instance, seclusion practices—such as the requirement that male guardians accompany them if they travel any distance from their neighborhood—restrict women's movements.

The traits associated with the most powerful women included being married to powerful or wealthy men in the town, who may be members of the local council or sheikhs. A powerful woman in Ba'adan center may or may not be well educated, but her sons and daughters go to school, a few all the way to university. These women have money and can own jewelry, houses, land, and cars, although "men have a say in how women handle [their money] and often its disposal is for the benefit of the family." A small number of these powerful women work outside the home, but "only in a government job as a teacher or nurse," where they do not have to interact with the opposite sex and potentially risk their reputation, safety, and family honor. The majority of Ba'adan center's most powerful women do not have economic independence and their influence is mainly derived from their spouses, family name, or their adept management of household affairs.

At the bottom step of the Ba'adan center ladder, women cannot express their opinions "and are totally dependent on men for everything." They are very poor, illiterate, and may have to work both "in and outside the house" to make ends meet. If they work outside the home, it is a sign of great economic stress in their households and they take low-status jobs as domestic workers or vendors. Some on the bottom step may earn an income at home from embroidery, hairdressing, sewing, and other activities. These women may have some more freedom of movement, but their husband's economic situation is not good and it is reflected in the entire family.

The Ba'adan center women's focus group identified four steps on their ladder. For the women on the middle steps, their assets and influence are more limited than those on the top step, but they enjoy some decision-making inside their households. They may also have some assets, thanks to inheritances, or work for pay within the limits of what is acceptable for women, for instance, selling goods to women door-to-door, teaching, nursing, or holding government jobs.

Much like the general traits of the ladder steps in other communities, women in Ba'adan center attached great importance to certain behaviors and attitudes as signs of power. Women on the highest step have "good morals and good reputations, have the experience and ability to solve problems, and have a lot of money and authority to express their opinions and [give] advice." Ba'adan center women on the lowest step, by contrast, have "weak personalities" and "are very tired. Their lives are full of suffering, deprivation, and daily misery."

In Ba'adan center, as in most of the communities in the study, the top rung of the men's ladder sits "higher" than the women's, and men's status is more tightly linked to their public roles and economic might. In Ba'adan center, these men are traders, elected officials, sheikhs, court employees, and "they get everything they want." Men on the bottom step are described as "tired. They work only for one or two days a month and are responsible for an entire family." In most communities, the men with the least power are jobless or rely on insecure daily wages.

To measure how things have changed in Ba'adan center, women put twice as many women on the top step (about 40 percent), compared to a decade ago. They indicated that women are moving up the ladder as they become better educated and find jobs; their husbands and children also have better jobs, which brings them status. Although they perceive they have greater power and freedom, these women's lives remain primarily in the domestic sphere.

The men of Ba'adan center reported the opposite trend about their agency: their *bottom step* doubled from 25 to 50 percent of the community's men over the past decade. The men spoke about no longer being able to work in other Gulf states or the United States, and the lack of stable jobs for workers in their town. And unlike the women, these men saw a large decline in the share of men on the top step over the last decade.[4]

A Representative Ladder

When we examine the general characteristics of the ladder steps, we see important consistencies across genders and contexts. Focus groups mentioned traits associated with economic assets and occupational status far more often than any other traits. Figure 4.1 provides highlights of the major characteristics that emerged in the ladder discussions.

To the men's focus groups, occupation and position of authority in that occupation mattered intensely to their perceptions of the stature a man commands in their community. The men on the top step of the ladders are at the pinnacle of local farming, business, politics, religious institutions, and sometimes civic groups. In addition to authority roles, they frequently described the most powerful men as very wealthy, commanding great respect, able to do whatever they want, and possessing excellent social skills and networks. Women attached an economic role to power on their ladders almost as much as men do. Even in traditional rural

Figure 4.1 Representative Ladder of Power and Freedom (Both Women's and Men's)

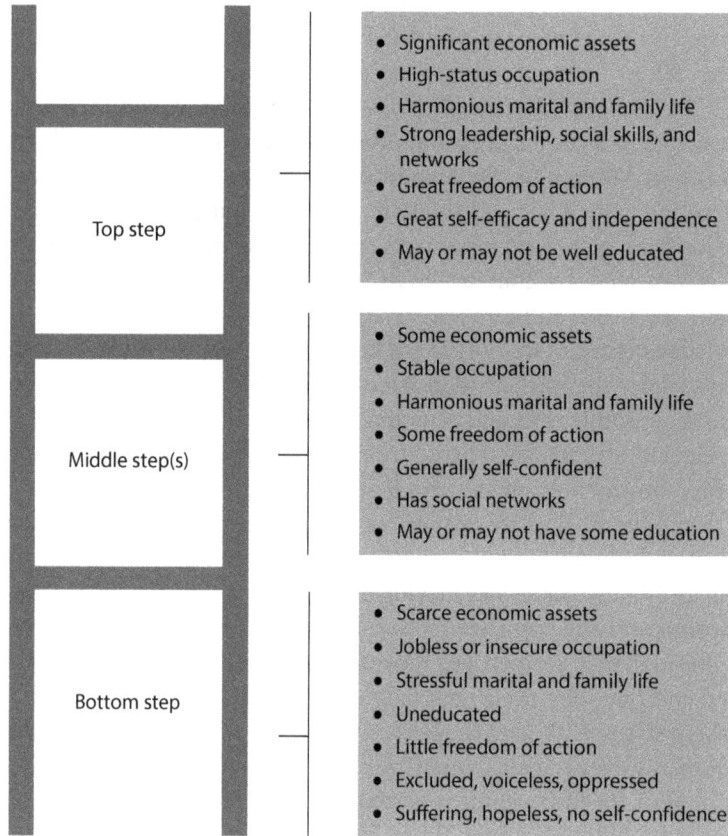

Top step
- Significant economic assets
- High-status occupation
- Harmonious marital and family life
- Strong leadership, social skills, and networks
- Great freedom of action
- Great self-efficacy and independence
- May or may not be well educated

Middle step(s)
- Some economic assets
- Stable occupation
- Harmonious marital and family life
- Some freedom of action
- Generally self-confident
- Has social networks
- May or may not have some education

Bottom step
- Scarce economic assets
- Jobless or insecure occupation
- Stressful marital and family life
- Uneducated
- Little freedom of action
- Excluded, voiceless, oppressed
- Suffering, hopeless, no self-confidence

communities, a woman on the top step may receive rental income from inherited land or have a nursing job; in urban settings, however, the most powerful women are doctors or lawyers. Women and men with little power do not work for pay or work in low-status jobs, for instance, as a domestic servant if a woman or a daily-wage hauling job if a man.

For both men's and women's ladders, education levels associated with power can be quite mixed, and this likely reflects the limited schooling opportunities that were available to most adults in our sample. Focus groups largely attributed a stable and agreeable family life to all but those on the bottom step. In addition, they attached great importance to conduct and attitude in their discussions of power and freedom. For example, men and women on the top step were frequently seen as driven, with strong leadership and social skills, while those with little power were more often described as unhappy, lacking confidence, withdrawn, or voiceless. Such assessments reflect what each community considered desirable values and behaviors to be admired and respected.

Where women's and men's ladders differ most is the important status that women derive from their gender-ascribed household roles; however, as gender norms change, these markers of status are also changing. In more traditional communities, focus groups often positioned women with many children on the top step and considered them influential due to their reproductive success; other focus groups, however, considered large families an attribute of the bottom step. Women may gain the top step if they have a powerful spouse or a strong voice in their household, even though, as in Ba'adan center, their physical mobility may be restricted. But in contexts where gender norms are relaxing more quickly, women on the top step may have important civic or political positions and enjoy great freedom of action.

Because women derive status from both domestic and productive roles, they arguably enjoy more sources of power on their ladders than men. In an urban community near Zorzor, Liberia, a woman on the top step may achieve that rung because she has 9 or 10 children (and "many more grandchildren and relatives"), because she is a community leader, or because she runs a big farm. Still, in the highly gendered playing fields of power, women's status remains subordinate to men's. The positions of authority, assets, and occupations that women on the top step command are almost always of less significance than the men's (on the top step) in the same community.

A large proportion of the participants assessed themselves as being on the middle steps, where their capacity to negotiate their interests is more in flux. Some women in Tanzania noted that:

> Most women are on the middle or second step. They can provide some income for their families, but depend on their husbands and their children. Their houses are always clean, but they do all the housework by themselves, with assistance from the children. Although they are the link between their families and other families, they have little time to concentrate on friendship because they are too busy trying to manage their household and family. They go to civic meetings, but they rarely speak out. They work hard, but a lot of their work is on the household farm or plantation, or at small tables where they tend small retail businesses in front of their houses. They are hardly employed. They get little cooperation or help from their husbands.

Before turning to the reasons why individuals can rise and fall on the ladder, it is useful to show the comparative findings on the change in positions of the 100 representative women and men on the ladders. Figure 4.2 breaks apart the dataset by urban and rural focus groups, with the first set of bars on the left displaying the share of communities where *both women and men* reported at least some upward movement over the past 10 years—or gains in power and freedom for their gender.[5] With 55 percent of rural communities and 42 percent of urban communities showing men and women advancing up the ladder, this is the most common pattern in our dataset, which we called "twin climbing." But women's and men's views are not always in sync. In 36 percent of the urban communities and 17 percent of rural communities, women are climbing the ladder, but men register zero or negative mobility. Declines in power and freedom by both sexes—"twin falling"—and men outperforming women are more prevalent in rural communities than in urban ones.

On Norms and Agency • http://dx.doi.org/10.1596/978-0-8213-9862-3

Figure 4.2 Outcomes of All Men's and Women's Ladders in Urban and Rural Communities

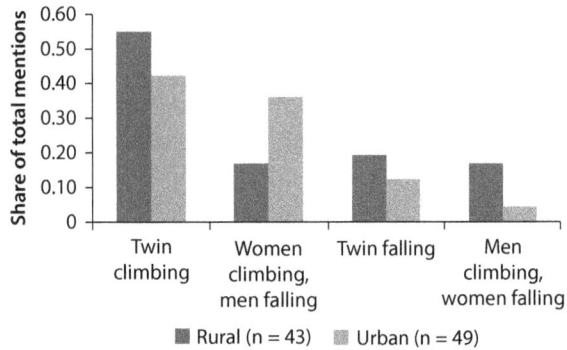

Note: Shares display outcomes from men's and women's ladders in 49 urban and 43 rural communities (or 184 ladders in all). Four women's and eight men's ladders did not register any movement, so were classified with the falling set. The five Sudanese communities are not included in this analysis because the women's focus group did not conduct the sorting exercise of 100 women at the end of their ladder discussions.

Importantly, the notion of "mobility" here and in chapter 5 refers to gaining or losing power and freedom—in other words, movements up and down the ladder of power and freedom—and not to the more traditional applications for assessing economic mobility. While there is significant overlap and emphasis on economic well-being, focus groups in this study did not completely associate accumulation of wealth or high-status occupations with great power. For example, elders, scholars, and religious or civic leaders of either sex may be poor, but they also are awarded great authority and respect by virtue of their benevolent deeds, wise counsel, or compassion for others. Alternatively, downward mobility may ensue from perceived misbehaviors and misconduct, some of which have a strong gender component. In rural Kim Dong District, Vietnam, women said loss of power can occur if women spend money "without discussing it with the husband" and make "the husband think he is unnecessary." We explore these and other triggers for climbing and falling in the next section.

Figure 4.3 also breaks out urban and rural samples, but instead presents the average rates of mobility on the ladders of the men's and women's focus groups. The "mobility index" captures the difference between the mean step now and mean step 10 years ago, and portrays the general direction and extent of change in power and freedom perceived by a focus group over the past decade. We find a striking contrast between urban women and men, with women seeing significant change in their power and freedom and men, on balance, reporting loss of control. The same dynamic does not translate to rural communities, where women and men show a more "twin rising" trend on average.[6]

From the accounts by the women's focus groups of what drives their sense of empowerment, urban women (and to a lesser extent, rural women) perceived that they have more voice and choices in their lives, and more space to negotiate and pursue goals. We expect urban women to feel more empowerment than rural women because cities offer more anonymity and freedom from confining norms, as well as more institutional outlets for exercising agency. Stronger trends

Figure 4.3 Average Mobility Index of Men's and Women's Ladders in Rural and Urban Communities

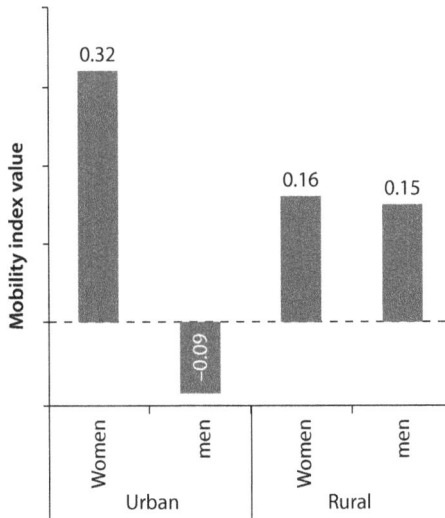

Note: Results from 189 focus groups reflect the mean step today versus the mean step 10 years ago. The 5 Sudanese women's ladders are missing from this analysis because they did not conduct the sorting exercise.

can also be felt in cities from universal education, promulgation and awareness of gender laws, investments in public services and infrastructure, the spread of communication technologies, and other forces. Women in the focus groups talked about how their lives are changing for the better, although exercising agency does not always require them to challenge and change gender norms.

Men did not register as much empowerment as women, which is to be expected, given that they are more accustomed than women to being in positions of power as a traditional norm of masculinity. Yet, many urban men reported feeling a loss of power and freedom to shape their lives. As shown throughout this study, urban and rural men commonly expressed difficulties with adapting to changes in their local structures of opportunities—and gender norms play an important role in constraining their agency and flexibility to adapt. From men's accounts, it is clear that, in their eyes, opportunities and other factors shaping aspirations and capacities to act are not equally distributed, and few available opportunities are considered suitable for them.

Perceptions of Factors Shaping Agency

This section presents the leading factors mentioned by focus groups for gaining or losing power and freedom in their communities. As with the ladder traits, the gender dimensions of the mobility factors are more remarkable for their similarities than for their differences. Nevertheless, the strong role that gender norms play in mobility processes will become more evident in the sections to follow, where we probe more deeply into and compare women's and men's ladder discussions in specific contexts.

But you cannot climb up from the very bottom. There is no way that you can even learn how to use money, if not only to drink. You cannot go to school anymore because there is no way you can understand what they teach you. So, once down, you are doomed to stay there.

—Urban man, Nsenene village, Tanzania

The weak woman can work as a warden serving coffee, at a sewing factory, or as a secretary, nurse, or teacher. The economic situation that forces her to work can make her strong.

—Village woman, Dirbas, West Bank and Gaza

Figure 4.4 Urban Upward Mobility Factors

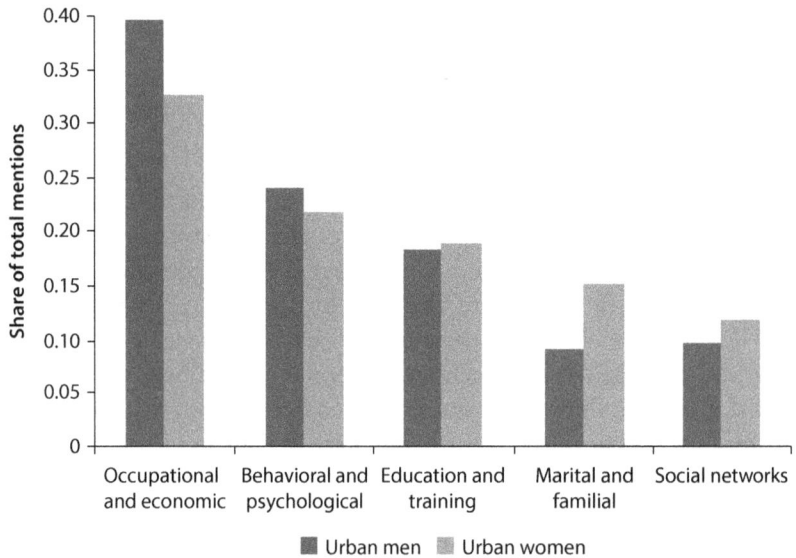

Note: Data from all 100 men's and women's urban focus groups.

Both men and women explained that they gain more power and freedom in their lives through *occupational and economic initiatives* that mainly include getting a better job and sound financial management. Among the four groups (men and women, urban and rural), economic activities account for about one-third of the factors mentioned (see figures 4.4 and 4.5[7]). In Ba Dinh District, Vietnam (a neighborhood of Hanoi), one way to move up the ladder is if "a man dares to borrow a big loan from different sources to open a business." Women in the same neighborhood said that what helps them climb the ladder is "getting promoted," "using money saved from a government job to buy land," or "being successful in the stock market." Across the focus groups, women and men not only stressed earning income, but also careful budgeting, borrowing,

Figure 4.5 Rural Upward Mobility Factors

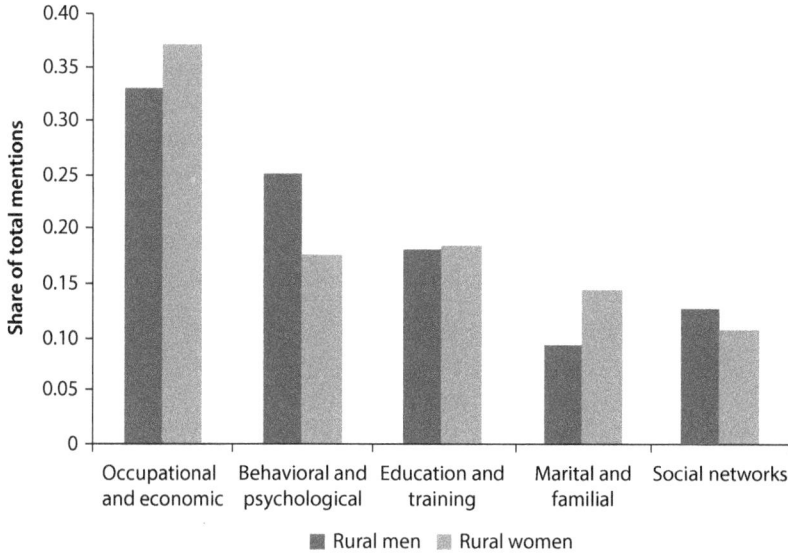

Note: Data from all 94 men's and women's rural focus groups.

and management of their finances to build savings. In rural Nagari Bukik Batabuah, Indonesia, women can climb, "but it doesn't happen quickly. We first have to save the wages that we receive from working in someone else's field before we are able to move up to a higher level."

Individual *behavioral and psychological factors* were the second most often mentioned factors that stimulate upward climbs, except by rural women (who mentioned educational factors slightly more). Both women's and men's explanations routinely indicated that ladder ascents require courage, sincerity, humility, service, temperance, spiritual guidance and growth, good reputation, hard work, consistency, positive mind-set, honesty, willingness to change, goal-setting, avoidance of alcohol abuse, utilization of individual talent, rejection of corruption or bribery, and optimism. In a village of Morobe Province, Papua New Guinea, some of the factors that allow men to climb the ladder included "the drive to start a business," a good character, and a "dream of being successful." A sense of self-efficacy and purpose—or capacity to aspire (Appadurai 2004)—were deemed to be vital: "A woman has to believe in herself, break through her fear, gain more self-confidence. Then everything becomes easier" (a woman, Justynowo, Poland).

More generally, the focus group narratives about behavioral and psychological factors revealed that both women and men fervently believed that their own positive mind-sets and self-confidence, as well as how they conduct themselves and treat others, matter greatly when it comes to gaining power and freedom. For many, power is associated with being respected by the community. Urban women in Zorzor, Liberia, warned that "money can't carry you up here [to higher steps], only how you talk to people and help pull them together." Focus groups mainly associated desirable behaviors and attitudes with moving up the ladder,

On Norms and Agency • http://dx.doi.org/10.1596/978-0-8213-9862-3

and undesirable or antisocial behaviors and attitudes with falling down the ladder. But these divides sometimes blurred: focus groups, on occasion, assigned movements both up and down the ladder to acts of selfishness or corruption.

As with the ladder traits, the role of *education and training* in gaining power and freedom is not as straightforward as conveyed in the figure because the frequencies of mention in the focus groups include contradictory reports that it is both necessary and unnecessary for upward climbing. While it is central to aspirations that younger generations described for their own lives, more than half of the adult focus groups neglected to mention education as a factor in upward mobility, while others often qualified its importance:

> Women on the highest step are supposed to be [educated], but the reality is that any creative, diligent, and aggressive woman is capable of influencing others. They can be community leaders. There are educated women in the lowest class, so education alone is not enough. Women should have other skills. (Village women's focus group, River Nile State, Sudan)

In Suakoko District, Liberia, the men advised that "education is needed, but in our area, people can do without"; and in Jakarta, Indonesia, the men explained that "some uneducated people have become big bosses. The important things are capital and ambition." Nevertheless, a strong cross-section of groups highly valued education and, where available, adult literacy and vocational training opportunities.

Ladder descents most often ensued from business failures, job losses, bad investments, and poor financial management (figures 4.6 and 4.7). Urban men and women stressed these risks more than their rural counterparts. The second

Figure 4.6 Urban Downward Mobility Factors

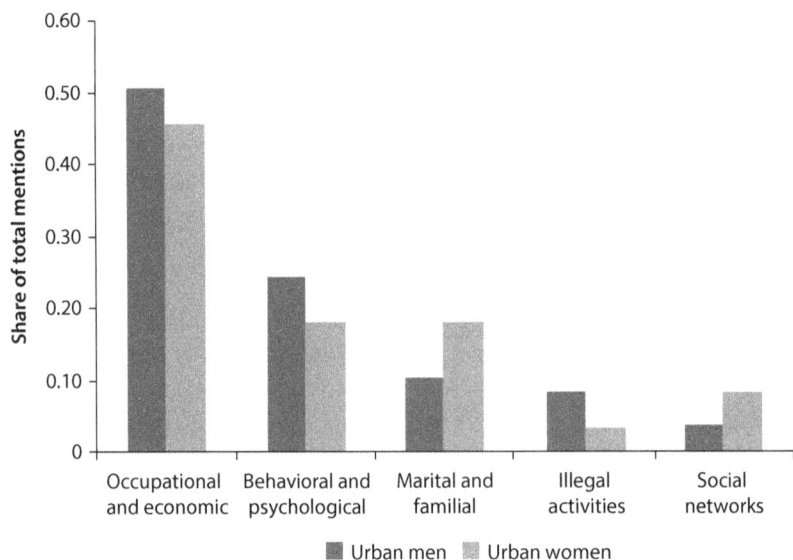

Note: Data from all 102 urban focus groups.

Figure 4.7 Rural Downward Mobility Factors

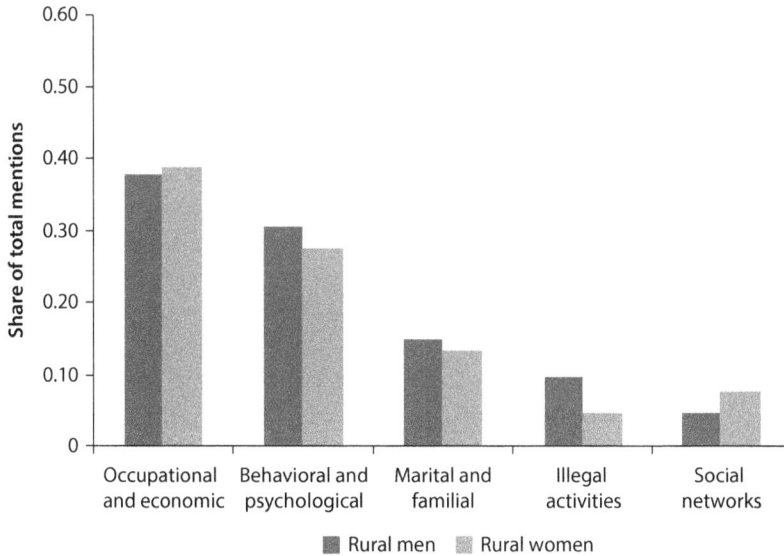

Note: Data from all 92 rural focus groups.

cause of descents, behavioral and psychological factors, can be triggered by dishonesty, prejudice, lying, conceit, wasteful spending, extravagance, corruption, cheating, jealousy, selfishness, laziness, infidelity, loss of trust, fights, disregard for the rules, and excess alcohol consumption (by men). These concerns were more often raised in the countryside and, again, it may be that behavioral factors are less prominent as a cause of losing power in urban groups because of the greater anonymity in urban environments.

Overall, factors related to *marital or familial relationships* were less frequently mentioned as triggers for climbing and falling. As expected, women mentioned the role of their spouse or other family members in their gains and losses of power more than men. "Marrying into a wealthy family" and cooperative couples and harmonious households bring clear advantages. In Zabibu village, Tanzania, for instance, a woman explained that to move up in her village a woman "needs to get a good and understanding husband, who allows her to go into business and engage in educational activities." Women from a more urban area (Nsenene village) in Tanzania agreed: "You can divorce a hopeless husband and marry a good one who can put you higher on the ladder." Dialogue and agreement between the couple were key for women from Saylla District, Peru, when it comes to leaving the bottom step.

Meanwhile, falling down the ladder can be triggered by any number of household problems, such as marital or family discord; widowhood; family dissolution or divorce; too many wives where polygamy is practiced; marrying "down"; sons who are unemployed, leave home, or engage in vices; and inability to bear children or bearing too many children. Rural men mentioned these hazards as often as rural women, and urban women much more so than urban men. In rural

Martynice, Poland, and elsewhere, women reported that being divorced or cheated on "is worse than his death." But it is urban women who displayed the greatest relative concern for marital and familial triggers. In urban Lambayeque Province, Peru, a woman explained that "when you separate from your husband, assets must be divided and this weakens you."

Nonfamily *social networks* are the last of the main factors in movements on the ladder (see figures 4.4 and 4.5), accounting for about one-tenth of the upward factors mentioned and less so for falling. In some cases, these connections can be instrumental in securing other determinants, such as economic gains, as suggested by a man from Tewor District, Liberia: "Make friends with people at the top step and ask for land." In other cases—mentioned by women—connecting with other women (informally or in formal organizations) can open information flows or build self-confidence and aspirations. In Old City of Hebron, West Bank and Gaza, "a weak woman can go up [the ladder] by hanging out with a strong woman"; in Umlazi township A of Durban, South Africa, a woman "must involve herself with other women" in order to climb. In the refugee camp visited in Al Fashir, Sudan, women said they can become more powerful through literacy and "training courses, workshops, and seminars, and interacting with active women leaders in society." In National Capital District, Papua New Guinea, getting involved in church activities helps women increase status and move up from lower rungs. Earning a good reputation through charitable works or taking a leadership role in self-help groups are sometimes mentioned as stepping stones for women and men alike. By contrast, women indicated that isolation from their community, self-help groups that lack cohesion, and "bad friends" who expect or owe loans can cause ladder descents.

Combinations of Mobility Factors

In surveying the narratives about movements up and down, two processes stand out. First, the bottom step of powerlessness is widely seen as the hardest of all to leave. Second, rather than describing one factor as more important than another, most focus groups conveyed that moving up the ladder requires mobilizing *combinations of factors.*

Those on the bottom step are widely perceived to face the toughest climb of all. Not only is great effort and sacrifice required, but some assistance from others or great luck are often seen to be needed as well. And these may well be less in one's control. In Umlazi township of Durban, South Africa, men say that "It is very difficult for a person to move out of step 1 because the majority of them are not educated at all. Maybe unless someone wins the lottery jackpot." Or, in University Quarter of Hebron in the West Bank, escaping step 1 takes "credibility, luck, and people's support." In a neighborhood of Monrovia, Liberia, women explained that "those that are down [the ladder] are not able to send children to school" and so their children, when they become adults, are less likely to be able to help them move up. In Olsztyn, Poland, the women's group thought that because those on step 1 "have nothing to invest," some of the only ways for these women to move up the ladder were to "win the lottery," a "wise wedding," or "organized crime." Scaling subsequent steps, by comparison, was seen to be more doable because each step potentially brings more earning power, assets, self-confidence, knowledge and skills, reputation for good work and honesty, and so forth.

In addition, the five upward mobility factors described above are seen to be interlinked, and it takes purposeful combining or sequencing of them to produce real gains in power and freedom. The introduction to part III mentions how their interconnections help open up pathways of empowerment and how some factors are necessary conditions for others to have an actual impact in triggering upward movement on the ladders. These pathways are not the same for men and women.

A man from Umlazi township B of Durban, South Africa, married three factors—related to better management and generation of economic resources and self-discipline—as necessary for leaving step 1: "If people work hard, save their money, and do not waste it on alcohol, they can manage to move up to the next level." In Floresti, Moldova, the men similarly noted that a man on step 1 can get to step 2 if he "finds a job or some possibility for earning money," but he also needs to "stop drinking and start taking care of his family," and to get "a good wife." In Paro, Bhutan, one man said that in order to climb, "a man has to be hardworking, reliable, and good at heart; be able to learn from others and help others; avoid indulging in alcohol; take good care of his family; not have extramarital affairs; and be positive in life." Numerous accounts about men needing to stop indulging in vices and focus on their family obligations to be a good provider revealed the extensive problems of jobless and deeply frustrated men in this dataset. In the Umlazi township B focus group, the men lamented how their lives have changed, compared to a decade ago: "Men had work before, now they have no job opportunities."

Women's combinations differed from men's for many reasons, including different gender norms and different positions and status in the communities and households. While economic factors featured broadly for women as well as men, women were less likely to mention problems with antisocial vices and more likely to speak about a need to become less passive and submissive, although these traits are often valued traits in a woman. In Lambayeque Province, Peru, a woman can increase her power and freedom but "she needs to take more initiative, take risks, begin a business and commit to it, take out a loan, be responsible and careful, and set goals."

In urban Ba Dinh District, Vietnam, women said that rising above step 1 may be possible if, among other measures, their husbands stopped beating their wives and if the women are able to get a loan to open a business "and improve the family economy." Domestic violence is a strong sign that women have little power and freedom. Economic initiatives are generally seen as ways for those on the bottom step facing difficult household circumstances to forge more voice and autonomy.

Climbing up the ladder, moreover, still means women have to tend to their household responsibilities even as they mobilize diverse assets and capabilities to fuel their ascent. In Firestone District, Liberia, women can become more powerful if they are extremely industrious and patch together different initiatives to build assets, but they cannot neglect their domestic duties:

> If you have a small farm, you make the farm bigger. If the crops come up, you sell the produce and make whatever business you want. But if you wash for one person, you can just as well wash for two or three people. In doing these things, you should tie your stomach [eat less] and ask your family to help you take care of some of your children.

Similarly, escaping the bottom step for women from urban Shirabad Ulya (Kabul Province), Afghanistan, also involved a flurry of initiatives that implicitly require carefully navigating old and new norms for women's conduct:

> Women must work hard and follow precisely the decisions made by the men household members. They must not quarrel with the men. Meanwhile they should consult their friends and get information and assistance from them. They must send their children to school, but must be careful about the expenses. They should avoid any extra, unnecessary spending. Whenever they have free time, they can go meet their friends.

Or, in the less traditional setting of urban Paro, Bhutan, a woman can climb up by being successful in business and by "being more responsible, emulating other people who work hard, and consistently working hard themselves; having a positive attitude and a desire to learn; being ambitious; and not indulging in bad habits." Yet, like elsewhere, a Paro woman's household role and domestic relationships may also be ingredients in her efforts to gain power, such as aspiring to be a "husband and wife [who] encourage each other and give moral support," or having "educated and independent children." Across diverse contexts, women reported climbing their ladders as they gain more voice and autonomy in their domestic roles; although, overall, women stress their own economic initiatives more than any other single factor as a reason for gaining power.

Downward mobility is also linked to intersecting causal factors that can send individuals spiraling out of control of their lives. The nexus of hardships mentioned often feature job loss or financial mismanagement that may then trigger undesirable or antisocial behaviors and marital or familial problems. According to a man from urban Emputa village, Tanzania, "you only have to drink a lot, hang out with women a lot, and sleep in bars and guest houses, and that will be the end of your power. There were rich men here who once had boats with engines, but now they are at the bottom begging." In Chiclayo, Peru, women particularly mentioned how a woman on the top step can fall down the ladder if she mismanages her business, makes a bad investment, or has problems with workers; although, women can also lose status in the village due to difficulties with their marriages or children.

In the next two sections, we look more closely at the gender dimensions of agency processes in an urban (Jaipur) and a rural community (Malangachilima), both with especially strong twin climbing. In each locality, women's and men's groups reported that many of them are gaining power. Unfortunately, twin climbing to the extent reported in these two communities is rare in our sample, but these contexts are nevertheless useful to examine more closely because they provide valuable insights into what strong agency looks and feels like for both sexes. They also clearly reveal the gender differences in the factors that underpin agency. A third section then assesses an urban community with a polarized mobility pattern, where the women perceived significant empowerment, but men reported falling down their ladders. Taken together, these localities display how men's and women's mobility on their ladders is interdependent, and the significant (albeit different) influence of gender norms and local institutions in their agency processes. We take up the latter themes more systematically in chapter 5.

Moving Up the Ladder in the City

Jaipur (Odisha), India, a growing town of 7,000, used to be mostly farms and pasturelands a generation ago.[8] With rapid urbanization, the town's level of poverty has plummeted over the past decade from 60 to 20 percent. The women of Jaipur have good jobs as teachers or administrative staff in private schools, as workers in tailoring and other industries, and as owners of big and small shops. The town's men work in daily-wage agricultural jobs, but there are also good jobs available in construction, stores of all sizes, travel agencies, computer shops, and the government.

The women's focus group from Jaipur described women on the top step of their ladder as having significant visibility in civic roles in their community and enjoying greater authority in their households. These empowered women participate in local meetings and interact with important community leaders. They also make substantive decisions related to their children (such as sending them to school, paying tuition) and do not have to seek permission from their husbands for everything: "She can go out of the house at will." At the other extreme, Jaipur women on the bottom step are depicted as having no education or economic independence, little voice, and no aspirations for themselves, and are secluded and isolated in their homes. (The full list of characteristics of women's top and bottom ladder steps from the Jaipur women's focus group are in table 4.1.)

With five steps on their ladder, the women in Jaipur provided a fine-grained analysis of the mobility factors and extent of changes shaping their lives. The group reported that 10 years ago nearly half the women of their community were on step 1, the bottom step, with little power and freedom. For women to escape the bottom step, the focus group suggested that they must aspire to get ahead and develop an attitude for "self-growth," improve their networks, and gain information and exposure by "meeting with other women frequently," and trying to have more say in their household. These are difficult hurdles for women on step 1, where gender norms for women's physical mobility and expectations of obedience and submission are at their strictest.

At the top of their ladder, they placed 25 percent of the women in their community on step 5, up from the respectable 15 percent of a decade ago. Women said that they can climb to the top step if they gain experience "dealing with community elders," learn more about mobilizing resources inside

On Norms and Agency • http://dx.doi.org/10.1596/978-0-8213-9862-3

Table 4.1 Top and Bottom Steps of Women's and Men's Ladders of Power and Freedom in Jaipur (Odisha), India

	Women's top step	*Women's bottom step*
General attitudes and behaviors	• Has good understanding of others' needs • Is the community's face (represents the community) • Has more exposure and is mobile • Is soft spoken and approachable • Is patient and tolerant • Can adjust and accommodate to everyone • Is determined and courageous • Takes initiative and responsibility for community concerns • Is trusted and looked up to by other women • Has awareness of community development issues, but is not well educated • Has vast experience and is seen as a guardian of the community • Able to speak in front of 10 people or to outsiders • Has good relationship with others and does not have vested interest • Turns cold shoulder to the women in community	• Does not interact or mingle in community; stays at home • Is not very expressive • Lets husband make all decisions, economic, future of children, marriage of children, education of children • Is not very responsive • Feels (internalizes) that they cannot understand anything because they are illiterate • Has no awareness of or interest in participating in community issues • Does not have decision-making power for self • Has high aspirations for children's education
Education	• Has an education • She completed 10th grade with honors • She completed a nursing course in Cuttack • Worked eight years before marriage • Has husband with university degree (BSc or MPhil)	• Is illiterate, did not complete primary education • Is less literate than husband
Jobs and specific community responsibilities	• Involved in community groups and is responsible for looking after financial management of those groups • Sometimes acts as midwife for poorer communities free of cost • Has time to devote to community causes and concerns	• Does not have a job • Mostly does housework
Family and household	• Has relationship with spouse where they trust and respect each other • Husband doesn't stop wife from being active in civic organizations or holding positions in the community • Aspires to raise daughters to be independent • Does not need permission from husband to go anywhere • Has equal voice in household's economic decision-making for small and large things	• Sees husband as the ultimate authority in making economic decisions • Husband is also in business • Submits completely to husband's decisions and demands • Reveres her husband
Savings and borrowing habits	• Saves through a self-help savings group or a chit fund • Has received a loan from a microfinance institution (MFI) and repaid it • Has a bank account in her name	• Has very little savings • Has only one member of family earning income
	Men's top step	*Men's bottom step*
General attitudes and behaviors	• Has money • Has political power • Donates money to the needy	• Has low income • Has no bargaining power
Education	• High school or university graduate	• Minimal or no education

table continues next page

Table 4.1 Top and Bottom Steps of Women's and Men's Ladders of Power and Freedom in Jaipur (Odisha), India *(continued)*

	Men's top step	Men's bottom step
Jobs and specific community responsibilities	• Is helpful to the community • Lets community members consult him and ask advice for free • Donates land for community development works, temple, school	Is a daily wage worker
Family and household	• Has politically oriented, supportive family • Motivates and grooms wife to take open seat reserved for women on the ward council	• Has a large family • Has many friends in the same economic situation
Political power	Is politically active and effective; can get work done for the community and individuals	
Financial power	Has their own business	Has no savings

and outside the community, and are "ready to provide a helping hand" to other women. These very same triggers are also on men's ladders, but these women's interactions with elites and local activism are more groundbreaking for their town.

The men's focus group in Jaipur paid most attention to assigning substantial economic and political roles to the men on the top step. Men on the bottom step, in contrast, have little earning power and education: "They are daily laborers and they have to fight every day to earn their livelihood." Unemployed men are also commonly found on bottom steps, but Jaipur's economy is unlike many in our sample because men can find sufficient jobs that they deem appropriate for them.

The men's ladder also features five steps, but most of the movement happens in the middle. The majority of men, on step 2 at the beginning of the past decade, rose to step 3, and the share on step 3 changed from 40 to 60 percent of the community's men. Due to education, better savings, and the assistance of self-help groups, many men in Jaipur on step 3 have been able to find better livelihoods over the past decade, working in the government or the private sector, or even running their own profitable businesses. The men's bottom step grew slightly, but stayed close to one-third of the community, similar to the women's bottom step.

Men attributed their bottom step and reasons for falling to troublesome behaviors that include "losing the trust of or not being accountable to" their self-help groups, not saving, drinking too much, and "not letting their women work." This last statement, implying that women's economic participation affects men's mobility processes, is a quite strong signal that Jaipur is undergoing real change in gender norms, not just relaxation of compliance with gender norms, as more women participate in the local economy.

Both the women and men of Jaipur, like many other communities in the study, spoke of the strong mutual support that defines the marital relationship on the top step. Women appreciated the presence of trust among these couples and the husbands' support for women's civic activities; the men's ladder specifically mentioned, for example, how powerful men groomed their wives to take advantage of the gender quotas for local council seats. No such harmony and cooperation are mentioned on the bottom step. The women warned that they could fall back down to step 1 if they "completely surrender to [their] husbands' authority."

The women in Jaipur are visibly gaining power and freedom, and in this process are changing some of the prevalent gender norms in the community. The most powerful women enjoy authority positions both inside and outside the home and have gained a significant presence in the formal economic, political, and civic institutions of their town. The men are moving up, too, and see their education, financial management, and self-help groups playing important roles. This simultaneous movement likely helps ease the way for local women to exercise agency and for men to accept the women's new conduct and roles.

Moving Up the Ladder in the Countryside

Malangachilima, Tanzania, is a large village of nearly 7,000. The village chairperson, a woman, estimates that poverty fell in the 2000–10 decade from perhaps 70 percent to 30 percent. She attributes most of the village's rising prosperity to the recent introduction of modern farming methods. Farmers are raising cattle and growing sunflowers, ground nuts, and grapes. Donated equipment for making sunflower oil stimulated the rise of a successful community cooperative for village men and women. The village also hosts a busy bimonthly market that draws buyers and sellers from across the area. Some of Malangachilima's smaller farmers have been through difficult times, however, due to swings in the area's economy, drought, and Rift Valley fever. And the village still has important development challenges. Most school-age children attend the local primary school, but only half go on to secondary school. There is no electricity, and most residents obtain their water from local stand-pipes.

When building their ladder of power and freedom, the women's focus group in Malangachilima described their most powerful women with these attributes:

- She works very hard.
- She harvests a lot.
- Most of her children go to good schools; some go even to schools in town or farther away.
- She completed primary and even secondary school.
- She is a leader; she gets involved in politics beyond the village.
- She has a good husband, but does not always have to have a husband.
- She can be rich and own cattle and land.

In stark contrast, they label the woman on step 1 "a slut," who "hardly has a husband; she simply gives birth to children who have different fathers. She is poor: she hardly owns a cow, possibly has a chicken. She has no land, unless it is inherited land." She also is "confined at home ... [and is too] poor to buy anything useful for herself. She never speaks in public." Polygamy is common in the village, which is especially disadvantageous for women on the bottom steps because their husbands are stretching resources across multiple households.

On Norms and Agency • http://dx.doi.org/10.1596/978-0-8213-9862-3

Powerful women take good care of their families, their husbands, and children. They are also very hardworking. A powerful woman will never say that there is nothing in her sock [store for food].

—Village woman, Malangachilima, Tanzania

What is surprising about Malangachilima is that the women felt that they have almost entirely escaped the agency-crushing bottom step. While they assigned an astonishing 95 percent of women on the bottom step just a decade ago, now only 5 percent are on this rung. On step 2, where most of the women now reside, women have their own farms and other ventures, most of their children are in school, and they worry much less about hunger.

Women said they can climb their ladders through hard work, leadership in local groups, saving money, buying cattle, and visiting their children in town and coming back "with good ideas." One woman explained that children send money from town, which has helped some villagers "become very powerful because nothing is disturbing them anymore and they have become busy in the community thinking about development issues." Although "nothing disturbing them" might be interpreted in different ways, women and men reported decreasing incidences of domestic violence. Also, once their children grow up, no longer require care and school fees, and start to give back, women generally have more time and resources to focus on themselves and become active in their community. To move up to the top of their three-step ladder, women need to "make their mind big" and "think how to change for the better." In reflecting on their growing strength, a woman declared, "I think that we have very few very hopeless women because we know what work means now, not like 10 years back when we were just following men. And in fact, we have many women now who are very powerful, manage their own lives, and are not at all dependent on men."

By comparison, Malangachilima's men have not been as successful at escaping the bottom step, but a good share are nevertheless on the move. The men estimated that their bottom step has shrunk from 85 percent a decade ago to about 50 percent still trapped there. The men on step 1 are described as letting their wives do everything for their families' needs and, when harvest comes, "he steals the crops. He is a lazy man." The leading reasons keeping men on the bottom rung (or descending to it) are too much drinking and too few assets "because the few cows they have are shared among the many wives they married." The village men also mentioned that these men on step 1 are the only decision-makers in their households and they may be "cheating a lot." And if you give a man on the bottom step a loan, "forget about getting it back." These men are "never trusted" and "will never have good ideas."

With half of the men in the village seen to be powerless and still on step 1, the Malangachilima community should be facing extensive hardship. Yet, the men's narratives also spoke of progress for the many men moving up. They described the men on the top step (which has grown from 5 to 20 percent of

On Norms and Agency • http://dx.doi.org/10.1596/978-0-8213-9862-3

the men) as commanding great respect in the community, helping others in need, having very strong family lives, and being good providers. For the share of village men who are finding ways to gain power, the men identified several factors: gaining confidence from their own education and educating their children, attending training courses and developing entrepreneurial skills, obtaining financial assistance, and improving their networks to get advice from other knowledgeable people who are considered powerful. One man elaborated, "Ten years ago, we rarely left the community; mingling with other people was very minimal. That is why our community was backward." In later discussions about community organizations, a man reported that now they have various outlets to obtain loans to expand their farming and other ventures, and that local men gather together in agricultural groups, carpentry groups, and beekeeping activities.

In fact, external groups seem to have played a valuable role in the village. Focus groups of younger women related that programs offered by nongovernmental organizations (NGOs) encouraged them to study and raised their awareness of their rights. And both women and men took advantage of NGO and governmental programs to mobilize their own farmer, producer, and finance groups and have reached out to external partners to strengthen their livelihood activities. For instance, a village woman noted that, "we can borrow money from our associations; we also have SACCOS [savings and credit cooperatives] from which we can get money. ... We had World Vision here, which has been a good resource for us." World Vision spent a decade working in the village and departed several years ago. Women and men have also rotated in and out of the local executive officer position.

In sum, gender norms seemed to have transformed very rapidly in this village. The large majority of women and a good share of the men of Malangachilima are rising off their very harsh bottom steps. They both are being helped by diverse factors, including their own economic initiatives, greater exposure to new ideas, educational opportunities, and collective action. Jaipur and Malangachilima are more hopeful communities than most in our study. Very often we find women climbing, but men are mostly stuck or falling on their ladders. Very often the men's focus groups are deeply discouraged by the poor condition of their local economy; problems of joblessness, frustration, and vices send more men tumbling than climbing.

Women Climbing, Men Tumbling in the City

As noted above, the general mobility trends on the urban ladders display a pattern of women perceiving significant empowerment and men seeing disempowerment. The forces driving this pattern mainly seem to be a consequence of communities in the study that have been hit hard by various shocks, which had heavier impacts on agency processes in our urban sample, compared to the rural. In a few cases where the role of shocks is less evident, men may be feeling emasculated by their exposure to new lifestyles or ways to earn a living that have raised their aspirations, but they do not have the means or local structure of opportunities to pursue such goals.

On Norms and Agency • http://dx.doi.org/10.1596/978-0-8213-9862-3

A quarter of the sample countries had been stressed by violent political conflict during the 10-year period of the ladders; other urban neighborhoods in peaceful countries reported significantly harmful effects from the global economic crisis of 2008 or other major economic shocks. Gender differences in responses to periods of turmoil are important for interpreting the patterns on the urban ladders. With the deterioration of economic opportunities, men struggle with identity issues as they strive to make ends meet and provide for their homes, often having to undertake economic activities that may damage their status or erode self-esteem (Schrock and Schwalbe 2009). Some men seem to become passive and opt for unemployment until better times. It is in these contexts where men's emotional struggles—and coping strategies that involve drinking, gambling, drugs, affairs with other women, and marital conflict—are often reported by women's and men's groups (although these are common problems for men on bottom steps even where shocks have not been reported).

Women in struggling economies, meanwhile, try their best to pick up the slack for their families. They begin new economic initiatives or intensify their existing ones, and carry their households through the difficult times. For some of these women, the grip of various gender norms relaxes due to the exigencies of these stressful periods. This relaxation, however, does not necessarily lead to a significant change in the overall climate for women's economic, political, and civic participation, as occurred in Jaipur and Malangachilima.

Ceadîr-Lunga, Moldova, illustrates the polarizing dynamics of economic stress on men's and women's agency. A city of about 23,000, Ceadîr-Lunga's economy has been weakening over the last decade and worsened during the global economic crisis of 2008 and 2009. Focus groups conducted in mid-2010 indicated that many men and smaller numbers of women have become economic migrants. Five of the eight men in the adult focus group in this town were unemployed at the time of our interviews. Unlike the men, most of the local women in the adult focus group had jobs. And in spite of the economic situation, this group of women mainly saw the past decade as favorable for their agency.

When asked about the best ways to make a living in Ceadîr-Lunga, the men identified diverse opportunities for both sexes, from working in the government and the private sector, running small- and medium-size businesses, to engaging in wholesale and winemaking ventures. Openings for such good jobs, they explained, are rare and few of them have the means to start their own business or to access the requisite finance. Some immigrated to find work in other European cities, but they do not speak highly of their experiences and reported that the men who are still working abroad are lonely and unhappy away from their families and friends.

The men also felt that women have better opportunities to get jobs in the city than men; local gender differences attached to the status of jobs clearly shape their perceptions. In response to questions about the worst ways to make a living in the city, for instance, the men identified digging graves and cleaning streets or houses; however, one of the men countered, "There is no such thing as a bad job. These are just insufficiently paid jobs, like watchmen, sweepers, cleaners."

On Norms and Agency • http://dx.doi.org/10.1596/978-0-8213-9862-3

Yet, another interjected that men would never take a cleaning job because it is so poorly paid and demeaning: "A man who respects himself will never accept such a job." They also said that local men would be unlikely candidates for administrative positions in firms. "They choose the woman [for a secretarial position] because she is more responsible and conscientious about the work she has to do," one man stated. These remarks about the gender appropriateness of one job or the other are not uncommon in other communities. The poor returns and potentially strong reputational harm attached to bad jobs or women's jobs (which may often be the same) seem to sap men's resilience in the face of deteriorating economic opportunities.

Women in Ceadîr-Lunga also mentioned struggling with the difficult economy, but they said this has pushed many of them into new jobs and expanded their income-earning role. They described the advent of more powerful women in their neighborhood, who did not exist a decade ago. The women on their top step are better educated, have fewer children, and work at professional jobs in the government or run their own enterprises. Some women have been able to launch businesses with funds that they earned themselves while working abroad or that their migrant husbands sent home. "These women are financially secure, smart, self-confident, good in business, but sometimes unreliable and unkind," they explained. A few of them climbed up the ladder by marrying rich husbands or taking advantage of market opportunities left by men who went abroad in search of better jobs. The focus group estimated that nearly 20 percent of the women in their neighborhood had pulled themselves up to the two top steps, which did not exist for them 10 years ago.

The much larger share of women still on steps 1 and 2 are also educated, may have jobs, and are raising families. Their husbands often are unemployed, so their households rely on the women's income. The Ceadîr-Lunga focus group estimated that 80 percent of the women in their neighborhood used to be on step 1 a decade ago, but this has now dropped substantially to 20 percent. Women on step 2, however, may well have been compelled to take a job due to the economic crisis, but this has strengthened their voice.

Men's and women's different coping strategies in the face of adversity affected their sense of agency in competing ways in Ceadîr-Lunga. When we asked the men about new gender laws taking effect in Moldova, one of them responded, "Mainly nothing has changed, especially for the good." Another elaborated, "It didn't change anything because the financial situation in Moldova is very bad. I think that women should stay at home and take care of the family, but when women go into politics, business, and so on, it is not a good thing." Unlike in Jaipur and Malangachilima, the men seemed loath to recognize women's expanded and important provider roles.

Beyond Ceadir-Lunga, economic factors also emerge as the triggers most often named that move individuals down their ladders. Falls can be precipitated by losing a business, being retrenched, losing property, losing a job abroad, going bankrupt, making bad investments, defaulting on loans, mismanaging money, dealing with national economic crises, facing war, and so forth. In rural areas, droughts, floods, pests, and diseases add further severe risks to livelihoods.

In our sample, urban men seemed to struggle the most with adversity. In many urban communities, where men's "good" jobs have grown scarce, they often perceived that women have easier access to work in certain sectors, such as service industries, because of the premium on "soft skills" and personal appearance. Whether this perception is accurate or not, it is clear that many urban men feel deep insecurity about their role as a provider and this is a source of great frustration for them.

The dataset also contains four economies affected by violent political conflict during the 2000–10 reference decade for assessing changes in power and freedom. The gender and conflict literature is bringing to light women's deep vulnerability to sexual and other violence in the case of war, but it also documents how periods of conflict force gender norms to relax as the institutional structures that control them are dismantled.[9] Women enlarge their public roles, but men go into retreat. These processes were especially on display in some of the sample communities in post-conflict Liberia. Women there widely saw their economic, civic, and political leadership strengthen in their communities, while many men reported feeling emasculated as they tried to recover their livelihoods since the war ended in 2003. Some of the men's narratives openly identified women's gains in power as challenges to their authority, if not causes for their loss of power. Women, on the other hand, voiced frustration at men's inability to adapt to women's new roles or to the changing economic and institutional circumstances in their communities. Gender relations in these mainly urban Liberian localities seemed very tense.

In Greenville, Liberia, for instance, the women mentioned that they have a new marketing association (established by their elected chairwoman), but the men are not helping make it a success. Rather, the men are leaving women alone to do the arduous work required to "cut palm nuts and brush on the farm." Women are gaining power, but men in Greenville are falling in droves down their ladder. Just half of the men were on the bottom step 10 years ago, but the men's group placed 90 percent of them there now. And this is how the men describe themselves on step 1:

> They are not working, there is no business. They cut palms and give them to their wives to sell so they can get food. They do the weeding and brush contracts; they collect kiss-me (tiny snails) to sell; they cut wood and make charcoal to sell. Any day they don't work, they have no food. They live in thatched houses and have a junior-high school level of education. They have a fine and happy family that goes to church together and sits together. ...

> [Some couples have a] fighting relationship; both women and men grumble and fuss every day. Even today, when we have gathered for the focus group, the wife is asking, "Why didn't [the man] go to the farm? Will sitting in that group give us our daily bread for today?" And that becomes another source of conflict between the man and woman today.

On Norms and Agency • http://dx.doi.org/10.1596/978-0-8213-9862-3

And in another Liberian town, Harper, where men also reported extensive disempowerment, they talked about how, since the war, women have taken over leadership positions at the local university and in the local market, while jobs that used to provide many local men with good and reliable income, such as at the port or with logging companies, have not been recovered. Like many urban communities in this sample, the men of Harper and Greenville feel voiceless and trapped, but women say they are finding their voice and building better and freer lives for themselves.

Men's and Women's Interdependent Agency and Gender Norm Change

The ladders highlight the fact that men and women recounted few differences in what drives their ability to gain more power and freedom in their lives. They most often stressed economic initiatives, although they acknowledged that attitudes, behaviors, and education also play roles in climbing the ladders, as do family relations and social networks. Yet, gender norms interact with local opportunity structures and individual initiatives to make processes of exercising agency quite different in reality for men and women. Women seem able to climb their ladders in good times or bad, and claim more empowerment whether they gain more voice in their domestic or public roles. Men's sense of agency, by comparison, appears to be much less multidimensional and more contingent on their status as providers and local economic trends.

The frequent uneven movement—where women gain a sense of power and freedom and men feel stagnant or see minimal movement—may have detrimental effects on the community as a whole. When men backslide and feel insecure, or perhaps even when they remain content not to climb, this may impede the functioning of local institutions and slow relaxation of and change in gender norms. Alternatively, when men see desirable outlets through which to exercise agency, it may be easier for them to recognize and welcome women's changing roles. And it is in this sense that men's and women's capacities to exercise agency in a community interact and together shape the prospects for the relaxation of gender norms.

In most communities, we observed a gradual process of norm contestation and negotiation. Women's aspirations are changing, but they are not necessarily finding promising openings for acting on them. In Ba'adan center women felt empowered, but their stronger agency continues to be heavily bound by traditional roles for their gender. Moreover, as explored in chapter 5, women who take on new public roles in very constrained environments may not necessarily derive greater agency like the women in Ceadîr-Lunga.

In the eight communities[10] similar to Jaipur and Malangachilima, however, where men are climbing the ladder in large numbers along with the women, we see gender norms relaxing quickly and local economic, political, and civic institutions becoming more accepting of women's participation and leadership. These sample communities with extensive twin climbing most often featured both sexes finding better livelihoods, becoming more active in local economic

"It is good for women to be strong, but the most important opinion is the man's opinion. He is the person who controls everything and has the power to make decisions in the family."

—Village women's focus group, Kharef District, the Republic of Yemen

"A person has to look for opportunity, take risks, push themselves, and fight to get ahead."

—Urban man, Lambayeque Province, Peru

organizing, and women entering local politics. These changes may send hopeful signals to other men and women about the potential for them to climb, and hence these contexts more reliably demonstrate rapid and significant institutional transformations in gender equality on the ground.

In his work on systemic shifts in inequality at the nation-state level, Tilly describes how the rhythm of social inclusion and democracy building can shift, almost unpredictably, from slower events of individuals breaking down barriers to exclusion (and only limited numbers of people climbing the ladder) to a much more rapid "categorical phenomena" where whole social groups suddenly find pathways to full citizenship in their societies (2007a, 64–70; 2007b, 35–50). Similar processes seem to be at play at the micro level. It may be helpful to conceive of extensive twin climbing seen in the focus groups as "innovative" moments in the lives of the communities, moments when more democratic markets, politics, and civic action become reinforcing—with greater gender equality as a core driver of this shift in institutional functioning. If this is the case, there may be potential for more holistic policy designs that can buttress both men's and women's agency and support their communities to make a shift to the more inclusive institutional equilibrium reported by study participants in Jaipur and Malangachilima.

Women's and men's accounts of the processes that increase their agency hinted at why their community institutions may function better with more gender-inclusive participation and leadership. The power holder perched on the top step of the men's ladder in Malangachilima "loves people" and does not discriminate; whereas the women on the top step remarked that they are now strong enough to approach a man with great power. Power is circumscribed by the norms of social interaction, as much as by physical, economic, or political might. Jaipur's most powerful and free woman "takes initiative and responsibility for community concerns," and is "trusted and looked up to by other women." Women on Jaipur's top step are also able to interact with the community elite and access public resources. In other words, as women find ways to climb their ladders, more and more gain entry into and benefit from the formal spaces of their communities. And in doing so, the attributes of greater power, identified by the focus groups, suggest that the presence of these women may help shift informal governance capacities toward more idealized normative codes of conduct.

Another crucial point is that a woman on the top rung can slip down if she "loses the trust of the people in the community," or "stops communicating with people lower on the ladder" or becomes arrogant. Leaders who display less than best behaviors are likely to be sanctioned by their communities. But this fundamental mechanism for local institutional accountability is far weaker in excluding environments. Where women can gain entry and influence, local institutions appear to become more responsive to serving the *entire* public good and not just the male half, or a small group of elites.

We note that women's and men's self-help groups and economic collective action are also present in the communities with extensive twin climbing. The power of civic networks in forging more-inclusive societies cannot be underestimated, especially their role in increasing women's empowerment. Appadurai's (2004) research on organizational efforts among slum-dwelling women in Mumbai, India, shows dramatic shifts in women's mind-sets due to the solidarity and awareness-raising of their organizations. When oppressed social groups see that the structures of their subordination are not necessarily immovable, they seem able to take bolder actions to help themselves—finding jobs and earning income, becoming active in civic organizations or politics, claiming a voice in their households—in ways that before were inconceivable. The women can then help one another to escape the bottom steps and marshal ways to mobilize and accumulate assets and capabilities.

Notes

1. See Petesch, Smulovitz, and Walton (2005) for a macro-level framework that inspires this community-level analysis.
2. Our tool builds on the "ladder of life" from the World Bank's global Moving Out of Poverty methodology (Narayan and Petesch 2005), which was designed to assess socio-economic mobility from the perspectives of men and women who had escaped poverty or remained trapped in poverty. While the ladder of life focuses on conditions that affect the poverty transitions of households, the "ladder of power and freedom" assesses factors that affect the "transitions" in the agency of individuals of the same gender.
3. The number of steps on each ladder varies according to what each group deemed was necessary to represent their community's reality. On average, three to five steps are defined, with rural communities typically adding fewer rungs than urban ones.
4. In Ba'adan center, the women's mobility index is a substantial 0.40, while the men's plunges to –0.85.
5. Figure 4.1 does not include the five men's and five women's ladders from Sudan because the women's focus group did not conduct the sorting exercise at the end of their ladder discussions. Figure 4.2, however, includes the five Sudanese men's ladders in the average ratings for the men's mobility.
6. If we used calculations based on the median mobility indexes for each sample group, urban men perform somewhat better, but the rural ladders become a more moderate

version of the urban ladders, with rural women's average mobility doubling the rural men's. The median, as opposed to average, mobility indexes for the urban ladders are 0.35 for women, but 0.0 for men. In the rural sample, the median mobility index is 0.20 for women and 0.10 for men.

7. Figures 4.4–4.7 present mobility factors mentioned by least 5 percent of the groups in the coding exercise. We do not, however, include the many factors coded under "other." Due to time constraints with informing the *World Development Report 2012*, it was not always possible to refine and clarify how the coders understood some of the factors coded as "other." A review of these factors reveals that a good share could have been coded under the already defined categories. We do not feel, however, that the overall pattern of findings would be much affected by a re-coding. Some of the additional factors under the "other" category that we did not code for include religion, sorcery, aging, and luck (winning the lottery).

8. This Jaipur is not the large city with the same name in Rajasthan State in India.

9. See, for instance, Petesch (2011); Menon and van der Meulen Rodgers (2011); Bouta, Frerks, and Bannon (2005); Bop (2001); Meintjes (2001); El-Bushra (2000); and Sørensen (1998). Petesch (2012) elaborates on the four conflict-affected countries in this sample in more detail than was possible in this study.

10. The communities with extensive twin climbing reside in Bhutan, India (three), Liberia, Peru (two), and Tanzania. Half are urban, half rural.

References

Appadurai, A. 2004. "The Capacity to Aspire: Culture and Terms of Recognition." In *Culture and Public Action*, edited by V. Rao and M. Walton, 59–84. Stanford, CA: Stanford University Press.

Bop, C. 2001. "Women in Conflicts: Their Gains and Their Losses." In *The Aftermath: Women in Post-Conflict Transformation*, edited by S. Meintjes, A. Pillay, and M. Turshen, 19–34. London: Zed Books.

Bouta, T., G. Frerks, and I. Bannon. 2005. *Gender, Conflict and Development*. Washington, DC: World Bank.

Dempsey, N. 2010. "Stimulated Recall Interviews in Ethnography." *Qualitative Sociology* 33 (3): 349–67.

El-Bushra, J. 2000. "Transforming Conflict: Some Thoughts on a Gendered Understanding of Conflict Processes." In *States of Conflict: Gender, Violence, and Resistance*, edited by S. Jacobs, R. Jacobson, and J. Marchbank, 66–86. London: Zed Books.

Epstein, T. S., A. P. Suryanarayana, and T. Thimmegowda. 1998. *Village Voices: Forty Years of Rural Transformation in South India*. New Delhi: Sage.

Fishburne Collier, F. 1997. *From Duty to Desire: Remaking Families in a Spanish Village*. Princeton, NJ: Princeton University Press.

Kabeer, N. 1999. "Resources, Agency, Achievements: Reflections on the Measurement of Women's Empowerment." *Development and Change* 30: 435–64.

Lomnitz, L. A. 1977. *Networks and Marginality: Life in a Mexican Shantytown*. New York: Academic Press.

Meintjes, S. 2001. "War and Post-War Shifts in Gender Relations." In *The Aftermath: Women in Post-Conflict Transformation*, edited by S. Meintjes, A. Pillay, and M. Turshen, 63–77. London: Zed Books.

Menon, N., and Y. van der Meulen Rodgers. 2011. "War and Women's Work: Evidence from the Conflict in Nepal." HiCN Working Paper 104, Households in Conflict Network, Institute of Development Studies, University of Sussex, Brighton, U.K.

Moser, C. 2009. *Ordinary Families, Extraordinary Lives: Assets and Poverty Reduction in Guayaquil, 1978–2004*. Washington, DC: Brookings Institution.

Narayan, D. 2002. *Empowerment and Poverty Reduction: A Sourcebook*. Washington, DC: World Bank.

Narayan, D., and P. Petesch. 2005. *Moving Out of Poverty: Understanding Freedom, Democracy, and Growth from the Bottom Up—Methodology Guide*. Washington, DC: Poverty Reduction and Economic Management Network, Poverty Reduction Group, World Bank.

Perlman, J. 2010. *Favela: Four Decades of Living on the Edge of Rio de Janeiro*. New York: Oxford University Press.

Petesch, P. 2011. *Women's Empowerment Arising from Violent Conflict and Recovery: Life Stories from Four Middle-Income Countries*. Washington, DC: USAID.

———. 2012. "The Clash of Violent Conflict, Good Jobs, and Gender Norms in Four Economies." Background paper for *World Development Report 2013*, World Bank, Washington, DC.

Petesch, P., C. Smulovitz, and M. Walton. 2005. "Evaluating Empowerment: A Framework with Cases from Latin America." In *Measuring Empowerment: Cross-Disciplinary Perspectives*, edited by D. Narayan, 39–67. Washington, DC: World Bank.

Schrock, D., and M. Schwalbe. 2009. "Men, Masculinity, and Manhood." *Annual Review of Sociology* 35: 277–95.

Sørensen, B. 1998. "Women and Post-Conflict Reconstruction: Issues and Sources." WSP Occasional Paper 3, United Nations Research Institute for Social Development, Geneva, Switzerland.

Tilly, C. 2007a. "Poverty and the Politics of Exclusion." In *Moving Out of Poverty: Cross-Disciplinary Perspectives on Mobility*, edited by D. Narayan and P. Petesch, 45–76. Vol. 1. New York and Washington, DC: Palgrave Macmillan and World Bank.

———. 2007b. *Democracy*. New York and Cambridge, U.K.: Cambridge University Press.

CHAPTER 5

Structures of Opportunity and Structures of Constraint

Both the women and men in our study recognized that certain factors and processes under their control can enhance their capacity to shape their lives. This chapter ponders factors that are also vitally important for exercising agency, but over which they typically have far less control: local-level institutions in the public sphere of their communities, and the normative climate for inclusion and accountability in these arenas. It is in the creation of structures of opportunities that are open and equal for men and women where policies have largely focused. And while changes have been implemented and more opportunities created that have translated to changes in endowments, economic participation, and aspirations, much hard work remains.

"Progress toward gender equality," in *World Development Report 2012* (World Bank 2012, 330), "entails shifts towards a new equilibrium where women have access to more endowments, more economic opportunities, and more ways to exercise their agency—and where this new arrangement becomes the dominant order." Chapter 5 draws on our dataset to probe the role that community characteristics play in constraining and enabling agency. Our initial focus is on local labor markets and then public and civic institutions, and especially how gender equality is reflected in legal frameworks. The constraints of gender norms, however, remain central because they so greatly shape aspirations and access to opportunities.

The traits associated by the focus groups with the ladder steps reveal that, as more and more women move up, a share of them are penetrating—perhaps for the first time in their communities—formal institutions and labor markets. For instance, in urban Karta-e-Bakheter (Parwan), Afghanistan, the women pointed out that on step 1 of their ladder of power and freedom, a woman is not working for pay (or cannot), but on step 2 she may be involved in "tailoring, embroidery, weaving carpets, tending home poultry." On step 3, a woman may be employed in a more remunerative job outside the home (e.g., earning income as a nursing aide or from livestock). And a woman on their top step is usually well educated, can be "nominated even for election," and "may be a doctor or teacher, and has

Education and development of the country also matter. If the country is rich, the people on the bottom can rise to a higher level. If [not], people are depressed, unemployed, homeless, and hopeless.

—Urban man, Dobrowice, Poland

a good economic position. They have freedom and power." Even in more traditional societies, such as Karta-e-Bakheter, greater participation of women in public spheres is displayed on the ladders. The basic question for this chapter is what role do institutional and normative factors play in shaping perceptions of agency. Do these three pieces move together? Or separately?

Gender norms influence not only women's (uneven) capacities for exercising agency—explored in previous chapters—but also the extent to which local institutions welcome women's participation and leadership.[1] This social context, which Kabeer (2001, 47) argues can be more aptly understood as "structures of constraint," means that individual women acting alone are unlikely to challenge and change the conservative elements of their local institutions: "The project of women's empowerment is dependent on collective action in the public arena as well as individual assertiveness in the private." While we observe many signs of individual women crossing gender boundaries throughout our dataset, signs of effective collective action (e.g., the women of Jaipur and Malangachilima in chapter 4) and institutional change in the gender order are relatively rare. This chapter looks at more typical communities, where local opportunity structures are less open to women's initiatives and chiefly appear to reinforce, rather than alleviate, gender inequalities. Gender norms in these environments prove more resistant to change.

The operations of markets and other institutions reflect local gender norms. The interaction between beliefs and attitudes, on one hand, and women's participation in the labor market, on the other, is tamed partly by the potential benefits women can obtain for themselves and their families, as well as by the norms within their households.[2] Escriche, Olcina, and Sánchez (2004) note the obvious changes in women's ability to work (outside the home) and in gender roles in the last 30 years—also seen in the decade changes study participants reflect on during the focus groups—including changes in attitudes toward women in the labor force. But we cannot really say whether these changes are due to adjustments in preferences and norms governing gender roles or due to a different socialization process for younger women and the transfer of preferences and aspirations from parents to daughters. It is not only the household and the market, but the overall structure of opportunities and normative climate in a community that helps or hinders women's and men's ability to negotiate gender-allocated roles.

Economic participation can be a strategic move to give women voice. But our dataset makes plain that, while communities may be growing or shedding jobs, the impact of economic trends on women's access to income opportunities and their sense of empowerment is far from linear. Social and cultural factors affect expectations of whether and under what conditions women may seek a job, as well as the types of work that they consider desirable and available to them.

In the first part of this chapter, we show how normative change is impeded by numerous factors, including the interplay between preferences and the local opportunities that combine to funnel women into less productive areas of the economy. For other reasons (explored later), women's economic participation in even dynamic markets may not be enough to challenge and change gender structures meaningfully. In the final sections of the chapter, we look at how better laws, political leadership, and community organizing provide other potential outlets for women to gain more power in their communities. Yet, our findings reveal that norms act as important constraints on these routes to empowerment as well.

Community Factors That Fuel Agency

Certain community-level conditions and trends, gathered from information from local key informants,[3] seem to be more conducive to men's and women's empowerment. To frame the comparative analysis, we sorted the focus groups' ladders into three categories, according to the extent of the mobility they reported: high, moderate, and downward. Figure 5.1 shows the average mobility for the three sets of men's and women's ladders, and table 5.1 presents the ladder distributions in each set by sex and location.

Figure 5.1 Average Mobility Index

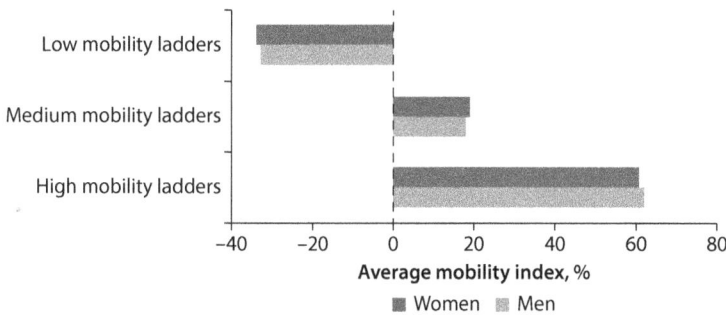

Note: The mobility index is calculated based on the difference between the mean step now and 10 years ago on each ladder. The distribution was divided into three groups according to the average distribution within each country set of communities. We used a tercile distribution function that classified the ladders based on the distributions of the mobility index for each country.

Table 5.1 Number of Ladders in Each Mobility Category by Sex and Location

	High mobility ladders		Moderate mobility ladders		Downward mobility ladders	
	Men's	Women's	Men's	Women's	Men's	Women's
Urban	4	27	21	14	26	9
Rural	12	14	17	14	17	14

Note: Results from 189 adult focus groups. The five Sudanese women's ladders are missing from this analysis because they did not conduct the sorting exercise.

At first glance, the average mobility indexes are quite similar for both men's and women's ladders in all three categories. However, when looking at the specific number of ladders located in each mobility set, more women's ladders are in the high mobility group than men's, particularly urban women's; and more men's ladders, also heavily urban, are in the downward mobility group. These patterns underpin the polarized urban ladders presented in chapter 4. One important explanation for why so many urban men feel disempowered or in limbo is that difficult local economic conditions provide few job opportunities for them. This—combined with their views of what constitutes an appropriate "male" job (which allows them to fulfill their provider role)—prevents men from adapting more easily to a changing environment.

Figures 5.2 compares local economic and poverty data with the ladder mobility categories. The focus groups' ladders that feature high mobility (more empowerment) correspond to communities that were more prosperous on average over the past decade and that have lower rates of poverty (as reported by key informants). We anticipated these findings for the men's ladders, but were surprised that favorable economic conditions and lower poverty levels proved equally important for women's perceptions of empowerment as well. We also find that men's and women's mobility is higher in communities where women currently serve as local elected leaders. The significance of the presence of civic groups and empowerment trends is more ambiguous.

The narratives in our dataset reflect the global trend of women's increasing participation in the labor force in the past decade. The rate of women working for pay has increased in most communities compared with a decade ago. This rate is the highest in the communities where the focus groups of both sexes reported greater gains in power and freedom (figure 5.3).

Whose Jobs?

In economic sociology, markets are as cultural as any other aspect of social life, and norms and values are a central part of their constitution and functioning (Spillman 2012; Wherry 2012; Zelizer 2010). Markets are not gender neutral; they are embedded in societies and take up (and reflect) their specific gender norms. Thus, when assessing women's agency, it is important to bear in mind that women's knowledge and evaluations of their actual chances in local labor markets are intimately shaped by the hierarchy of values to which they adhere, as well as the values of their community, family, local leaders, and employers. In other words, whether jobs are plentiful or not in local markets, they may or may not be open to women, or women may not see existing opportunities as appropriate for them. Norms and values not only act here as external secondary factors brought in as part of the black box of individual preferences, but are fundamental to, for example, how employers define potential or ideal employees.

World Development Report 2012 documents the rapid expansion of women participating in the labor force in recent decades together with a more slowly

Figure 5.2 Mobility on Ladders in More Prosperous and Poorer Communities

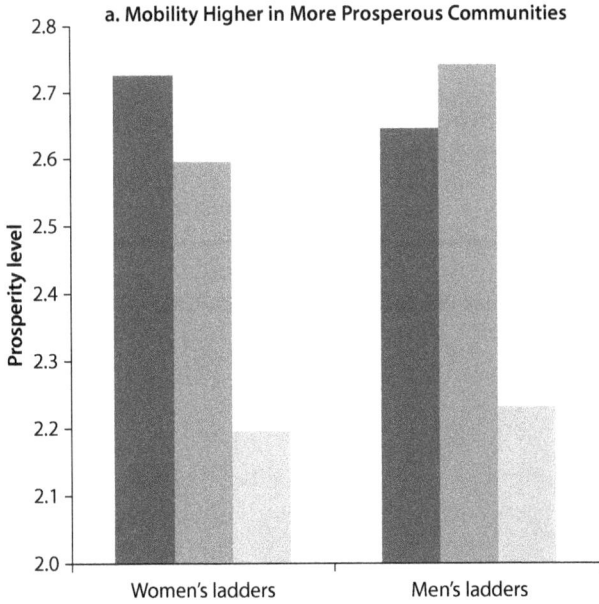

a. Mobility Higher in More Prosperous Communities

Note: Respondents scored the prosperity level of the community compared with a decade ago on a scale from 1 to 3, with 1 = less prosperous, 2 = prosperity remains the same, 3 = more prosperous.

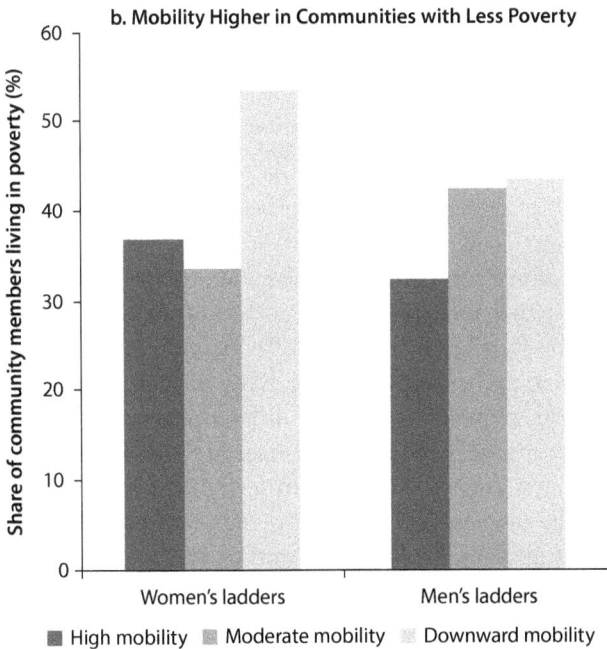

b. Mobility Higher in Communities with Less Poverty

■ High mobility ■ Moderate mobility ■ Downward mobility

Note: Data from 189 adult focus groups. The five Sudanese women's ladders are missing from this analysis because they did not conduct the sorting exercise. Respondents provided the estimated share of community members living in poverty conditions.

On Norms and Agency • http://dx.doi.org/10.1596/978-0-8213-9862-3

More women are making business now and can do anything for themselves.

—Rural women's focus group, Suakoko District, Liberia

Women study to be teachers or pedagogues because they love children. Men often inherit a private business.

—Urban women's focus group, Belgrade, Serbia

Figure 5.3 Rates of Women Working for Pay with Twin Climbing and Falling

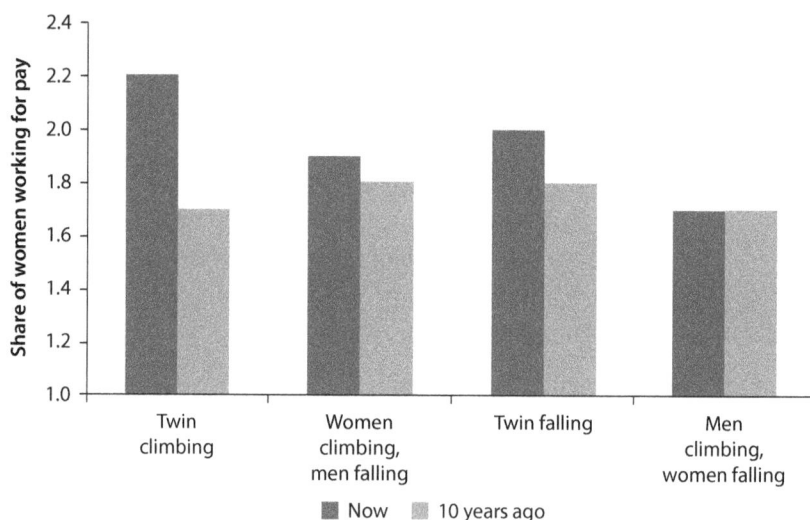

Note: Data from 184 adult focus groups. The five men's and five women's ladders from Sudan are missing from this analysis because the women's groups did not conduct the sorting exercise. Respondents scored the extent to which women work for pay in the community on a scale from 1 to 3, with 3 = majority work for pay, 2 = some work for pay, 1 = rare for women to work for pay.

declining occupational segregation by gender across the world. Women continue to be over-represented in less productive sectors of the economy and in positions of lower authority (see Tzannatos 1998). To explore how gender norms may be affecting economic agency and the desirability of particular local jobs on offer, we asked the focus groups to reflect on differences in men's and women's economic roles and capacities and key challenges in their labor markets.

Discrimination in general is a problem for both sexes in the study, although women see gender discrimination against them as a stronger barrier than men do. It is a factor that influences which jobs women and men can get. Men reported discrimination against men and against women, but both women and men reported more discrimination against women. In Kalahandi District (Andhra Pradesh), India, a woman explained simply, "We are female. That is why we get lower wages." It is relevant that young men and young women have the strongest views regarding discrimination.

On Norms and Agency • http://dx.doi.org/10.1596/978-0-8213-9862-3

Opportunities for jobs vary significantly by gender; in fact, when asked to sort the "best" and "worst" ways to earn a living for workers in their localities, the focus groups, across countries and communities, identified about 50 percent of the jobs they mentioned as gender-specific ones (either men's or women's jobs). Individual accounts of the factors that determine their ability to get a job reflect these gender differences. Normative perceptions, as well as predominant gender roles within a society, define a job as male, female, or gender neutral. And not only are jobs gender specific, but the skills jobs require are as well. Men in the study, for example, believe that having good connections is important, and they mention this more than women (figure 5.4)—as well as give more relevance to information sources about job opportunities. Women depend more on the demand for gender-specific abilities such as soft skills for "female" jobs (such as education, nursing, or retail). The ability to balance work and family life and having previous job experience matter more for women than for men. But both equally recognize that education is a central factor at the time of finding a job.

Gender discrimination——as shown in figure 5.5—plays a role in the types of jobs women can find, because it influences perceptions of women's abilities and the opportunities that are open to them. Again, jobs requiring "feminine" skills in social relations—better at conversation, more attentive—are deemed better for women, but jobs involving authority, technical knowledge, strength, or public safety often remain solely for men. Young men in the sample felt that women can find jobs more easily, while young women had the opposite opinion.[4] "I browse through the newspaper ads in Belgrade looking for work, and I see more demand for girls to work in cafés and pizzerias, boutiques, counters, everywhere—for them it is easier," remarked a young man from Sumadija District, Serbia.

Figure 5.4 Most-Mentioned Factors Affecting Access to Jobs in the Local Labor Market, According to the Men's and Women's Focus Groups

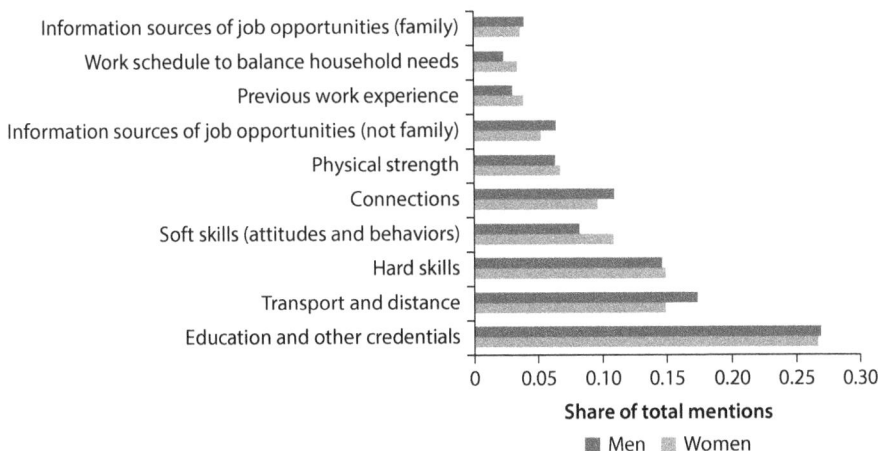

Note: Data from 388 adult and young adult focus groups.

On Norms and Agency • http://dx.doi.org/10.1596/978-0-8213-9862-3

Figure 5.5 Perception of Discrimination by Sex in the Labor Markets

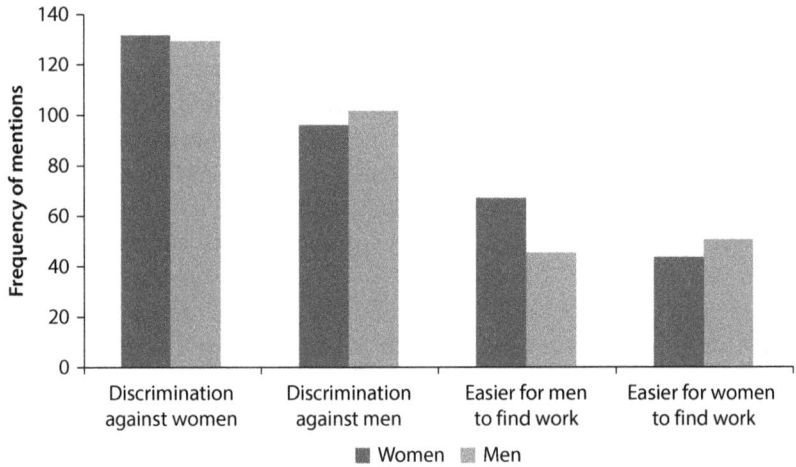

Note: Data from 388 adult and young adult focus groups.

Figure 5.5 shows how women and men recognize that there is more discrimination in the market against women than against men. But a significant number of views also points to some discrimination against men. Women more often perceive that in line with this discrimination, it is easier for men to find a job. Men are more evenly divided over which gender has better job prospects.

"Women excel in health, education, and housekeeping. But men excel at everything else, like engineering and police," suggested a woman in Rafah, West Bank and Gaza. In Karta-e-Bakheter, Afghanistan, a woman said that "tailoring, embroidery, and carpet weaving are for women, and construction, metal work, carpentry, and jobs in the government are for men." In Monrovia, Liberia, where gender norms are more relaxed than in West Bank and Gaza and Afghanistan, women are servers at "drinking spots," while men purchase supplies and handle the cash. In Lambayeque Province, Peru, where the tourist industry is booming, men are the chefs in the city's world-class restaurants that cater to the tourists, while women, who have less access to training and opportunities, are sometimes cooks in smaller establishments and catering companies. In Tandjouaré Prefecture, Togo, a young woman explained that jobs requiring "physical force [are] for men, and courage and patience are for women."

Social norms, and the institutions that support them, determine to a large extent the types of jobs, and their particular working conditions, that women and men can apply for, as much as the views the communities hold about specific jobs (Morrison and Jutting 2005). These views take several forms. A detailed look at the data suggests three specific ways that norms and jobs are in constant dialogue for women.

First, we see that the *women must negotiate their work choices around the different constraints and norms governing a woman* to avoid female-inappropriate work and potential risks or difficulties—verbal, physical, and sexual harassment, physical injury, and more. (Most of these norms follow the attributes of a good woman, advanced in chapter 1.) In the process of searching for work, women in the study not only considered salary and status (which everyone takes into account) but also had to factor in the potential threats to their moral integrity and their family's honor. In communities that still tightly hold to more traditional norms for women and gender roles,[5] some jobs considered inappropriate or immoral for a woman are perfectly acceptable for men. For example, any job in trade, which involves dealing with strangers, or in services that require interaction with men, or a job with night hours, often are off-limits to women.

In all the Sudanese focus groups, one of the worst jobs for women was hawking tea, coffee, and homemade food because it required women to "work long hours on the street and deal with different types of people who may treat them indecently." They mentioned that tea sellers under age 40 can be treated like prostitutes and even older women are harassed as well. Unmarried women doing domestic work for other families risked sexual advances that "deprived a girl of modesty." Women's jobs cleaning schools and selling in telecom centers and shops are also deemed undesirable in Sudan, but are considered acceptable, good-paying jobs for women in many sample communities in Sub-Saharan Africa and elsewhere. Similarly, call-center jobs in Hyderabad (Andhra Pradesh), India, are not well considered, in spite of the potential economic gains: "Actually, there is good money in call-center jobs, but society doesn't consider this a decent job. Women engaged in such jobs are not considered respectable because it has night shifts and the workplace is full of young men who have fat salaries." In these communities, women approach the labor market with already constrained choices and miss out on good opportunities for employment.

In more conservative communities, such as those in West Bank and Gaza, the Republic of Yemen, and Afghanistan, for example, where women's physical mobility is restricted, it is not surprising that the women are less attractive as potential employees. Similarly, women who have the qualifications for a job, but who need their husbands' or father's consent to work, are considered less reliable, even if more qualified than male colleagues. Sometimes, women from the sample communities where no childcare services were available—for example, in the Dominican Republic—self-censored their work choices (as much as employers do) when faced with the possibility that household demands may compete with their work hours. The whole set of social relations that makes up the labor market is affected by the gender norms of a community, and not only the part pertaining to gender relations in the household.

Second, a *good job for a woman has to be flexible.* How women internalized or appropriated the norms of their communities shows in the way they described what constitutes a desirable job for women. These jobs tend to mesh well with domestic work and childcare in terms of location and time flexibility, and do not involve physical strength. "Safe and easy jobs are best for women" pointed out a woman from Jaipur (Odisha), India, meaning the best jobs are not physically demanding, are close to the woman's house, and allow them to devote time to housework.

On Norms and Agency • http://dx.doi.org/10.1596/978-0-8213-9862-3

Flexibility is one of the main reasons why being a small business owner is frequently mentioned by the focus groups as a suitable job for a woman. It provides some freedom in the allocation of time and does not require traveling long distances away from home. Women's search for flexibility solves both self-imposed limits (to accomplish the many household tasks they have more easily) and ways to adhere to social norms. While some women find jobs that conveniently complement their domestic duties, others face demanding physical work in fields or factories in addition to their housework and are aware of the price they pay. "Selling coconuts is the worst because women have to climb coconut trees, cut the nuts, husk them, and then carry them to the market to sell. Women do all the hard work and men come home and find dinner ready and served to them each evening," pointed out a young woman from East Sepik Province, Papua New Guinea.

Third, *economic need is stronger than traditional norms*, so the norms have to adjust. In East Jakarta, Indonesia, selling carpet used to be only a man's job, particularly because it requires travel around the city. But today, being a female itinerant carpet seller is considered a good job, although "it wasn't a few years ago. But because of poor living conditions [and economic stress], it must be done—by men *and* women," noted a young woman. It is obviously better if a woman can sell from home and take care of the house, but when both wife and husband have to work to feed their children, norms relax and adapt. In Serbia, women do construction work under the same conditions as men, rain and snow. And in Liberia, opportunities opened up for women during and after the war, and they began running businesses, farming, and selling cash crops.

Clearly the choices women make when it comes to work vary, depending on several factors, and so does the way they negotiate social norms. For some women in the study, taking a particular job is a response to certain restrictions in their choices; for others, it is an expansion of their ability to choose. In rural areas, as Agarwal (2003) reports, nearby farm work, household gardening, or small livestock tending can help women increase their agency because the jobs are accessible, manageable with their domestic work burden, and within their mobility restrictions; require less education; and do not need assets or investment. Some women feel motivated to work to reach specific aspirations or goals. All of them are acting as economic agents and expressing their preferences to earn income, perform their domestic (gender) roles, safeguard their reputation, and more (Kabeer 2000).

It Takes a Village: Local Economic Dynamism and Empowerment

Having a job that offers the possibility of generating an income and accumulating assets is at the core of both men's and women's accounts of what helps them gain power and freedom. Economic well-being is one of the main attributes they associated with being on the top step of the ladder. For men, having a job so they can be a good provider is the identity of their gender and meets the expectation that they will be a good husband. For women, a job and its income are means to increase their bargaining power inside the household. But men and women alike

I worked in Zastava [a factory] for 24 years and then I was fired. I automatically lost everything. I lost any freedom and power I had. Everything was lost.

—Urban man, Kragujevac, Serbia

Unfortunately, the economic situation has a big effect on an individual's personality. … If [the man] is able to provide for his family, his personality will be stronger.

—45-year-old urban man, Old City, Hebron, West Bank and Gaza

are largely dependent on the structural conditions of their local economies in the pursuit of employment.

The links between empowerment, norms, and economic dynamism are not clear in this study. As women become more economically active, they gain a sense of empowerment. The exceptions are contexts where norms are deeply discouraging or desirable job choices extremely scarce. Here we provide additional evidence from our study that women perceive empowerment from their economic initiatives, regardless whether their economies are growing rapidly or moderately, or shrinking. Looking at market trends described by the focus groups, however, gender norms do not keep up with women's changing roles. This variability means that perceived changes in empowerment and gender norms cannot be assumed to be complementary forces or direct and universal consequences of economic dynamism.

To explore these interactions more fully, we examine some weaker local economies in the study against a more dynamic one to see what happens to local norms around women's paid work. In these contexts, the variation in the stringency of norms does not correspond with the state of the economy in the community or with how women are able to handle both norms and employment opportunities.

When Choices Disappear or Stay Poor

The traditional gender division between a household's productive and reproductive tasks assumes that there are sufficient economic opportunities for men to find paid employment or other productive activities to support the household. But reality is not always that accommodating. What happens to women's agency in weak economic situations where there are not many jobs available, and where lack of economic dynamism takes a toll on men's opportunities? The answers vary, but it is clear that normative views are shaping women's sense of their choices, along with the stressful market conditions.

Among communities that have seen less growth, economic need is forcing a relaxation of gender norms. In the least dynamic communities where everyone is struggling, especially men who cannot continue providing for the household, women spoke of being thrust into the market to earn an income. They end up competing for and working in whatever jobs are available. The market registers

On Norms and Agency • http://dx.doi.org/10.1596/978-0-8213-9862-3

There is no work. Nobody is doing anything. If you find a job, you cannot hold it. And the jobs which you do find are the worst ones.

—Urban young woman, Kragujevac, Serbia

fewer differences between genders when needed workers are unskilled and eager to work. There is little self-selection out of a job, except for some clear gender differences, such as physical strength (from which norms were derived), but even that does not keep women from working in construction or agriculture. In agriculture, men do the jobs that require plowing or heavy lifting, while women seed, weed, harvest, and pack. Choices of jobs, according to the focus groups, are more often constrained by availability, and job selection may not be strategic or based on a sense of self-efficacy or empowerment.

In Serbia, Poland, and Moldova (as discussed in other chapters), women's presence in the labor force has a longer history; nevertheless, it too segregates jobs by gender, similar to contexts where women's economic participation is more recent. In the East European communities, as elsewhere in the sample, women opt for careers in the humanities and teaching, while men go into sciences, engineering, and business. "Women are less capable in business than men," and "women study to be teachers or pedagogues because they love children more" is the view among Serbian women in Belgrade. Yet, men and women from this region voiced growing disenchantment about which jobs can be found and kept in their weak local economy. The type of job may vary, from domestic work for young women to factory work for young men, but the feeling seems pervasive that opportunities are limited at best.

In some communities, like rural Floresti District, Moldova, opportunities are deteriorating for both genders. The community had good stable jobs for both women and men that disappeared when the greenhouses and dryers closed, the state-owned enterprises were liquidated, and some private companies went out of business. Floresti District is poorer than it used to be, and many people grow vegetables and raise small livestock to survive. Perhaps not surprising, women reported disempowerment on their ladder. Men, by contrast, said they have moved off their bottom step in large numbers by finding stable work locally or with temporary migration, which has allowed them to "find a good wife" and "stop drinking and start taking care of the family." In line with their gender role, these factors allowed men to escape the bottom step in this village (box 5.1 presents the particularly difficult case of Roma men in Serbia struggling to overcome a harsh economic and social climate).

For Floresti District's women, by comparison, the local jobs still on offer strain their gender roles, identities, and expectations. Their discouragement is high, although they face little gender discrimination in job opportunities or in equal income. For example, a recent renovation of a local school employed about 30 people, of whom 12 were women; all received equal pay regardless of the specific tasks performed. Moldovan men and women work equally in good and bad jobs

On Norms and Agency • http://dx.doi.org/10.1596/978-0-8213-9862-3

Box 5.1 The Roma of Kragujevac: Where Disadvantages and Strict Norms Overlap and Trap

Kragujevac is one of the oldest Roma settlements in Serbia. Small in size, its population is dense with a high unemployment rate. Multigeneration families have at least three children and 95 percent of the inhabitants are poor. Many people have been laid off in the last decade in the economic downturn. Men find it hard to reach employers and get a job. They mainly engage in manual labor and agricultural and seasonal work, collect secondary raw materials, or work for the local garbage disposal company. Some find work through the National Employment Service and personal contacts.

Women work to a lesser extent than men: a small number of them clean other people's houses, work for the municipal gardening company, or pick fruit in season. Most women do not receive fixed salaries. The few girls who finish school actively seek jobs, but have difficulties finding regular work. Kragujevac does not present a very uplifting panorama.

"Men and women have a lot of free time because, among other reasons, they cannot find anything to do for pay," related a young woman of Kragujevac. Even when they find a job, in their free time men tend to socialize with other men, gamble, or drink. The younger men, who have lost their motivation and aspirations, do the same. "Most young men in the community have a lot of free time. There are a lot of idle guys who do nothing; they look for work, but hope not to find it," explained a young man.

Women, as traditional, are in charge of the housework, whether they are working for pay or not. When men don't work, they sleep late and spend their time with their friends, away from their homes. "He only comes home when he is hungry. He brings no money. How could he bring money when he does nothing? We receive child support, which is not enough, but what can we do when there are no better opportunities? Our families help us a little, as much as they can afford to," commented one woman. Women notice that men, unlike them, find it harder to accept the loss of work, given the pressure they feel to provide as breadwinners. Even though they would like to have more work and better business opportunities, however, when faced with unemployment, men would rather be idle than do "female tasks" and contribute to the care of the household.

and get similar earnings. Their discussion about local jobs portrayed men as truck drivers, metalworkers, and locksmiths, while women clean and cook, as well as work in construction and agriculture.

And while some gender specialization is evident in the jobs the focus groups listed, women are competing for and taking men's jobs that require strength, despite almost universal preference that women do less arduous work. For example, men clearly saw strength as a factor that should favor men in construction work: "Jobs that imply physical work are harder and men are better at those kinds of jobs, for example, construction. Moreover, men are braver and therefore take more dangerous jobs." While women see construction as "one of the worst ways of making a living" because "it is very physically taxing" and pays poorly, it is nonetheless viable if it is the only job available.

On Norms and Agency • http://dx.doi.org/10.1596/978-0-8213-9862-3

Women in Floresti District defied gender differences and restrictions outright. They challenged the concern for their safety and risked traveling at night if they needed the job. Safety became a secondary issue when it came to getting a job, as some young women noted: "In our situation now, it is more important to find a good job with a wage that covers commuting expenses. I prefer to work closer to my home in order to save time and money, and my husband prefers this for me too. But if I don't have a choice [with a distant job], he will not forbid it." These women are not abiding by traditional norms, but are they increasing their agency in the process? Not always, as they made clear when discussing their ladder of power and freedom. To move up, they needed either to start a small business or "find a more prestigious job."

Even though these women are well educated, the limited desirable opportunities seem to be holding back more rapid change in gender norms. Some young women expressed progressive views in terms of aspirations of freedom and productive use of their acquired skills: "I studied and if I find a job opportunity to use my education, then I don't want to stay home just taking care of my children." But as so commonly found in our dataset, this view sits side by side with other women's opinions that highly value the mother's role. Nor have more flexible norms changed young men's mind-sets: "I consider it better for the entire family if the woman stays home and takes care of the children until they are 3 to 8 years old." Although some local women have been working in jobs outside the home for decades, norms remain parked between community disapproval and endorsement: "There are some people who say that a working mother has abandoned her children"; and "it may be, though, that when a mother leaves her child and gets a job, then she is in a difficult economic situation and that is what she needs to do."

Sometimes the need for cash in a household and the demand for unskilled workers in nearby markets together unlock doors to women's economic participation. They may even cross, and change, the boundaries of gender-appropriate work, and open up job possibilities for other women. But in contexts where choices are limited or deteriorating, the process of norm relaxation is slower than in more economically dynamic communities (see box 5.1). In sum, in Floresti District, where previous economic opportunities and education levels have raised expectations, where desirable economic options are now scarce, and where old and new norms coexist, not just any job will lift women off the bottom ladder step. "I didn't succeed in finding a job I wanted," lamented a 19-year-old woman in her focus group, "so I decided to stay home and take care of my children and household."

Hato Mayor, a secondary city in the Dominican Republic, is another local economy that is losing jobs. Unemployment and poverty in the sample communities jumped when the free-trade commercial zone they depended on was hit by a downturn. Today, it is difficult for workers to find stable jobs and the local market is less active. But compared to rural Floresti District, there are enough work outlets for many informal workers and entrepreneurs in Hato Mayor to make ends meet. Perhaps surprising, both women and men perceived upward movement on their ladders and singled out their initiatives with their own businesses and better financial management as central to these gains. Women, for instance, said they can move up the ladder by opening their "own small businesses selling food, making and selling sweets, selling second-hand clothes, and cleaning streets." These women see themselves as empowered and "willing to push forward" to contribute to their families' well-being during the difficult times.

Yet local opinions about women's dual roles appear to be even more contested in Hato Mayor than in Floresti District. The women's focus groups support working mothers and their attempts to reconcile productive and reproductive demands, but they were also aware of the opinion this generates in the community. When a working mother leaves her children, people think and say that she is going "to prostitute herself." Moreover, women reported discrimination and physical risk at their jobs: "Women get paid less for more work and they get abused." And they do not dare work at night due to unsafe streets. In their focus groups, the men were clearly more conservative than the women. Despite the women's changing roles, men made plain that gender differences should remain intact and women should not go after or take male jobs, for instance, working construction and driving motorcycle taxis. Younger men were as conservative as older men and echoed these negative views.

When Choices Grow

Chapter 4 looked at Jaipur (Odisha), India, a rapidly urbanizing town, and Malangachilima, Tanzania, a village moving into commercial agriculture. These two communities were in the midst of particularly fast change, and both women's and men's focus groups presented clear evidence of a strong relaxation of gender norms for women's public roles. Jaipur and Malangachilima give us a valuable look at how quickly women's roles can sometimes change, when local opportunity structures support their economic initiatives. In most other sample communities with dynamic local economies, however, gender norms are more resistant and do not shift as quickly.

In Umlazi township B, a community of 3,000 outside Durban, South Africa, a local official interviewed for the study estimated that perhaps 80 percent of the women currently work outside the home, mainly as teachers and nurses, and some in offices, retail, or the police. Just 10 years ago, few women earned any income at all. "Women are no longer regarded as just housewives," a young woman remarked, pointing to a shift in the predominant association of women with their domestic role. In this suburb of Durban, women generally have more education than men, with young women attaining the highest levels. Women in Umlazi township B feel empowered; they placed 75 percent of the women in their community at the top of their ladder and characterized them as being "powerful women who can afford anything. They own vehicles and houses. They are single parents and are independent. They do not wait for men to do things for them. They send their children to university. They have lots of money. They have everything they need and can eat whatever they feel like eating."

Young women here do not see themselves as bound by any restrictions when it comes to finding a job: "Nothing [prevents us from getting a good job].

Now women can go out to work and hold a high-ranking job, even in the army and the police. This is a great change since our parent's time.

—Urban young man, Khartoum, Sudan

In today's world, women fit anywhere as long as you have the right qualifications." They listed highly skilled work—some conventionally masculine jobs—as suitable for women, desirable to them, and available not only to men. They asserted that they can be police officers, lawyers, and doctors, just the same as men. They also remarked that they want to be like their fathers and "have prestige like him, and get [public] exposure like him." For these young women, domestic work and care giving are not attractive jobs.

But while their hopes for the future include professional careers, they also want marriage, recognizing that pursuing both has a cost: "If you are a married woman, it is even more difficult [to work far from home] and it can destroy the marriage. Men cannot wait for a woman. If you are gone too long, by the time you come back, he may have moved out to live with someone else." These young women are forced to hang on to this dual role of professional worker and proper wife to accommodate male peers who may or may not welcome their income-earning role. "Yes, it is acceptable that they have the right to work," noted a young man, "It is good because they can assist their husbands in meeting household demands. In some households, you find that the man is unemployed and only the woman works and supports the family." Yet, another young man disagreed strongly, "It is not acceptable because a woman needs to be at home caring for the children. Most of the time, working women are promiscuous and don't respect their husbands." Unlike the communities that are struggling with limited jobs and high levels of poverty, these young women at least can take heart in the ready availability of desirable jobs and the prospect that some men are broadminded enough to welcome this development.

As quickly as women's public roles are changing in Umlazi township B, traditional gender identities continue to frame desirable jobs. Other young women consider construction jobs as more suitable for men due to their greater strength. And when men are employed in healthcare, "male nurses are discriminated against and people call them homosexuals." Gender stereotyping allocates such jobs as nursing and office administrative work more often to women and authority positions to men: "If the school principal is a man, the school is highly respected because men are known for enforcing discipline."

In Ouagadougou, Burkina Faso, the market has become more dynamic, but it is still not easy for men or women to find jobs. Education remains a distant objective for everyone. Some young people aspire to technical and professional jobs, but they are not attainable by local workers. Indeed most of the good jobs are clearly manual skilled labor that is highly segregated by gender: mechanic's work, carpentry, and construction for men, and sewing and housekeeping for women. A female mechanic will be hired "only if she has real experience and because women mechanics are very scarce," noted a man, but women "don't have the strength to carry bricks," so they should not work in construction. The Ouagadougou focus groups also mentioned that they avoided illegal or risky jobs because they threaten people's honor, which appears to be very important to men and women alike.

The qualities of desirable and unappealing jobs, as well as the determinants of access to them—norms of femininity, flexibility, and need—vary when considered in the context of specific communities. The Umlazi township B community has a more dynamic economy, so young women are reaching for and expecting better opportunities than their mothers had, which are less defined by traditional gender norms than in urban communities experiencing tougher economies. Young women in Hato Mayor, the Dominican Republic, are completing high school, for instance, but their local economies are stressed and discourage women from conceiving of, much less pursuing, professional jobs as part of their future (table 5.2). In Ouagadougou, Burkina Faso, jobs also remain scarce and traditional norms continue to segment the labor market and dampen aspirations.

In his review of the literature on youth aspirations in Africa, Leavy and Smith (2010) finds that higher poverty rates and the lower socio-economic status of rural communities limit the hopes of young people. In our rural sample, however, there are village economies with enough vitality and growth that young people can imagine better futures for themselves than what is immediately available. In other communities, norms are relaxing and reinforcing women's economic initiatives. A case in point is Firestone District, Liberia.

Firestone District, a rural town described by a key informant as poorer than a decade ago, is still recovering from the recent downsizing of its Firestone rubber plantation and processing plant. This event sent men looking for work in other

Table 5.2 Desirable and Undesirable Jobs in Three Urban Communities

	Dynamic labor market: Umlazi township B, South Africa	Middling market: Ouagadougou, Burkina Faso	Slow labor market: Hato Mayor, Dominican Republic
Desirable jobs	Nurse[a] Teacher Police officer Lawyer Plumber (men)	Trader Tailor (women) Gardener (men) Mason (men) Mechanic (men) Carpenter (men)	Mototaxi driver Construction worker (men) Retail and shop clerk Security guard Concierge
Undesirable jobs	Drug dealer Taxi driver Security guard Caregiver (women)	Pickpocket Drug dealer Prostitute (women)	Waste picker Domestic service worker (women) Day worker in agriculture Street cleaner Drug dealer

a. All professions not marked were considered gender neutral by the focus groups.

On Norms and Agency • http://dx.doi.org/10.1596/978-0-8213-9862-3

communities or in alternative livelihoods, such as starting small businesses, and propelled women into the labor market to assume the role of provider or augment income that used to be generated solely by their husbands. Rather than the traditional unskilled jobs of fixing hair and dealing in second-hand clothes, the women discovered better options for paid work in the private sector, such as selling fish or charcoal, making and selling soap, refining palm oil, running a taxi service, and renting properties.

The need for women in Firestone District to support their families—and their new autonomy—has changed women's views of their own capabilities. As a result, younger women are completely disregarding the gender assignment of jobs, do not automatically assume that unattractive jobs are only for women, and do not feel forced to take whatever work is available, like their mothers did. Inspired, too, by the successful and educated women on the upper rungs of the Firestone District ladder, the young women are finishing their education and envisioning good jobs not currently available in their community.

This growing empowerment of the women, vis-à-vis the men's (which is more moderate), is permeating other areas of their lives and influencing how they envision the future. The women not only are working and saving but are engaging in what other communities term exclusively male activities, such as going out in the evening or with friends, having affairs, and financially supporting their households. Even though many in Firestone District disapprove of women stepping out of their traditional space, and even though these activities can indeed cause them to fall down their ladders, the younger women's attitudes denote freedom from normative constraints.

Sometimes changes in market signals induced changes in individual behaviors of the focus group participants, which may slowly modify social norms around jobs. But the relationship between market trends, agency, and norm change is mediated by a complex set of deliberations that include valuations of material benefits, time costs, and reputational risks for different individuals in a household.[6] In harsher contexts, the gains of women's economic agency are not at all clear, and the norms that surround these gains are more resistant to change.

In countries and communities in the study, where context allows for more economic choices, young women were as likely as young men to feel both constrained and empowered to find a job. Women looked to their parents, partners, siblings, and peers for advice and saw in their experiences notions of what is possible for them. And they make choices weighing similar factors as men—opportunity, economic need, returns from their labor, and the best use of their talents and skills. In these more inviting contexts, young men and women alike expressed their desire to be independent, but are aware of responsibilities toward their families. "Nowadays both parents [mother and father] are working [and] ... women also spend most of their time at work," explained a young woman from Umlazi township B in Durban. While another from this focus group elaborated, "Nowadays women no longer have to care for children by themselves. Their husbands and boyfriends are also accepting the responsibilities of caring for the children."

On Norms and Agency • http://dx.doi.org/10.1596/978-0-8213-9862-3

Impact of Laws and Local Civic Action on Empowerment

Markets are not the only structures that influence what is possible on the ladders of power and freedom. National policies, local governing bodies, state agencies, and community-based organizations also play a role in shaping local opportunities and the climate for women's inclusion and influence in the public sphere. We unfortunately had limited time with the focus groups to explore these pathways for exercising agency and how they may interact with gender norms. What was shared, nevertheless, indicates a good deal of unrealized potential for policy action.

We begin by reviewing focus groups' accounts of their understanding and implementation of gender laws. As part of institutional attempts to alter practices by directly sanctioning them, laws represent one of the resources for states to challenge prevalent norms. Next we move to discussions about the (limited) resources that are available to couples facing disagreement and conflict in their marriage or union. Viable exit strategies are central to reducing domestic violence. A final section discusses local political leadership and collective action.

Equal Rights for Women?

Facilitators asked the focus groups about their awareness of their country's gender laws and any impacts from them. A majority of groups had at least some knowledge of one or two laws (see figure 5.6.a). Participants mentioned domestic abuse laws most often, but they also displayed varying degrees of knowledge about women's rights to resist forced or early marriages; to obtain a divorce, custody of children, and child support; to own and inherit property; to claim equal pay and take family leave; to vote and run for office; and to access family planning. For most, however, awareness was extremely limited. "We have never heard of these laws," stated a woman from Briceni District, Moldova; another in her group added, "School teachers probably know something about this." Overall, the urban adult women's focus groups demonstrated the most specific knowledge: "Yes, we are aware of the laws. There is the act against dowry and there is also the act against domestic violence. We learned about all these acts by going to self-help group (SHG) meetings. TV also tells us about the acts," explained a woman from Nellore (Andhra Pradesh), India.

As expected, women viewed the new laws and their impacts more favorably than men (figure 5.6.b). "Men used to beat us and everything would just carry on as normal. But now we can report them to the police," announced a woman from rural Ngonyameni, South Africa, when asked about her knowledge and views of the new gender laws in her country. Another from her group countered, however, that "we just hear about the laws on the radio, but they do not apply in this community." Like other progressive forces, local awareness and passive or active support for laws may co-exist alongside normative views that accept, for instance, violence against women or men's claims to full property rights in

We understand that there are laws establishing the rights of women, but most of us do not take them seriously. As men, we are the heads of the family. In the past, no one knew about these laws, and women respected their husbands. Now, because of these laws, women try to control their husbands, which is not good.

—Village man, East Sepik Province, Papua New Guinea

I've heard of parental leaves for the fathers. It's good when men take on some of the responsibility of caring for the children. I think they will make use of it in our generation.

—Rural young woman, Martynice, Poland

cases of inheritance or divorce. In some contexts, nevertheless, women perceived the laws as helping them. According to young women in Paro, Bhutan, "there is less harassment of women now and men have to think twice before they divorce their wife or have extramarital affairs. Such behavior may come with a big cost for them because of the law."

Young women from rural Malangachilima village, Tanzania, could recall several of their rights: "Yes, we all have to go to school. We can inherit property like men. Men should not beat us and, if they do, we can take them to court. We can be politicians." Yet earlier, when we asked this focus group about control of assets and inheritance, they explained that men control most possessions in a household and that "the eldest son is the chief heir." Any land a woman may inherit from her family is taken care of by the eldest son (or next man in line) because women leave their village to marry, have children, and cannot manage the property. In this sense, the new laws may embody ideals that are quite removed from the actual choices and possibilities for women.

Still, in Liberia and other countries in the sample, some men openly admitted that they no longer beat women because they fear going to jail. "Every day, there used to be an incidence of rape, but now there is less. The use of fast-track courts has made it more alarming for men to be associated with rape. Most men violated young girls through 'cash violence,'" stated a young man from the capital city of Monrovia. In Emputa village, Tanzania, urban women proclaimed that the new laws mean they are investing more in their assets: "They [the laws] have assisted us because we have worked hard and now don't lose everything. For example, when you leave the man's home, you divide the property and can go with something to begin your new life." But another woman from Emputa village made clear that she has been waiting for three years for the government to take any action against her violent husband.

On Norms and Agency • http://dx.doi.org/10.1596/978-0-8213-9862-3

Figure 5.6 New Gender Laws

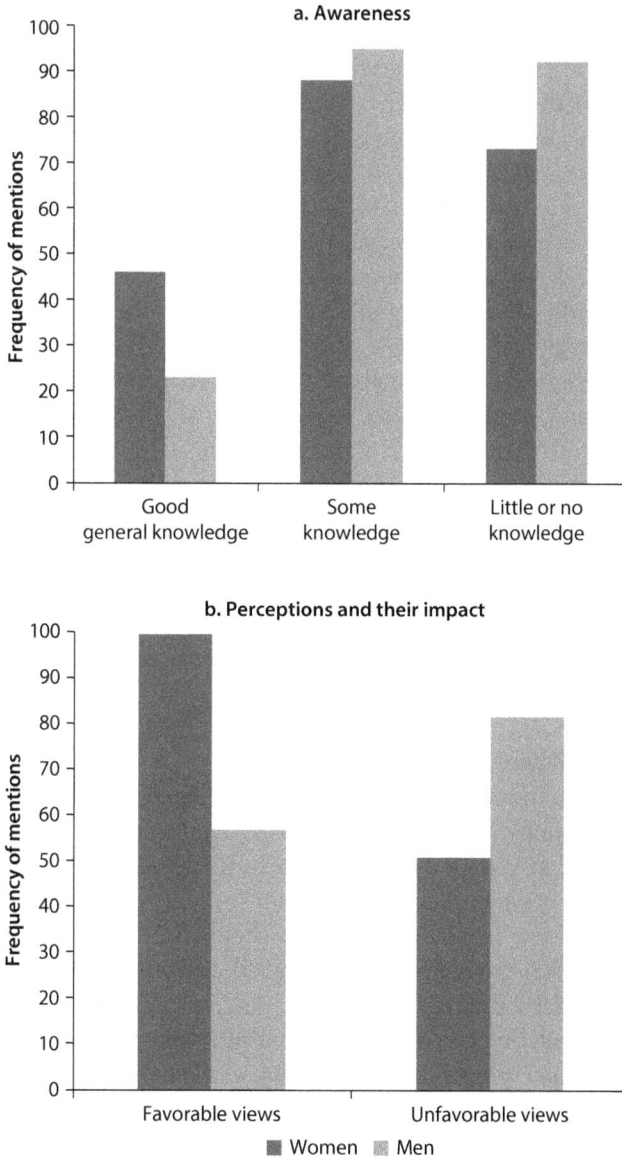

a. Awareness

b. Perceptions and their impact

■ Women ■ Men

Note: For both figures: Data from 388 focus groups.

The men's focus groups, along with a number of the women's, expressed mixed views about the laws, often indicating that they were ineffective or disregarded. "Just show me, please, a man who has been punished for his violence—no one," affirmed a man from Moldova. In Levuka, Fiji, a village man contended that the laws "may be implemented in towns and cities, but not here." Women in Tanzania and Sudan described weak enforcement of laws prohibiting female genital cutting and, in Poland, women reported that equal pay rules are "ignored so often. The men always receive more. They receive all the add-ons [benefits] and bonuses." A man from Nsenene village, Tanzania, maintained that "for me, I think such laws have spoiled our women. They have become big-headed and unmanageable at home and in society. And their daughters are learning the same. If we want respect and discipline, we need to revise such laws."

However, not all is discouraging news. There is a desire for gender equality that springs from the influence of changes occurring in both the private and public spheres. For some of the focus groups, the notion of gender equality is simply lauded as a constraint on misbehavior and harm, but the majority perceived that gender equality embodies the highest ideals of their societies. For women in Samte, Bhutan—Sisum's village, whose story opens part I of the report—who reported problems of violence against them, gender equality "means everything a woman dreams of; it is a dream come true." Others in this group added that gender equality would bring a "better life," "peace and less domination," and shared decision-making. Some of the focus groups, mainly rural men and to a lesser extent urban men, felt that the notion of gender equality violates cherished values and traditions, and perhaps fuels rather than eases violence against women. Yet, overall the focus group narratives suggested that, with investment in stronger enforcement combined with building greater awareness about the need for and intent of the laws, there is significant unrealized potential for gender legislation to alter women's and men's views of gender equality.

Do Institutions Work? Where to Turn for Help

The focus groups offered discouraging accounts about the enforcement of laws and other community resources for addressing family conflict, such as divorce or disagreements, that cannot be resolved behind closed doors. When the focus groups were asked where local couples turn for help with marital disputes, the number one response was family members (figure 5.7), followed by formal state institutions or local governments, although their presence is more marked in urban than in rural settings.

Specifically for divorce, for example, both young adult and adult focus groups across the sample indicated that getting a divorce is difficult or simply unacceptable for couples in their communities. This local institutional reality, where informal mechanisms and traditional gender norms still prevail, is important for understanding just how limited women's possibilities are for exiting abusive relationships. The pressures to resort to family or other informal networks are also why central government laws, policies, and programs—as important as they are for gender equality—often have less effect than expected. Rather than using the formal justice system, which may not even have a physical presence in or near many of the study communities, most participants explained that parents, in-laws, extended family, community elders, and local "reconciliation committees" (specific to Vietnam) all try to mediate to avoid a temporary or permanent separation due to violence in the home.

On Norms and Agency • http://dx.doi.org/10.1596/978-0-8213-9862-3

There is no divorce, unless the husband kicks out the wife.

—Urban man, neighborhood of Kragujevac, Serbia

Figure 5.7 Where People Turn for Help with Family Conflict

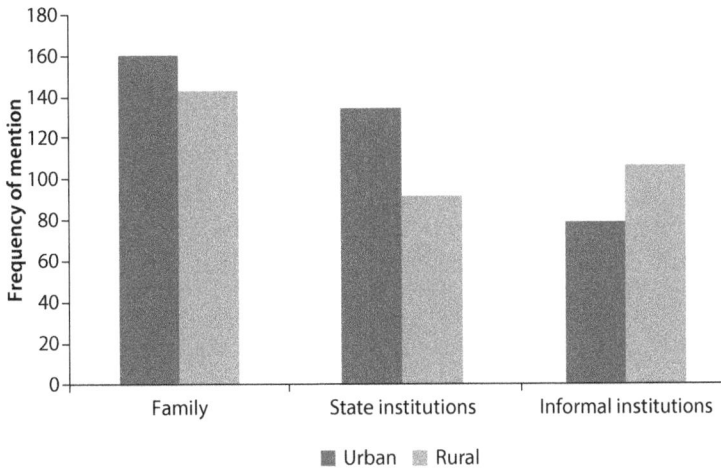

Note: Data from 388 young adult and adult focus groups.

In a semi-rural community of Ngonyameni, South Africa, according to the women's focus group, the new gender laws "have changed nothing here. We do not have any job opportunities, our husbands assault us, and most of the time the tribal court favors the man. So really nothing has changed. These laws apply only to urban areas." Similarly, in rural East Sepik Province of Papua New Guinea, women said that neither the police nor the churches will get involved in domestic violence matters. And while they mentioned that non governmental organizations (NGOs) can help women get access to the courts, a young woman claimed that "most women are afraid of their husbands and do not pursue claims in the District Court for maintenance." In Sigatoka, Fiji, women reported that "nobody divorces in our village. You can't just fight with your husband and then want to divorce. This is a Fijian village. There is always a way to solve marital disagreements."

Focus groups of both women and men made plain that individuals or couples seeking temporary or permanent separation are strongly discouraged by peer pressure, community opinions, and threats of unfair treatment. Women face complete destitution, permanent separation from their children ("the children don't belong to her, they belong to her husband"), and lasting ostracism from the community. Bride price and dowries that pass assets across family networks and down to husbands or wives further complicate divorce processes. In both Papua

On Norms and Agency • http://dx.doi.org/10.1596/978-0-8213-9862-3

New Guinea and the Republic of Yemen, women referred to bride prices and expensive dowries as impediments to divorce: "It's hard for a woman to get a divorce in this community because if the bride price is paid it makes it difficult for the woman to leave" (a women's focus group in Western Highlands Province, Papua New Guinea). Religion, both Christianity and Islam, imposes restrictions on divorce in a number of the sample countries.

Where official channels are an option—mainly in some of the better-off urban communities—focus groups indicated that they are employed only as a last resort, when family and other informal local institutions have been tapped and failed, and then only for the most extreme circumstances. "A justifiable reason is if a woman was terrorized by the husband. In this case, a woman can go to her parents' home. She can call the police or some social service, but these actions are justified only in case of great violence," explained a woman from urban Kragujevac, Serbia. A young man from Hoang Mai District, Hanoi, Vietnam, hinted that the reluctance to use formal mechanisms, until all other options had been exhausted, was less because of distrust in the formal civic institutions than because of the economic cost of involving them:

> Many couples who get divorced negotiate with each other for child custody and property because otherwise they have to pay fees if the court is involved. In cases where they cannot reach an agreement, they look for help from relatives or friends. Women often turn to the Women's Union for help if relatives fail. In the end, if nobody can help solve the dispute, the court makes a decision according to marriage, family, and other laws.

Men and women made clear how essential local institutions are for delivering gender equality in difficult situations. In the many contexts where local power inequalities are strong, and credible threats of violence to women underpin them, women's access to formal institutions may often be tightly restricted. Yet, the continued reliance on the traditional informal mechanisms to uphold laws and resolve disputes so often leaves women persistently disadvantaged and vulnerable. Taken together, these are key processes by which inequitable and excluding power structures resist change.[7] Thus, even where a nation's constitution may guarantee equal rights, and laws and regulations have been enacted that are strongly in the public interest and enjoy widespread support, local structures and normative behaviors that perpetuate gender inequalities may nevertheless endure. Without strong state capacities for enforcement matched by broad-based knowledge of the laws, formal legal, legislative, and regulatory reforms are unlikely to be effective.

Whose Voice Counts? Local Political Leadership and Civic Action

Many women's ladders in our sample conveyed that—in addition to participating in their local economies and feeling empowered by this—women are gaining more and more access to the formal political and civic institutions in their communities. In the 97 communities of the focus groups, 24 urban and rural women were elected leaders, up from a total of 10 a decade ago. Opportunities for

Sometimes having better education or better access to political leaders or local officials also helps you move up the ladder [from step 1 to step 2].

—Urban woman, Nellore (Andhra Pradesh), India

collective action also appear to be flowering, especially for women, but the link between collective action and empowerment is not as clear-cut as women's political inclusion.[8]

A quarter of the 24 elected women in the focus groups hailed from Liberia. The young women and girls in these focus groups frequently named their president, Ellen Johnson Sirleaf, as their role model. And in urban Firestone District, men noted that 10 years ago not a single woman held a local position of authority, but now, "people attend community meetings and women are very much involved. ... The level of development now is enhanced by women's participation." And, in Tewor District, Liberia, young women reported that, although their town is now more than 20 years old, it only started building a new high school when a woman became the local commissioner. A woman in Thimphu, Bhutan, also pointed out benefits of women in political power: "Women representing their community as local leaders have also helped bring issues related to women into public forums." In the ladders of the Indian focus groups, a common attribute of women on the top step is holding leadership positions in their village or neighborhood self-governance institutions. Beaman *et al.* (2009, 2012) find that a community in India with a decade of experience with women leaders (who emerged after gender quota requirements were enacted in 1993) can erase the bias in men's perceptions that they are automatically better leaders than women and close the gender gap in educational outcomes.

The contributions of civic networks to movements up the ladders are less clear-cut in our dataset. From key informants' reports to the field researchers, we find a median of 14 different local civic groups per community in the urban sample, and a median of 10 in the rural sample, but the numbers vary significantly. In urban Mongar District, Bhutan, women said that the factors that help them move up their ladder include "exposure [to successful women and information]," "advocacy," "nonformal education [such as training]," and local development projects that have gender targets. As discussed in chapter 4, focus groups also mentioned informal rotating savings groups (like the savings and credit cooperatives [SACCOs] in Malangachilima) and more formal SHGs, and leadership roles in them, as helpful for climbing the ladder. But overall, these civic supports are not that prevalent among the mobility factors.

With the exception of religious institutions in some contexts, economic groups generally outnumber other forms of grassroots organizations in our sample. Beyond the ladder exercise, focus group responses to specific questions about sources of credit and local producer or trade groups revealed gaps and disappointments. The large majority of focus groups indicated that economic groups were absent, ineffective, or accessible to only a few residents in their communities. And, even when they perform well, the economic groups are often more helpful to women than men. In Comendador, the Dominican Republic, for instance, the women said, "There are associations, but they have no economic projects and they don't help women." In Nsenene village, Tanzania, where women are outperforming men on the ladders, a man remarked, "Women get loans from institutions, such as FINCA, PRIDE, and local SACCOs. They can borrow money and do business. We men can have nothing to do with such initiatives, so we are left behind." Many women's and men's groups, in fact, commented on how the men are excluded from many lending and savings opportunities. One woman in Nellore (Andhra Pradesh), India, stated, "Men don't get loans these days. If they need a loan, they are asked to bring their wife for a guarantee." Another in the same group added, "Men have no credibility these days."

In the eight "high mobility" communities with extensive twin climbing, like Jaipur and Malangachilima, there are many reports about the vitality of local economic organizations. In Cusco Province, Peru, a village with twin mobility on the ladders of its focus groups, they described a farmer's group comprised of women that meets three times weekly to take their produce to the nearby town market. And a governmental Vaso de Leche [Glass of Milk] program, which provides nutritional support to poor young children and pregnant mothers, is run by local women. In Koudipally Mandal (Andhra Pradesh), India, another community where both women and men are climbing in large numbers, there are 22 SHGs, which receive support from external governmental, civic, and private sector agencies and are widely considered an important resource for local women's awareness-raising, solidarity, and economic initiatives.

In Kalahandi, a tribal village in Odisha, India, also with high twin mobility on its ladders, the women said that they are moving up their ladder because, unlike in the past, they are now saving money and taking out loans in their SHGs. The women also reported that their SHGs help create strong bonds between women of lower and higher castes, when before they would not sit together in meetings.

The mixed reports about economic groups are also reflected in performance on the ladders. At first glance, figure 5.8 reveals that, as with civic groups in general, there are more economic groups present in urban settings. In the cities in our sample, the focus groups with ladders showing twin climbing described numerous economic groups, which may also be present (albeit in smaller numbers) in sample locales where both men and women perceive disempowerment. In rural communities where women are rising on the ladders, economic groups are more numerous, but they practically disappear where women report disempowerment. No clear patterns emerge for rural men.

When we asked the focus groups about their hopes for their communities and their children, the call for jobs and economic interventions emerges by far as the top desire. In Nellore (Andhra Pradesh), India, a woman argued, "Life can be very different if there is marketing assistance for the products a woman can make

Figure 5.8 Median Economic Groups (Producer, Trade, and Finance) in Different Empowerment Contexts

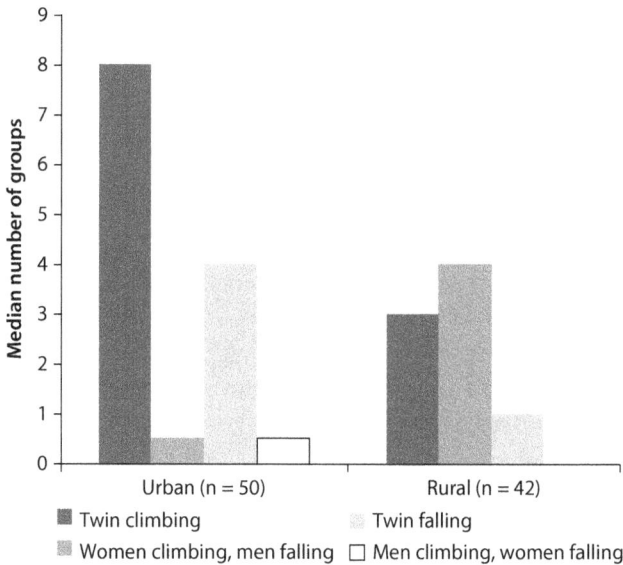

Note: Data from 184 adult focus groups. The Sudanese ladders are missing from this analysis because the women's focus group did not conduct the sorting exercise.

at home." And in rural Koudipally Mandal (Andhra Pradesh), India, a woman expressed hope that a factory will be built nearby, "so that the younger generation will have better job opportunities." Help with farming is the wish voiced by a young man of rural Sumadija District, Serbia: "A lot depends on the local government, if only they would invest in agriculture and in the villages. This is where my hope lies." In rural Kharef District, the Republic of Yemen, where girls are now attaining more education, women believe that "education will improve our status in the future," and they hope "our children find jobs and our daughters become teachers."

Focus groups also wanted better public services in their communities, calling variously for schools, health clinics, clean water, roads, public transportation, and police. In Floresti District, Moldova, like other communities, women wished for free and accessible education and more job opportunities for their daughters and sons. In the village of Naw Da (Parwan), Afghanistan, where there is no school for girls, an adolescent girl suggested, "If there is vocational training for young women in the community, we will learn something. With this, we can earn an income and change our lives." In River Nile State, Sudan, women hoped for legislative policy to address problems of "women facing harassment while moving around the community and region." In East Sepik Province, Papua New Guinea, a young woman lamented that her village did not pool funds to sponsor students seeking higher education, and another one spoke of educating daughters so they "do not make the same mistakes" or "get pregnant early and miss out on opportunities." In Thimphu, Bhutan, a young woman pointed out that "education and awareness may be the right tools to make both men and women use more family planning services." And both younger and older women expressed a need for daycare.

Some focus groups called for interventions to increase awareness of and support for women's rights, or to reduce the problems facing men that perhaps prevent more empowerment for women. To strengthen their village, for example, women of Zabibu village, Tanzania, hoped to "stand for office and participate in various forms of leadership in our community and country at large." Or in Kim Dong District, Vietnam, women wanted to see "more policies to ensure women's rights and more job opportunities for women." In rural Ngonyameni, South Africa, young people face heavy school dropout, joblessness, drug problems, and early pregnancies. In addition to more economic opportunities, the young men's focus group there thought sports or other recreational facilities may help them stop their risky behaviors and take their education more seriously. Similarly, in a village of Red Sea State, Sudan, young women wanted their community to offer handicraft projects for them and build a sports club for the men. Focus groups also desired the happiness and safety of their families and communities. In the remote village of Jahran District, the Republic of Yemen, the young women's "greatest wishes are marriage and employment."

Men's and women's aspirations for the future and their activities have to be congruent with their gender identity (see box 5.2). These identities develop in relation to each other. As discussed in chapter 1, a good husband prefers that his wife not work. If she does, his role of provider—his masculine duty and thus status—may be questioned by the community. "Now we need to find work and jobs. ... Based on the present economic situation of the community, there is no work for men. If someone wants to help the community, the first step is to help the men because they are responsible for food and the overall maintenance of the family" (adult men, Boyina Bagh, Afghanistan). Likewise, women's identity is built around being a housewife or a mother and, when it comes to work for pay, women's identities and associated duties take precedence or get translated into specific goals or jobs that align with such identities.

In Naw Da, Afghanistan, the women placed 80 percent of themselves on the bottom rungs of their ladder, because women "do not have jobs, freedom, or education. They cannot go anywhere. They do not have income sources, nor is there a school they can attend. They cannot make decisions and their husbands are uneducated." None of them has found a way to climb up their ladder in the past decade. In order to have more power and freedom, they felt that they needed to be supported in their efforts by the "government, NGOs, village elders, and the local mullah, who should know the rights of the women and push the men to accept these rights. In the present situation, we do not see any chance for women to change their lives." These powerless and isolated women recommended that interventions start by changing men's mind-sets.

Box 5.2 Public and Private Power

The important shifts made by women into positions of public power, where they are possible, seem to occur independently of what happens in their private lives. Women carefully hold their public power in check when they step into their homes; they find they are unable to translate potential gains from their public roles into their personal lives.

A 53-year-old woman from urban Ba Dinh District, Vietnam, explained this dilemma for women: "It is not that, if you are powerful in society, you should also have power at home. Of course, if you have power in society, you gain respect from your husband and children. But a woman should use her power properly, at the right time and in the right place. You should not bring power home and apply it in your family because then you may not be happy. Some women are powerful outside, but not in their family."

In fact, gains in power outside the household do not always translate into domestic power. Sumitra is a 37-year-old woman from a village of Phulbani municipality in Odisha, India. She is the ward member of her village and a member of the local *panchayat* (council), and also participates at the district level. But in most ways her life is no different from any other woman's in her community. Her day begins at 5:00 a.m. with all the household work; after finishing that, she goes to her daily wage work under the National Rural Employment Guarantee Scheme or to the rice paddy. Her husband also does daily wage work, but whatever he earns he spends on alcohol. The household is run on her income. Her evenings are frequently filled with verbal and physical abuse: "I don't remember one day that has ever ended peacefully. Most of the time, I and my children go to bed with empty stomachs because my husband throws away the cooked food in anger. This is the life I am living and yet people say I have political power."

Her journey into politics started with the 2007 election, when members of the community nominated her to run for a ward seat on the council. For her own and her community's benefit, she ran and won the position as ward member. However, she is discouraged. She says that nothing has changed in her life nor she has contributed anything to her community in the past four years. She regularly attends her ward council meetings, for which she is paid INR 30 (Indian rupees) per meeting, but she does not see herself as empowered. "We women have power in name only. We cannot contribute to improving our lives or the lives of community members." She also noted, "If I don't work for a day or two, my family will starve. … My elected position has not improved my life in any way." She will not run in the next election.

On the other side of the spectrum is Mrs. Latata, from Fiji, who is 71 years old and "the most senior member of the village women's group" (which has five members). She worked as a primary school teacher for 42 years, beginning her career when she was 24, and has become an agent of change by providing information about laws and assistance for women in her community who do not know about their rights or the legal system. Latata also teaches young girls to be critical, but not aggressive, in the solution of disputes. She feels that young girls can at least be introduced to thinking about things critically. "To be a leader, they need to have the 'know-how' to handle problems. They need to know that when you have leadership skills, you can solve problems amicably and don't have to make a big deal about it. You don't have to be aggressive [to get your point across]; there is a way to deal with things and make your point, and to give your help in a way that respects other views."

box continues next page

On Norms and Agency • http://dx.doi.org/10.1596/978-0-8213-9862-3

Box 5.2 Public and Private Power *(continued)*

Latata not only promotes peaceful dialogue skills, which can be used as much in public as in private, but also teaches girls about their rights and legal issues. She recounts the story of a young woman "who, after she finished school, looked after her elderly parents. Her father eventually passed away, but told her that she would be able to survive on his pension, which was held in superannuation funds in the capital. The woman found out later that her father had not legally left his pension to her and had no clue how to access the money her father had left her. [The young woman] told me that she knew I was the only one who could help her." Latata contacted the proper offices in the capital on the young woman's behalf and facilitated the payments. "These are the sorts of deeds Latata feels she is able to do from the knowledge and the confidence she has learned from being part of a women's community group," explained another woman.

Change Women Need

When looking across this large dataset, it is clear that women's life choices remain more restricted than men's and that markets, local politics, public services, and civic action—in most communities—mainly reinforce rather than ease these inequalities. Weak local institutions and restrictive norms blunt the effects of broader progressive forces on women's power and gender equality. On balance, though, we see more evidence of rising aspirations and relaxation and change of norms in contexts where local markets are reported to be more dynamic. Women's local political leadership also emerges as a significant force for women's empowerment and gender norm change. And while community-based groups do not receive high marks on balance from focus groups, a strong presence of economic collective action can make a difference, especially when paired with other supportive conditions.

Women's ability to work for pay, which most women participating in our study aspired to, may be one of the most visible and game-changing events in all communities. Women's work, as the focus groups showed, has the potential to alter traditional definitions of gender roles, duties, and responsibilities, as well as the main components of the identity of both men and women. Yet, empowerment and agency do not directly result from economic participation, but are supported by what women experience when leaving the home to join the market. Women gain a greater sense of self-efficacy, broaden their aspirations, and forge ways to reconcile their identity as workers with their identity as mothers. In Samtse, Bhutan, Sisum's mountain village, a young woman saw herself "completing law school and looking for a job as a lawyer" and another one believed she can be "a successful government servant."

Throughout this study we learned from the communities that the interplay of three forces influences gender equality: changes in the capacity to identify new opportunities and aspire to them, changes in the capacity to act and actively pursue those ideals or the use of those opportunities, and changes in the structure of opportunities and normative frameworks that constrain individuals. These three areas do not always move together. Nor, necessarily, do men's and women's perceived trends in empowerment grow in parallel. Also, women may feel more empowered, but there is little evidence in our data that this perception is matched by greater influence in their relations with men. Further complicating the linkages between the three forces, some norms may become more fluid in stressful economic times, and women's new freedoms may again narrow when their households and communities become more prosperous, or when the political climate changes for women's roles. As Kabeer (1999) notes, access to new resources may open up new possibilities for women, but the use of such possibilities is not necessarily uniform. Women, as they revealed in their focus groups, are still heavily influenced by the normative elements inherent in what affords them status and a good reputation with their families and communities; in their social relations; and in their individual (and other women's) histories, beliefs, and identities.

There seems to be no simple pattern of more flexible gender norms routinely developing alongside the creation of more and better economic opportunities in our study communities. Neither do we necessarily find a stronger adherence to traditional norms among the sample communities that have seen fewer changes or experienced reversals in their economic situations. In the less vibrant communities, the market requirement for unskilled labor is opening doors for women and men alike, and this can sometimes break the grip of traditional gender norms. Gender norm change is also sometimes possible, independent of local market and institutional forces, and women's own actions. For example, in contexts outside of our sample, such as in Senegal, community-based public awareness campaigns have been able to stop the accepted practice of female genital cutting (Mackie 2000); and in Afghanistan, community awareness projects have successfully reduced the incidence of early marriage (Malhotra *et al.* 2011).

While an individual woman's view and ability to act is relevant, sometimes a critical mass is needed to break a cycle. As Fogli and Veldkamp (2008) show in their study of the transition of women into the United States' labor force in the 20th century, local transmission of information generates change. Women learn from other women's experiences: as the women's focus groups told us, they learn from their mothers, their mother's peers, and their own peers. They learn from what happens to other women's children, and in others' households, and in communities.

The process of gender norm change appears to be uneven and challenging. When only a few women manage to break with the established norms, uncertainty reigns and traditional norms are not challenged and may even be reinforced. Also, the easy co-existence of new and old norms means that households in the same community can vary markedly in how much agency women can exercise, and that women often feel less empowered when the opinions and values shared by their family members and communities stay with traditional norms. Moreover, the lack of gains in women's empowerment is not always due to overt resistance to it; in many cases, it is due to a passive, underlying view in the community that "this is just the way things are here." This view commands adherence and we find it acknowledged again and again in accounts by different communities in the study. Even if actual practice has changed and is different (e.g., many women claimed some measure of economic independence), and even if many have let go of the norm (men must be the sole providers), the persistent belief—and reality—is that status and respect continue to be governed by the traditional gender norms. These dynamics keep change from happening.

The women's stories explored here in both more and less dynamic communities unrelentingly show that, although many women have higher expectations and more chances to work, to run for elected office, or to engage in community organizations, all too often they must still accommodate their public roles to conservative gender norms. At the same time, other women who have limited or poor opportunities to participate in the public life of their communities may be able to negotiate gender norms in ways that increase their agency, and eventually, some other outcomes, too.

Notes

1. See Fehr and Hoff (2011) for a thoughtful discussion of the literature on circumstances under which norms and preferences may be more malleable than often recognized.

2. Also noted by Duflo and Udry (2003); Guiso, Sapienza, and Zingales (2006); and others when looking at household bargaining and female labor force participation. Both studies highlight the impact that beliefs and preferences have on economic behavior and thus economic outcomes. Also see Munshi and Rosenzweig (2006) for an example of how traditions surrounding men's caste-based occupational networks in Mumbai limit young men's returns from education more than young women's.

3. Most of the key informants interviewed for each sample community were local officials, elected leaders, or civic leaders, although business leaders and teachers sometimes worked with our teams and completed the surveys, too.

4. This difference is not as stark among older adults in the study.

5. Specifically West Bank and Gaza, the Republic of Yemen, and Sudan, but also Umlazi township A in South Africa, Hyderabad in India, and East Jakarta in Indonesia.

6. Gary Becker (1981) conceives of economic models that account for household specialization of human capital and division of labor. For wider reviews of this literature, see Doss (2011), Alderman et al. (1995), and Dasgupta (2000).

7. See, for example, North, Wallis, and Weingast (2009).

8. In their extensive review of community-driven development programs, Mansuri and Rao (2012) find extensive problems in targeting the poor and meeting performance objectives, but they also mention more promising results from "a couple of recent studies of community-based projects, which provide microcredit, cash grants, and business- or livelihood-related training..." (11). Their review of community-driven development evaluations finds elite capture in communities that are "remote from centers of power, have low literacy, are poor, or have significant caste, race, and gender disparities" (6); and local social capital that "tends to melt away when the [project] incentives are withdrawn" (11).

References

Agarwal, B. 2003. "Gender and Land Rights Revisited: Exploring New Prospects via the State, Family, and Market." *Journal of Agrarian Change* 3 (1): 184–22.

Alderman, H., L. Haddad, J. Hoddinott, and R. Kanbur. 1995. "Unitary versus Collective Models of the Household: Is It Time to Shift the Burden of Proof?" *World Bank Research Observer* 10 (1): 1–19.

Beaman, L., R. Chattopadhyay, E. Duflo, R. Pande, and P. Topalova. 2009. "Powerful Women: Does Exposure Reduce Bias?" *Quarterly Journal of Economics* 124: 1497–540.

Beaman, L., E. Duflo, R. Pande, and P. Topalova. 2012. "Female Leadership Raises Aspirations and Educational Attainment for Girls: A Policy Experiment in India." *Science* 335: 582–86.

Becker, G. S. 1981. *A Treatise on Family*. Cambridge, MA: Harvard University Press.

Dasgupta, I. 2000. "Women's Employment, Intra-Household Bargaining, and Distribution." *Oxford Economic Papers* 52 (4): 723–44.

Doss, C. 2011. "Intrahousehold Bargaining and Resource Allocation in Developing Countries." Background paper for *World Development Report 2012: Gender Equality and Development*, World Bank, Washington, DC.

Duflo, E., and C. Udry. 2003. "Intrahousehold Resource Allocation in Côte D'Ivoire: Social Norms, Separate Accounts, and Consumption Choices." Working Paper 857, Economic Growth Center, Yale University, New Haven, CT.

Escriche, L., G. Olcina, and R. Sánchez. 2004. "Gender Discrimination and Intergenerational Transmission of Preferences." *Oxford Economic Papers* 56 (3): 485–511.

Fehr, E., and K. Hoff. 2011. "Tastes, Castes, and Culture: The Influence of Society on Preferences." Policy Research Working Paper 5760, World Bank, Washington, DC.

Fogli, A., and L. Veldkamp. 2008. "Nature or Nurture? Learning and the Geography of Female Labor Force Participation." NBER Working Paper 14097, National Bureau of Economic Research, Cambridge, MA.

Guiso, L., P. Sapienza, and L. Zingales. 2006. "Does Culture Affect Economic Outcomes?" *Journal of Economic Perspectives* 20 (2): 23–48.

Kabeer, N. 2000. *The Power to Choose: Bangladeshi Women and Labour Market Decisions in London and Dhaka*. London: Verso.

———. 2001. "Reflections on the Measurement of Women's Empowerment." In *Discussing Women's Empowerment: Theory and Practice*, 17–57. Sida*studies* 3. Stockholm, Sweden: Novum Grafiska AB and Sida.

Leavy, J., and S. Smith. 2010. "Future Farmers: Youth Aspirations, Expectations and Life Choices." FAC Discussion Paper 13, Future Agricultures Consortium, University of Sussex, Brighton, U.K.

Mackie, G. 2000. "Female Genital Cutting: The Beginning of the End." In *Female Circumcision: Multidisciplinary Perspectives*, edited by B. Shell-Duncan and Y. Hernlund, 245–82. Boulder, CO: Lynne Reiner.

Malhotra, A., A. Warner, A. Gonagle, and S. Lee-Rife. 2011. *Solutions to End Child Marriage. What the Evidence Shows*. Washington, DC: International Center for Research on Women (ICRW).

Mansuri, G., and V. Rao. 2012. "Can Participation Be Induced? Some Evidence from Developing Countries." Policy Research Working Paper 6139, World Bank, Washington, DC.

Morrison, C., and J. Jutting. 2005 "The Impact of Social Institutions on the Economic Role of Women in Developing Countries." Working Paper 234, OECD Development Centre, Geneva, Switzerland.

Munshi, K., and M. Rosenzweig. 2006. "Traditional Institutions Meet the Modern World: Caste, Gender, and Schooling Choice in a Globalizing Economy." *American Economic Review* 96 (4): 1225–52.

North, D., J. J. Wallis, and B. R. Weingast. 2009. *Violence and Social Orders*. Cambridge, U.K.: Cambridge University Press.

Spillman, L. 2012. *Solidarity in Strategy: Making Business Meaningful in American Trade Associations*. Chicago, IL: University of Chicago Press.

Tzannatos, Z. 1998. "Women and Labor Market Changes in the Global Economy: Growth Helps, Inequalities Hurt, and Public Policies Matter." Social Protection Discussion Paper 9808, World Bank, Washington, DC.

Wherry, F. 2012. *The Culture of Markets*. Oxford, U.K.: Polity Press.

World Bank. 2012. *World Development Report 2012: Gender Equality and Development*. Washington, DC: World Bank.

Zelizer, V. 2010. *Economic Lives: How Culture Shapes the Economy*. Princeton, NJ: Princeton University Press.

Final Thoughts

World Development Report 2012 showed that gender equality and economic development can reinforce or hinder each other through complex social and economic processes. The opportunities available to women and men—and their ability to take advantage of them—are determined by social norms, gender roles, beliefs about their abilities, and their assets, as well as by the social expectations of the communities and countries they live in. While we see significant progress in many places, gender disparities are still evident, particularly regarding empowerment and agency.

Data analysis from standard nationally representative surveys has not provided much information on norms and their effects, which *World Development Report 2012* identified as resistant to change and potentially hindering the advancement of gender equality. In our study, given the nature of our data, we were able to look deeper into social norms, and found that gender norms affect decision-making at the household and individual levels, as well as the functioning of markets and formal and informal institutions. Also, just observing changes in outcomes, such as increasing female labor force participation, does not always reveal the effects of these norms and raises more questions. Are more women working due to increasing labor market opportunities and their gains in education, despite rigid gender norms? Are gender norms dynamic and relatively flexible depending on the economic context?

We began our qualitative research into gender norms to explore the relationship between social norms and women's and men's agency. We hoped to identify a few simple patterns suggestive of causality that could also help practitioners identify missing or new areas for interventions to encourage gender equality. In this respect, however, our research proved too ambitious and we did not find any "silver bullets" for development intervention.

We did, however, illuminate a range of variables and complex interactions that determine the space for renegotiating or "bending" the gender norms that influence behaviors and affect the pace of change and growth of men's and women's agency. When households and communities find ways—or the need—to relax and change inequitable gender norms, we saw that men's and women's individual and collective agency can increase and reinforce one another.

One of the more consistent findings across the 97 research sites is the universality and resilience of the norms that underpin gender roles. Given the diversity of the communities and people participating in the focus groups, we expected to find a wider spectrum of attitudes and roles, and in particular expected to observe more flexibility in gender roles in areas with greater economic dynamism. While we did uncover some softening of norms in urban areas relative to rural areas, and by younger generations relative to older generations, these differences were less striking than the similarities across sites. In every research location, women and men of all generations identified the dominance of women's domestic role and men's breadwinning role as absolutely core to female and male identities.

The good husband defined by the focus groups is almost entirely characterized by his income-earning capacity and household authority role, and the negative behaviors he should not engage in "too much," such as drinking, womanizing, and gambling. On the other hand, the good wife is strictly defined by a long list of submissive qualities and household tasks, including being nurturing and gentle mannered; tending to the house; caring for the children, the husband, and the elderly; cooking well; and also contributing to the household income if and when needed. The idealized visualization of a good wife (or a good husband) is almost impossible to find in a single woman (or man); for women, such a stringent definition, and the demand for adherence to it, may be due to high levels of stress and poverty, and for women and men alike, the profound attachment of the man's identity to a job and income are key.

Some of the focus groups gave evidence of gender norms changing, albeit slowly and incrementally, with new economic opportunity, markets, and urbanization (chapter 2). In some locales and among younger age groups, participants described relaxation of gender norms where the structure of opportunities that increase women's access to jobs does not curtail men's opportunities and occurs with other changes, such as improvements in public institutions. Economic roles for women often creep into their domestic role, and in some places, younger men even take on some narrow domestic responsibilities. What is striking is the glacial pace of this change relative to the pace of change in contextual factors. Gender norms are being contested, bent, and relaxed, but not necessarily broken fully and changed. Younger people may delay compliance to a later point in time, but the norms and the expectations around them do not change.

The process of changing gender norms is not always peaceful or harmonious, and the uncertainty around prospective change may lead to gender-based violence or new forms of gender inequality. At the household level, we saw that space to negotiate a shift in norms in order to intensify agency is most commonly expanded in the constant dialogue among men and women implicit in everyday life. Tension is commonly associated when a woman participates as an equal in these exchanges, and we chiefly focused on relaxation of norms that permit women's roles to expand into men's roles in the household rather than the reverse. (There is little opposition within a household, for example, if a man opts to take on more domestic work.) Sometimes this tension can become violent. Violence and the threat of violence or abuse play a role in reinforcing the status quo and in discouraging women's efforts to challenge existing expectations and norms.

Despite the resilience of gender norms, our study found evidence of women's agency increasing in some strategic life choices (chapter 3). The most powerful results in terms of norms evolving toward gender equality and resulting in greater agency are in the expansion of education for girls (and women). However, they remain more constrained by household preferences and strict gender roles in how many years they can attend school and which fields they can study. Younger generations of women are also demanding more control over marriage and child-bearing than older generations, and they are participating more and more in these decisions. And, while in many cases this control does not translate into outcomes, young women—and young men—harbor different aspirations than their parents, such as having fewer children, getting more education, and marrying later. The structure of opportunities and the social pressures surrounding them do not always allow their aspirations to materialize, but often they achieve a middle point.

Exercises in the study to look at levels of, and changes in, power and freedom suggest positive progress for women, but less for men (chapter 4), which is partly explained by their different starting points. Men as the traditional power holders are accustomed to having more freedom than women. Men report fewer improvements in their sense of agency, but they benchmark their gains and losses against a higher base line. When compared to men, women in our study in general feel more empowered than 10 years ago. The rising availability of economic opportunities, increasing levels of education, and growing control over reproductive choices have been central in enabling women to gain more decision-making power in their lives.

Looking at the ladders of freedom and power created by the women and men in the study, we found that men tended to equate power more directly and more narrowly with their economic success. In this respect, many have been disappointed in their ability to find jobs they want to do and acquire the incomes they aspired to. Communities where both men and women feel more empowered now than 10 years ago were a small fragment of the sample, but they generally experienced more rapid economic growth (and consequently more job opportunities) and had more women in decision-making positions in public institutions and private organizations.

Given that norm change is slow and incremental rather than seismic, what role is there for development interventions to influence movement toward gender equality and normative change? Earlier chapters detail examples of the variables and combinations of variables that expand or constrain the space for renegotiating norms. The focus group discussions suggested that the interplay between desire for change at the individual level, the opportunities to effect change at the household level, and the support or lack of support for changes in norms at the community level represent a critical set of interactions that can accelerate or delay shifts in attitudes. On the individual level, women's desires to operate outside prescribed norms may be high, low, or non-existent. Within a home, depending on the personalities and views of household members, tolerance for behaviors outside the norms may be considerable or absent. A community may actively show support for or sanction those pushing against traditional norms of behavior.

A motivated woman or man in a household with high tolerance for bending traditional norms in a community where others are doing likewise may more easily incorporate making decisions and choices outside the normal range for their gender. The same woman or man in a more traditional household may face considerable domestic unrest or violence. The same man or woman in a community that is resistant to behaviors that threaten traditional roles may find themselves isolated and without social capital beyond the boundaries of the household. It is not enough to generate change in a single area. As women learn and benefit from new gender norms, their intra-household bargaining position must also improve at the same time. Women's aspirations need to be accompanied by opportunities to realize them and interventions that facilitate the accumulation of assets and capabilities. Empowerment thus requires a combination of factors to become a reality. And individual attempts to change norms may fail more often than not, especially if they try to reallocate power.

At the individual level, education, self-efficacy, and the ability to aspire emerged from the focus groups as important factors with respect to the capacity to negotiate change for greater agency. In particular, the education of boys and girls—beyond its role in building human capital—is crucial in shaping norms. In multiple discussions, adolescent boys and girls described how education exposed them to new ideas and knowledge, enlarging their capacity to analyze and encouraging critical scrutiny of established gender relations and the status quo. These discussions reaffirmed what is already known about the intergenerational transfer and reproduction of norms within households. Education fosters learning away from the household environment where gender roles are played out in every interaction and action. The research team realized the importance of ensuring that school curricula offer gender-neutral learning opportunities.

Several sections of the research probed nearly universal patterns that emerged among young people's aspirations. They wanted higher levels of education than the current average in their communities, better jobs than commonplace in their communities, marriage at an older age than normal in their communities, fewer children at a later age than usual, and so on. When prompted to further describe what they thought were realistic outcomes, their predictions fell somewhere between current practices and their aspirations. This capacity to visualize a different path from the existing, accepted course to even a pragmatic midpoint is a positive feature that development interventions can build on.

Women's and men's success in achieving what they aspire to often depends on factors outside the individual's control (see the second part of chapter 4), mostly in social and political structures. Evaluations of development interventions indicate that projects targeted at young people can profoundly affect their ability to aspire and, by extension, to make decisions that may be more empowering.

The threat of violence or abuse reinforces the status quo and discourages women's efforts to challenge existing norms. The team, during the research, recognized that action to reduce violence and abuse within the households had both short-term and long-term benefits. Lowering the threat immediately improves physical and psychological welfare in the household, and also introduces a safer environment for women to participate in household discussions and decisions on household actions that can shift the balance of power in the household. We also found many cases, however, where laws promoting gender equality were in place, but implementation in practice was deficient, making women feel even more disempowered.

The norms that uphold women's heavy domestic workload are powerfully reproduced in the household, where girls mirror their mothers' unending responsibilities and long, isolated hours at home. In contrast, men spend work and free-time hours in activities outside the household, which are reflected in boys' time-use patterns and easy interactions in the community and wider world. Even when girls go to school and boys help out a little in the house, the girls' workload in the house does not change or lessen. The time that women and girls must spend on domestic responsibilities constrains their time available for activities outside the house: earning income (which gives women more voice and clout in the household), socializing and engaging in public institutions (which puts them in contact with extended social networks that support non-traditional behavior), and attending school (which enhances their knowledge and nurtures their aspirations).

At the community level, the focus groups pointed out that the impact of moral support—whether from a community or a social network—for women is critical for women's empowerment and perseverance to gain agency. Their efforts to bend roles in their own households are less stressful when they can talk to a neighbor and get constructive advice, for example, about "getting a husband or mother-in-law to agree to let them work for pay outside the household." Even when change is resisted by husbands or extended family, if other men and women in the same community are allowing women more control over assets and diversification into economic roles, then there is some sense that they can "ride a wave" in their negotiations for change. This sense that a critical mass is developing can help accelerate reforms and has growing credibility in development project design.

By extension, we expected that communities with vibrant local organizations would show a stronger sense of collective action in support of gender "norm-benders." As chapter 4 suggests, however, community-based groups have a mixed record in supporting improvements in agency for women and men, despite their potential as networks for change. Development interventions work frequently with community groups, so the question arises whether they are the best places to generate a critical mass of support for women and men pushing the boundaries of entrenched norms around gender roles.

We found that regulations and laws promoting gender equality promoted some change when they were well-publicized and well-enforced, but outreach and public understanding of the laws—whether they criminalize gender-based violence, permit divorce, or support women's inheritance rights—were very uneven. In general, people in urban areas had more knowledge of such laws and women were more in favor of these regulations than men. In none of the sample countries did we find either men or women to be really well-informed of their rights, entitlements, or obligations with respect to key laws intended to promote gender equality. Clearly, the countries in our research need more, and more effective, awareness-raising campaigns to promote knowledge and enforcement of these laws.

Overall, our research offers new evidence that increasing women's agency involves constant dialogue between social norms, empowerment, capacity to aspire, and the structure of opportunities. These findings strongly support *World Development Report 2012* and suggest that direct intervention in all these domains can accelerate the improvements in agency offered by economic growth.

Methodological Note

The field work behind *On Norms and Agency* (conducted under the title *Defining Gender in the 21st Century*) reached 97 urban and rural communities of Afghanistan, Bhutan, Burkina Faso, the Dominican Republic, Fiji, India, Indonesia, Liberia, Moldova, Papua New Guinea, Peru, Poland, Serbia, South Africa, Sudan, Tanzania, Togo, Vietnam, West Bank and Gaza, and the Republic of Yemen. Nearly 4,000 individuals from three generations participated in the study between June 2010 and March 2011.

The rapid assessment explored trends in gender roles and norms and what the women and men participating said drives their major decisions for education, economic participation, and family formation. We set up small, same-sex discussion groups and asked their members to reflect on questions about these decisions, for example: Why and how did they decide to end their education? Are men and women better at different jobs? Do women and men save differently? What makes a "good" husband or a "good" wife? We employed qualitative methods, which are appropriate for examining these questions because they permit exploration of multidimensional factors that need to be traced over time, as well as contextually grounded for sound interpretation of their meaning and significance in the lives of the sample women and men and their communities. These methods are the preferred approach for researching "how" and "why" questions given that they "allow investigators to retain the holistic and meaningful characteristics of real-life events" (Yin 2003, 3). Our research design also enabled us to explore commonalities and combinations of factors that affect gender norms and individual agency across sets of communities (Ragin 2008).

We selected countries for the global study based on three criteria: First, we chose at least two countries in each world region.[1] Second, we chose countries where World Bank country units had strong interest for the work to be conducted there and wanted to learn from the study and incorporate findings into their policy analyses and guidance activities. And the third criteria were countries where a local research team with the required expertise on qualitative data collection could be identified. Although the study samples are small and not representative of their general country or regional contexts, we designed them, at the community level, to capture a mix of urban and rural contexts, as well as more modern and traditional gender norms. In every country, research teams fanned out into both middle-class and poorer neighborhoods of cities and towns, and into prosperous and poor villages. The final sample of communities is listed in table A.1. (Names of the communities in the study are pseudonyms or are referred to by districts.)

Within the study communities, five different data collection tools were used: three structured focus group discussions (an interview guide was prepared for each age group: adults, young adults, and adolescents[2]), one key informant interview centering on a questionnaire about the community with close- and open-ended questions, and one mini case study.[3] (See table I.2 in the Introduction, which summarizes the general topics covered with each method.) Focus groups lasted 2.5–3 hours on average.

Because bias can sometimes be introduced by focus group dynamics, such as when more assertive group members dominate discussions, facilitators received training in additional measures to foster inclusive discussions that would capture a range of attitudes and experiences common in the community. We also set up single-sex focus groups of roughly similar ages, so participants would feel safe and comfortable and answer frankly. Further, on some key questions, focus group members had opportunities to respond in private and then volunteer to discuss their responses in the open (same-sex) group.

Local researchers with extensive country knowledge and qualitative field experience led the focus groups. The field team members recruited to conduct the focus group discussions and interviews were generally experienced facilitators who received supplemental training and a detailed methodology guide in preparation for their field work. The methodology guide reviewed the study's conceptual approach and sampling procedures, presented each of the study instruments, and discussed documentation and analysis techniques.

As part of the field work in each site, facilitators interviewed local key informants to complete a community questionnaire, which provided extensive background information about the sample community. Key informants were community leaders, government officials, politicians, important local employers, business or financial leaders, teachers, or healthcare workers. The selection of the participants for the adolescent and young adult focus groups was based on specific age criteria. The field teams also received instructions to compose the groups, as much as possible, to reflect the range of educational and livelihood experiences common in the community for that age group.

We reiterated to the teams from the onset that this was a cross-country study. The teams had to balance concerns for responsiveness to the issues and pace of a specific group's discussion with the global study's need for a core set of data that could be compared systematically across all the focus groups across all the countries. The teams were trained by the core World Bank study team to follow standard methodological use of each data collection tool. Both facilitators and note-takers pretested all data tools, including country-level additions and adaptations. We asked the facilitators to stay as close as possible to the interview

Table A.1 Communities in the Sample

Country	Location	Name of community
Afghanistan	Rural	Boyina Bagh (Kabul Province)
	Urban	Shirabad Ulya (Kabul Province)
	Urban	Karta-e Bakheter (Parwan Province)
	Rural	Naw Da (Parwan Province)
Bhutan	Urban	Thimphu District
	Rural	Paro District
	Rural	Samtse District
	Urban	Mongar District
Burkina Faso	Urban	Ouagadougou (capital city) : two different communities interviewed in the same city
	Rural	Sanmantenga (province)
	Rural	Barsalogho (province)
Dominican Republic	Urban	Santiago de los Caballeros (large city)
	Rural	Comendador (municipality)
	Urban	Hato Mayor (municipality)
	Urban	Santo Domingo (large city)
Fiji	Urban	Suva (capital city)
	Rural	Naitasiri (province)
	Rural	Sigatoka (province)
	Urban	Lautoka (large city)
	Urban	Levuka town (old capital of Fiji, city)
	Rural	Labasa (province)
India[a]	Rural	Koudipally Manda/Kowdipalle (district, Andhra Pradesh state)
	Urban	Nellore (large city, Andhra Pradesh state)
	Rural	Velugodu (district, Andhra Pradesh state)
	Urban	Hyderabad (large city)
	Urban	Bhubaneswar (city, Odisha state)
	Urban	Jaipur (city, Odisha state)
	Rural	Kalahandi (district, Odisha state)
	Rural	Phulbani (municipality, Odisha state)
Indonesia	Urban	East Jakarta (large city)
	Urban	Tangerang (large city)
	Rural	Sungai Puar (district)
	Rural	Nagari Bukik Batabuah (district)
Liberia[b]	Rural	Tchien District
	Rural	Tewor District
	Urban	Buchanan (large city)
	Urban	Greenville District
	Urban	Firestone District
	Urban	Harper District
	Urban	Monrovia (large city)
	Rural	Suakoko District
	Rural	Zorzor
Moldova	Urban	Balti (large city)
	Rural	Briceni District

table continues next page

Table A.1 Communities in the Sample *(continued)*

Country	Location	Name of community
	Rural	Floresti District
	Urban	Ceadîr-Lunga (large city)
Papua New Guinea[c]	Urban	National Capital District
	Rural	Morobe Province
	Rural	Village near Buka (capital city of Bougainville District)
	Rural	Milne Bay Province or Alotau
	Rural	Village near Wewak (East Sepik Province)
	Rural	Western Highlands Province
Peru	Urban	Lambayeque Province
	Rural	Cusco Province
	Rural	Chiclayo (large city)
	Urban	Saylla District
Poland	Rural	Justynow village
	Rural	Martynice village
	Urban	Dobrowice (city)
	Urban	Olsztyn (large city)
Serbia	Rural	Sumadija District
	Urban	Belgrade (capital city)
	Urban	Kragujevac (large city)
	Urban	Pomoravlje District
	Urban	Sjenica (city)
South Africa	Urban	Umlazi township A
	Urban	Umlazi township B
	Rural	Rural community (Ngonyameni area, Kwa-Zulu Natal)
	Rural	Semi-rural community (Ngonyameni area, Kwa-Zulu Natal)
Sudan (North)	Urban	Khartoum (capital city)
	Rural	River Nile State
	Rural	Blue Nile State
	Rural	Al Fashir (capital city of North Darfur State)
	Rural	Red Sea State
Tanzania	Urban	Emputa village (Bukoba municipality)
	Urban	Nsenene village (Bukoba municipality)
	Rural	Malangachilima village (Dodoma region)
	Rural	Zabibu village (Dodoma region)
Togo	Urban	Assoli Prefecture
	Rural	Ave Prefecture
	Urban	Lomé (capital city)
	Rural	Tandjouaré Prefecture
Vietnam	Urban	Ba Dinh District (Hanoi)
	Urban	Hoang Mai District (Hanoi)
	Rural	Hung Yen District
	Rural	Kim Dong District
West Bank and Gaza	Urban	Neighborhood, Rafah Governorate
	Urban	IDP camp (internally displaced persons), Rafah Governorate
	Urban	Neighborhood, border area, Rafah Governorate

table continues next page

Table A.1 Communities in the Sample *(continued)*

Country	Location	Name of community
	Rural	Dirbas, Hebron Governorate
	Urban	University Quarter, Hebron
	Urban	Old City, Hebron
Yemen, Rep.	Rural	Jahran District (Dhamar Governorate)
	Rural	Kharef District
	Urban	Aden (large city)
	Urban	Ba'adan (city)

Note: Community names have been replaced with pseudonyms and/or moved to the next administrative level (municipality, district, or governorate) when the research site is smaller than 2,000 inhabitants. For cities, the name of the city is used to replace the name of the specific neighborhood. In the case of large cities, when possible, municipality or large neighborhood or other level was added as identifier.

a. Two states were included in India, each one treated as a country with four communities each.

b. Liberia was a pilot country. Double the number of required communities were surveyed.

c. More communities were included due to diversity of provinces in Papua New Guinea.

guides, so that they posed the same questions and created the same visuals. The facilitators also kept to the particular sequencing of the modules.

With our encouragement, facilitators had license to probe more deeply into specific issues that cropped up in the focus groups. We asked them to let focus group participants reflect on and reply to more general questions first before exploring a subject in greater detail. For broad questions—such as, what does it mean to be a powerful woman in the community?—we gave them specific guidance on how to allow an open flow of answers, instead of guiding responses in particular directions. If participants met questions with silence or a subject appeared to be too sensitive for open discussion in a group, facilitators either (a) moved on to the next question and perhaps returned later to the topic, or (b) found alternative ways to address the issue, such as allowing them to answer in private or write confidential replies. We also deliberately designed the order of discussions to present more sensitive questions in later modules when greater rapport and trust had developed among members of the group.

The facilitators introduced all focus groups and informants in the study to the objectives of the assessment, explained the type of information being solicited and how it would be recorded, emphasized that participation was entirely voluntary with no adverse consequences for those who did not wish to participate, and described how they would ensure the confidentiality of participants' answers (the data) and their anonymity. We made certain that participants understood that the study was not intended to directly change any policies or services affecting their communities and that they would not receive compensation, financial or otherwise, for joining the study.

Some parts of the data collection required the study participants to reflect on earlier periods of time, and we identified a specific period. When facilitators asked participants to reflect back 10 years ago, they could assist their recall by substituting a fixed reference year for the term "10 years ago" and linking the baseline year to a major national event to strengthen their memories (for example, a natural disaster, a change of government, the end of a conflict, or an epidemic).

We based several data collection modules on specific visual displays or material to encourage richer discussion, such as the ladders of power and freedom created by each group, list of characteristics for a good and bad wife and husband, and causes and consequences of domestic violence. For contexts where participants' literacy was limited, the research teams substituted symbols for text. For example, a face with a big smile was used to represent "very happy" to respond to a question on happiness in one of the modules.

The closed-ended questions included in the focus group guide required individual responses from the group members, rather than a consensus response, so that the members of a group could not bias each other's responses. The responses to these questions were recorded in a standardized spreadsheet (Microsoft Excel).

We also electronically taped many focus group discussions, but due to limited budgets and limited time for full transcription, note-takers attending the discussions recorded the majority of the documentation. Regardless of recording, all focus groups included note-takers, and their notes were added to transcripts of focus groups findings. The note-takers, as well as facilitators, were the same sex as the participants in each focus group.

The final dataset from the field work is narrative and numerical data. The study's principal findings rest on systematic analysis of the content of the narratives, comprising more than 7,000 pages of text in the global dataset. The text was treated like a single database and coded with NVivo9, a social science software. We populated thematic nodes with portions of narrative text following a predetermined node tree designed by the lead research team. In addition, free nodes were inductively coded according to specific categories: generational differences, relevant information, notable case (or gem), rural-urban differences, and gender or generational differences.

The closed-ended questions (where all participants gave their own opinions on a set scale of possible responses) were treated as a numeric dataset, where we used weighted frequencies and averages. Similar treatment was given to the database generated by the community questionnaire. Throughout this report, we give coding frequencies derived from NVivo—both the number of focus groups and number of mentions of a specific study topic—as guidelines for findings on certain themes.

In order to understand specific pathways for explaining the change in levels of power and freedom (from the ladder of power and freedom activity presented in chapter 4), we developed a model for qualitative comparative analysis (QCA). QCA is based on a Boolean method of logical comparison that represents each case (which in this study was a community) as a combination of causal and outcome conditions (Ragin 2008). The analysis allows identification of different combinations of conditions that produce a specific outcome; in our study, this was the perceived changes in power and freedom during a 10-year period for women and men in a community.

A separate tercile analysis was also undertaken with the ladder outcomes and presented in chapter 5. We applied a STATA tercile distribution function to the dataset of mobility indexes (calculated as the difference between the ladder mean step now and mean step 10 years ago). The terciles were assigned on a country-by-country basis.

The global analysis phase of the rapid qualitative assessment was launched with an interactive writing workshop that brought together 18 of the 20 country team leaders with the study's global assessment team at the Rockefeller Center in Bellagio, Italy, in September 2011. The opportunity to share country findings, to collaborate intensively on identifying important themes for the global report to address, and to reflect on strengths and weaknesses of the study methodology greatly facilitated the analysis of patterns, as well as the vital context-specific dimensions of gender norms, aspirations, and agency.

Notes

1. As defined by the World Bank: Sub-Saharan Africa, East Asia and the Pacific, Europe and Central Asia, Latin America and the Caribbean, Middle East and North Africa, and South Asia.

2. Adults were 25–60 years old, young adults 18–24, and adolescents 12–17.

3. This was a detailed report of a finding that emerged as important for understanding gender norms or structures shaping economic decisions in that locality.

References

Ragin, C. C. 2008. *Redesigning Social Inquiry: Fuzzy Sets and Beyond*. Chicago, IL: University of Chicago Press.

Yin, R. K. 2003. *Case Study Research: Design and Methods*. 3rd ed. Applied Social Research Methods Series, Vol. 5. Thousand Oaks, CA: Sage.

Environmental Benefits Statement

The World Bank is committed to reducing its environmental footprint. In support of this commitment, the Office of the Publisher leverages electronic publishing options and print-on-demand technology, which is located in regional hubs worldwide. Together, these initiatives enable print runs to be lowered and shipping distances decreased, resulting in reduced paper consumption, chemical use, greenhouse gas emissions, and waste.

The Office of the Publisher follows the recommended standards for paper use set by the Green Press Initiative. Whenever possible, books are printed on 50% to 100% postconsumer recycled paper, and at least 50% of the fiber in our book paper is either unbleached or bleached using Totally Chlorine Free (TCF), Processed Chlorine Free (PCF), or Enhanced Elemental Chlorine Free (EECF) processes.

More information about the Bank's environmental philosophy can be found at http://crinfo.worldbank.org/crinfo/environmental_responsibility/index.html.

green
press
INITIATIVE

www.ingramcontent.com/pod-product-compliance
Lightning Source LLC
Chambersburg PA
CBHW080609270326
41928CB00016B/2984